RURAL FRANCE

RURAL FRANCE

The People, Places and Character of the Frenchman's France

JOHN ARDAGH

CENTURY PUBLISHING
LONDON

Contents

Contributors

Anthony Burton
Waterways

Peter Graham
A Village in Cantal

Roy Malkin
Jura; Fontainebleau; Ile-de-France Writers and Artists;
Forests and Wildlife; Rural Châteaux

Pierre Marchant
Dordogne; Alsace

Michael Schwab
Savoy; Rural Cuisine

Steven Spurrier
Wines

First published in Great Britain in 1983
by Century Publishing Co. Ltd,
76, Old Compton Street, London W1V 5PA

ISBN 0 7126 0101 5

**Designed and produced by
Quintet Publishing Limited, London**

Editorial Director
Clare Howell

Editor
Hilary Dickinson

Art Editor
Christopher White

Designer
Martin Atcherley

Cartographer
John Mitchell

Phototypesetting and black-and-white illustration origination by
Dorchester Typesetting Group Limited, Dorchester

Colour illustration origination by East Anglian Engraving Limited, Norwich

Printed and bound in Italy by L.E.G.O. Vicenza

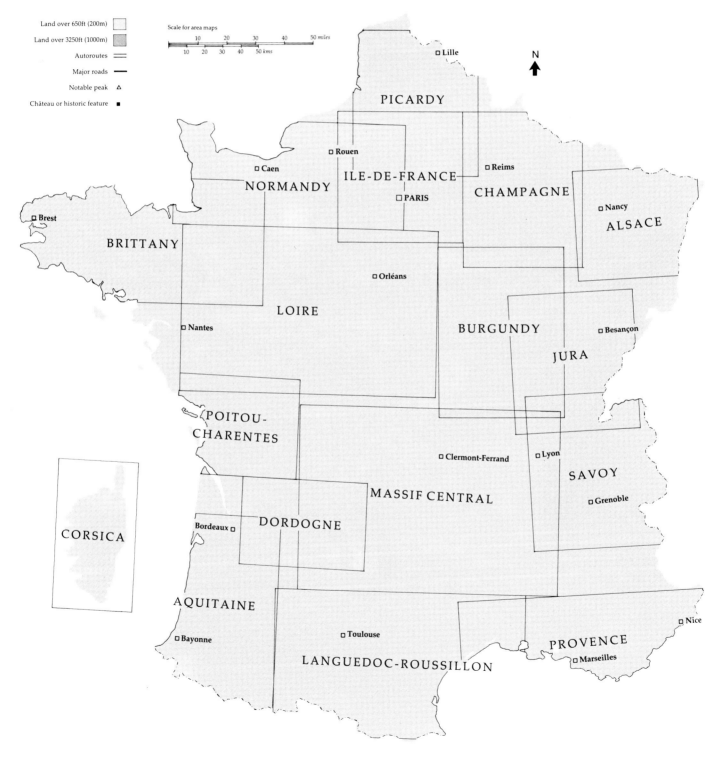

Land over 650ft (200m)
Land over 3250ft (1000m)
Autoroutes
Major roads
Notable peak △
Château or historic feature ■

Scale for area maps
10   20   30   40   50 *miles*
10 20 30 40 50 *kms*

N

Lille

PICARDY

Rouen

Caen

NORMANDY

ILE-DE-FRANCE

Reims

CHAMPAGNE

Nancy

ALSACE

PARIS

Brest

BRITTANY

Orléans

LOIRE

Nantes

BURGUNDY

Besançon

JURA

POITOU-
CHARENTES

Clermont-Ferrand

Lyon

SAVOY

MASSIF CENTRAL

Grenoble

CORSICA

Bordeaux

DORDOGNE

AQUITAINE

Bayonne

Toulouse

Nice

PROVENCE

LANGUEDOC-ROUSSILLON

Marseilles

RURAL LIFE

France, and certainly rural France, has changed radically since World War II. It has moved from an agriculture-based to an industry-based economy. Its number of farmers has dropped by three-quarters. Most of its cities have doubled or trebled in size. And yet, though smaller villages may be depopulating, and though the old-style peasant culture may be dying, rural France retains immense strengths.

By western European standards France is a relatively large country, four times the size of England, with some 30,000 villages. It is a land of immense diversity, and this makes generalization hard – a diversity alike of scenery and climate, of kinds of farming, of life-style, of temperament and even of race. For France belongs both to northern and southern Europe; it is a nation welded from many different cultures. The people of sunny Languedoc, volatile yet easy-going, are very different from stolid Normans, just as their little stone red-roofed houses are quite unlike Normandy's cosy timbered cottages, and the slow rhythm of their life as vine-growers is not the same as the meticulous toil of the Norman dairy farmers. Breton villagers, with their dreamy Celtic legends and folklore, and their own Celtic tongue, are a world apart from Alsatians whose traditions and dialect resemble those of nearby Germany. And the big prosperous wheat farms of Picardy are far removed from the poor small-holdings of the Massif Central. Yet all of this is rural France.

It is a land where the sense of place, and of local loyalty, is strong. A villager may consider another village a mere ten miles away as alien territory. And if he migrates to a far-off city in search of work, he will not forget the *pays* of his birth, nor lose touch with it; often he will return there to spend his old age, to die and be buried there. Many of the villages are highly picturesque, in a variety of styles; and despite the massive post-war drift to the towns, fewer buildings are in decay than might have been expected. This is because one of the positive trends of the past decade or so is the French awakening to the need to preserve their rural heritage: many farm-houses, cottages and manors have been lovingly restored either by local country folk or by well-to-do weekenders from the towns.

Since World War II, rural France has undergone what most experts describe as a 'revolution'. Six million people have moved off the land, which today employs only 8 per cent of the active population, against 35 per cent in 1945. Post-war technical improvement on the farms made economic nonsense of the huge peasant community, while new industry was easily able to provide jobs for the emigrants during the boom years of French expansion. Those who remain on the land have developed entirely new attitudes. The peasantry used to be a world apart, passive and archaic. After the war, however, there arose a new dynamic generation of modern-minded young farmers, and they have steadily transformed French agriculture, or large parts of it. The old reactionary peasant, alcoholic, half-illiterate, living scarcely better than his animals, does still survive in some poorer areas, mainly in the west and south-west; but he is a dying species.

The peasantry used to be a society apart, but sociologists today agree that 'the peasant' is ceasing to exist. Farmers today are more like small businessmen; they have integrated at last into local society, they have lost their old inferiority complex, and their children are hardly different from town children. 'This used to be considered a decadent profession', said one Breton farmer,

7

Rural Life

(Left) A street market in
L'Isle-sur-la-Sorgue, Vaucluse
(Provence).

(Opposite above) Despite the
post-war drift of people from the
country areas to the towns,
buildings in the villages are
being preserved and restored.

(Opposite below) In some rural
areas, traditional crafts such as
barrel-making have been
preserved and even revived.

'but now we have prestige. I no longer envy city folk.' So the old notorious gulf between *paysan* and *citadin* is at last fading away. In the old days, a town girl would rarely accept marriage with a farmer. This would have meant a life of drudgery and a fall in her social status, but today over a third of young farmers' wives are the daughters of non-farmers. Moreover, on more than half of French farms, at least half of the family income comes from a member who has a non-agricultural job – maybe teaching, or hospital or factory work. Thus rural and non-rural economies are becoming more closely intermeshed.

It follows that the nature of village life has been changing too. Now that farmers have cars, they are much less likely to use the nearby small village as their main centre, but will go instead to the nearest country town or large village. Social, commercial and other activity is thus being regrouped in these larger places, with the result that a remarkable polarization has been taking place. In a word, a village of under, say, 500 inhabitants is likely to be dying; a village of over 1,000 or so is probably booming. Many a smaller village has lost its *curé*, its school, its post office, almost all its shops and cafés, and its population may well have halved since the war, unless it happens to be in a tourist area or within commuter range of a city. By contrast, a large village is likely to have many of the amenities of a town. Older people too, when they retire, may choose to move from their small village or farmstead to a villa in a small town to have amenities close at hand. These trends are likely to continue.

The rural and city *milieux* are today moving far closer together. As the farmers develop urban styles, so also the townsfolk penetrate the countryside, to live and even to work, as they rarely did in the old days. And as the farmers become less numerous, so they become a less important part of the total rural population. Rural France is alive and well, but it has become far less of an exclusively agricultural community. This trend has various facets. Above all, city dwellers, irked by urban life, have been buying up empty farmsteads, or building villas in the country, and using them for weekends, for summer holidays or for retirement.

This movement is especially prevalent in Provence and within a 100-mile radius of Paris, where in the Yonne *département* (northern Burgundy) 20 per cent of all housing falls into this class. With over two million of these secondary homes, France holds the world record: one family in nine has one, against one in 15 in the United States, one in 140 in Germany, one in 200 in Britain.

In some cases, artisans or artists have moved from the cities to the peace of the countryside, hoping to make a living there. In an area such as Provence, in many a village one sees little signboards, *'poterie'* or *'sculpture'*, indicating that some young hopeful is running a boutique there, probably above the modest studio where he (or she) works at his craft – and he may well be from Paris, or indeed from Hamburg, Amsterdam or Chelsea. At the same time, the big villages have been filling up with little enterprises that service the newly modern farms and other residents – garages, farm toolshops, veterinary clinics, banks and specialized shops of all kinds.

Rural Life

The old village of Limeuil in its hilltop setting near the confluence of the Dordogne and Vézère rivers is typical of many rural areas which have become popular for people buying holiday homes.

(Opposite) French farms vary greatly in size and wealth, from small hill-farms where old-fashioned methods are still used, to large modern cooperatives.

All this is the new rural France. And it has involved a great deal of new building, of villas and workshops. Perhaps surprisingly, these on the whole have spoilt the landscape less than one might have feared. True, there are some eyesores: but mayors and other authorities generally make sure that the new building harmonizes with local style – in Brittany, white walls and grey slate roofs, in Provence, plain stone walls and red-tiled roofs.

Until twenty or thirty years ago, the average French village was run by an élite of local dignitaries (*notables*): the *curé*, the schoolteacher, the lawyer, maybe the *châtelain*. These educated people acted as intermediaries between the peasant and the rest of society and the state. But since the war the *notables* have been leaving the villages or losing influence; the calibre of teachers has declined and so has the *curé*'s role. At the same time, now that the peasants are far better educated, they have less need of these *notables*, or else they want more sophisticated help, from people such as accountants or agronomists who live in the towns. The new forceful generation of farmers have also been taking matters into their own hands to form their own élites. Far more of them than in the old days are mayors or even *conseillers généraux* (the equivalent of county councillors) and now wield a great deal of local influence.

The bottom tier of local government is the *commune*. The country is divided into some 36,300 of these, which cover the entire territory. Some are big cities; most are small villages plus their surrounding hamlets. Each *commune*, however small, has its locally elected mayor and council. The mayor with his sash not only officiates at weddings and other ceremonies: he is also legally the delegate of the State in the *commune*, responsible for its management. Even in centralized France he thus has quite a lot of power – and this has been increasing since the Socialist government's devolutionary reforms began to come into effect in 1982. These abolish the prefect's control over local budgets. They also transfer from prefect to mayor such matters as the right to grant building permits. The new-style farmer-mayors are thus now playing a governmental role that was inconceivable in the old days. In one large Breton village, a mayor of this breed whose father had been a peasant smallholder is now in charge of such tasks as building a primary school and preparing a new public drainage system.

Local politics in rural France follow national lines. That is, mayors and councils are seldom elected on a fully independent ticket: nearly always they belong, or are affiliated, to one or other of the big national parties. France is a highly politicized country, and this extends down to the villages. As might be expected, rural areas tend on the whole to be rather more right-wing than urban ones, but this is by no means the rule. If the Vendée and most of rural Alsace and Brittany, for example, remain bastions of the right, by contrast large parts of the Midi have long been in the hands of the left, and many villages there even have Communist mayors. Paradoxically, small farmers, though strongly individualist, will often vote Communist out of a general sense of grievance against the rich ones – and the Communist Party in its turn cynically courts them by extolling the virtues of the mini-capitalist private family farm!

Rural Life

Though the influence of the Church has declined since the war, it still plays a key role in many villages, especially in traditionalist areas such as Alsace. This village is Riquewihr (Alsace).

(Opposite) The town hall at Puy l'Evêque. Local politics are important in rural areas. Every commune has an elected mayor and council.

Rural politics have other odd aspects too. For example, in the same valley, one village may traditionally vote left, while another five miles away and just as poor may always vote right, for no apparent reason, except that local personalities count for a lot. In the north, in a conservative area such as Normandy, some feudal attitudes still survive among the peasantry, such as an innate respect for inherited wealth: thus, in one village, the rich local *châtelain* is always unquestioningly re-elected mayor even though he is manifestly incompetent or out of touch with the needs of his *commune*. In the south, politics are more theatrical, but though passions may erupt violently, tensions do not run very deep and are easily soothed over a friendly glass of *pastis* between rivals. In some Languedoc villages, a cosy Don Camillo/Peppone sparring will often persist between political foes who will cheerfully abuse each other in public yet also be on friendly '*tu*' terms.

One kind of feuding that today has largely faded away from rural life is the old historic one between Catholics and anti-clericals. In pre-war days, the inhabitants of many a village used to be ranged into two camps: the 'Whites', led by the *curé*, and the 'Reds', led usually by the left-wing local teacher. These tensions still persist in some country districts. In most cases, however, they have become obsolete, now that the Church has lost so much of its influence and this weakening of clericalism has led to a softening of anti-clericalism too, since the clergy are no longer seen by the left as such a 'threat'. Moreover, many of the clergy themselves have today moved over to the left, while quite a number of Socialist mayors today are practising Catholics – so the old battle-lines have become confused. In some villages, the *curé* and the local Socialists are today in alliance against the older conservative farmers and the tradesmen. This re-alignment has been due in part to the rise since the war of a new style of militant Catholic action. The Church used to be closely identified with the right. But many post-war Catholics, clergy and laity alike, now lay the accent less on liturgy and church-going than on social justice and on applying Christ's ideals in practice. These people often vote Socialist and even help to activate the Socialist Party – in the villages, as in the towns.

Today, social life in the villages and on the farms is low-key; people are usually working too hard to have time or energy for sociable leisure pursuits. The older men sometimes sit in cafés playing cards, or they enjoy a game of *boules* in the village square, especially in the

Rural Life

Midi. Younger men often play football, and some teen-agers will go to the local youth club which may have an amateur music or drama group. Social clubs for the elder-ly, which hardly existed 30 years ago, are now active in many villages. In summer there is the annual village fête, maybe lasting three or four days; and on winter weekends there are hunting parties. But generally people tend to spend their evenings at home, watching tele-vision, having a leisurely meal, then going to bed early; and on Sundays there is still the ritual of the large, copious family lunch.

Neighbours and friends are less likely than before to invite each other home for a meal or even drop in for a casual drink. This used not to be the case in pre-war days, when villagers and farmers were bound together in a closer and warmer community; their very poverty, and isolation from the world outside, created a sense of soli-darity. Today, prosperity has changed all that, bringing new forms of entertainment such as television and plea-sure motoring. Many people are conscious of a certain loss in human terms, and will often talk about it. Maybe they *do* romanticize the 'good old days' and forget their darker aspects – the drudgery, the lack of comfort, the disease and malnutrition. Yet they are probably right in

(Left) While family life remains strong in country areas – especially the ritual of Sunday lunch – social contact between neighbours has lost some of its old community warmth.

(Above) Older people in many parts of rural France regret the changing patterns of life of recent years since the advent of mass entertainment and increased prosperity.

(Right) Many villages hold an annual fête when traditional instruments and costumes are still used.

believing that there has been a loss. Today, one hears the same kind of lament in many regions, from Provence to the Auvergne to Brittany.

In one Provençal village, a man of 40 said, 'When I was a boy, in the 1950s, people would still gather together in each other's homes in the evenings, to tell stories, sing local songs, play Provençal music with our traditional instruments. But television has killed all that.' And in a nearby village a woman gave the view, 'Until the late fifties we were incredibly poor – no electricity or running water, and meat a once-a-week luxury. Yet I regret those days, because we had a warm feeling of togetherness.

Rural Life

(Opposite) The market-square has always been a popular meeting-place, particularly in rural communities.

(Right) Grape-pickers having a picnic lunch during the wine harvest in the Hérault département (Languedoc).

(Right) A fête at Mèze, in the Hérault.

We'd stroll round the village in the evenings, gossiping, flirting. Today each family sits on its own at home, in front of the television.' In the Auvergne a farmer recalled his boyhood: 'At harvest-time there'd be noisy parties and dances every night in the village hall. Today the job's done by two men with a combine-harvester, and we've little social life left here. In the evenings we watch television or drive to visit friends who live miles away.' And in Brittany, where 30 years ago young people would draw round the fire on winter evenings to hear grannies reciting Celtic legends, a farmer said: 'We are far better off than my parents were, but I think we have less fun. We visit and meet together less – and we're all aware of a loss of sense of community.' In some areas, one hears also the complaint that prosperity has brought with it a less generous and more mercantile spirit. 'When we were poor,' said a farmer in Normandy, 'we'd all help each other for nothing. But today, if a farmer gives another a hand with the haymaking for an hour or two, he'll clock-watch, and expect to be paid. It's sad.'

Today, some pioneers are at least making efforts to revive rural traditions and to prevent the old folk-cultures from dying out. Generally, this takes the form of creating new folk-groups, who at the summer fêtes will put on the traditional costumes and perform the old folk-dances of the region, with local songs and music. Very often the initiative for this has come not from the villagers themselves, but from local intellectuals such as the schoolteachers, or from students living in nearby towns. This trend reflects a broader movement in France for a new urban generation to seek renewal of contact with its rural roots. The villagers do at least follow this movement quite gladly, and so the local fêtes have found a new lease of life, and new folk-groups have sprung up everywhere. It may be an artificial revival, but clearly it is better than letting the old traditions disappear.

Rural Life

It is time to look more closely at French agriculture itself since that is the real basis of the country's rural life. Here there is a striking paradox: while socially the villages may have been losing some of their old community spirit, professionally French farmers have been learning how to group together, so as to make better use of their resources for mutual profit. The old-style French farmer was a stubborn individualist; warm and friendly with his neighbours, yes, but deeply suspicious of entering into any financial association involving trust.

However, the modern farmers have become aware of how short-sighted these attitudes are. Since the war, they have developed big cooperatives, which in many cases sell direct to the retailers, thus by-passing the profiteering middlemen. Many of them have also been grouping locally to buy shared equipment, with the help of state loans. This may seem normal common sense in a modern agriculture: but it cuts across rooted French peasant habits. Another state-backed scheme facilitates the enlargement of farms by enabling the land itself to be jointly owned. This generally succeeds when the owners belong to the same family. But joint ventures between mere neighbours are far more rare, and often they fail. 'I tried to form one', said a Breton farmer, 'but we found we didn't really trust each other, especially the wives, who are the ones who do the accounting.' Individualism dies hard. So, in such cases, the farmers continue to inflict on themselves more drudgery than they need. In western Normandy, one small dairy-farmer and his wife have to milk and tend the cows twice a day every single day of the year, with never the shortest holiday or break, simply because they cannot persuade their neighbours to work with them on any kind of rota basis.

Farmers have also had to grapple with the problem of land parcellization. Much of rural France is split into a crazy quilt of thin strips: a farmer may have twenty or thirty little fields, not next to each other but widely scattered, and this has hardly made it easier to operate large modern machinery. Since the war a policy of *re-membrement* (re-grouping) has been embarked on, with the government giving grants to farmers willing to make rational swaps. This has brought results, and some 30 million acres have been thus *remembrés*. But the scheme is not imposed on a *commune* unless over half the farmers are in favour. And often it has run up against the conservatism of the older peasants, who have resisted it through emotional attachment to their own bits of soil. A farmer may finally accept the idea in theory, but when the work starts he will be struck with sentimental horror, and refuse to give up the field where his father taught him to plough or the pear-tree his grandmother planted. This helps to explain why, in many poorer *départements*, less than ten per cent of the *communes* have been *remembrées*. In the Lozère, one goat-breeder has 85 acres split into 50 far-flung parcels.

French farms today vary enormously in size and wealth. The range of incomes is higher than in industry, with some farmers earning up to forty times as much as others. Many farms are still too small to be viable under modern conditions, so therefore it is right that the drift

from the land should continue, at least in those areas – such as Brittany and Poitou-Charentes – where there is still some rural over-population. Today the exodus has slowed right down, but it is expected to go on for another ten years or so, until the numbers employed in farming finally level off at about 5.5 to 6 per cent of the French active population (in Britain it is 2.8 per cent). This is thought to be a reasonable figure, as a basis for viable family farming.

Nowadays, France produces more food than she requires for her own needs or can reasonably hope to export. Therefore, it can be argued that many of the less fertile areas should no longer be used for farming at all, but for something else. As the drift from the land continues, more of these remoter areas will become semi-

In many parts of France, small farms are expanding as parcels of land are grouped together. At this farm near Saint-Avit-Sénieur in the Dordogne, the old farmhouse is surrounded by the newer cowsheds and tobacco-drying barns.

(Below left) Stubble-burning near Tursac in the Vézère valley, Dordogne.

(Below) Sunflowers, such as these between Arles and Tarascon, are almost as common a feature of Provence today as they were when Van Gogh painted them.

Rural Life

deserted, and more villages will die. France's network of 30,000 villages today appears a picturesque anachronism, a left-over from a bygone peasant age. And yet, they cannot simply be left as ruins, troubling the landscape. There are many people who argue that it is essential to preserve the human tissue of hamlets and farmsteads that has existed all over France for millennia.

The solution to the problem seems to lie in the extension of the multiplicity of activities already being conducted in a rural setting. Today, more people want to live and work in the countryside, if they feasibly can. But few of them will be involved directly in farming. Instead, other activities will continue to develop, for which there is a vast potential – forestry, crafts and artisan work, small-scale modern industries and rural tourism.

One shining example of how an enterprising farmer can diversify is to be found in the lonely Cévennes. Here a Protestant couple with a fifty-acre upland dairy farm had three sons aged 17 to 23 who wanted to stay on the land, so the family saw that the only chance was to expand the farm and vary their activities. One son is a trained carpenter, another a locksmith. In winter, the

family make lampshades and various metal ornaments, using sophisticated machines, and sell them via the local handicrafts cooperative. In summer, they pick wild bilberries which they make into tarts and *crêpes* and then go and sell to the tourists who visit Mont Aigoual, the local beauty spot. The family have also elegantly converted an outhouse into two *gîtes* (rural guest-lodgings), which are booked by paying visitors all summer. All this has added greatly to the farmer's income, and has enabled the family to stay together in its homeland.

As the new technology gathers pace, bringing with it smaller, cleaner industrial units, needing less manpower, so it will gradually introduce a new mobility that could revolutionize rural life, in France as elsewhere. The post-industrial age will move back to reclaim its rural heritage, and transform it. Already in the past forty years rural France has changed more than in the preceding 400. It will always remain beautiful, serene and charming, for that is the gift of its landscape, climate and traditional architecture. But its way of life, by the early twenty-first century, may be as far removed from that of the 1930s as the 1930s were from the Stone Age.

(Opposite) Hay-making in the Charente.

(Left) White Aquitaine cows in the Dordogne.

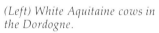

Vines being sprayed in the Hérault (Languedoc). This département *has over 400,000 acres of vineyards, more than any other in France*

21

BRITTANY

France's only Celtic province retains a strong sense of its separate identity, and in some ways has more in common with Wales or Ireland than with the rest of the French nation. It is a vast granite peninsula jutting into the Atlantic, a land of legend and mystery where the menhirs and stone calvaries bear witness to a special religious past. Yet today it is also a land of modern-minded traders and farmers, hard workers more than mystical dreamers, struggling tenaciously to preserve Brittany's new-found prosperity.

The 2,000-mile coastline is everywhere jagged, with many rocky headlands. But near the sea there are fertile plains where agriculture today is well organized and successful. This coastal belt is thickly populated, with several major ports – Lorient, Brest, Saint-Malo. The central hinterland is quite different again – a wild upland massif where the soil is thin and many farms are still poor, and the gales howl across the moors. Here the forestland has been eroded, and the fields are divided by low walls of rough granite slabs. The climate of Brittany is typical of the north-east Atlantic – mild but wet, and changeable. As in other Celtic lands, the continual alternation of sun and storm may help to explain the mercurial temperament of the people.

The earliest known inhabitants were a race of Iberian stock who have left behind them thousands of menhirs and dolmens, notably around Carnac on the south coast. The first Celts arrived in the sixth century B.C. and took over these menhirs for their own druidic rites. They gave their new homeland the name still sometimes used, Armorica, 'the land by the sea'. Then came the Roman conquest which made little lasting impact on the province. Then the main Celtic invasion came from Britain in the fifth and sixth centuries. These Celts elaborated the tales of Merlin, of King Arthur and his knights which Bretons today associate with the forest of Broceliande, now thought to be the forest of Paimpont near Rennes. Arthur more probably held court on the north side of the Channel, not the south: none the less, these legends today remain a basis of Breton mythology, as do those of Tristan and his Irish love, Isolde.

Bretons soon adopted the name '*la petite Bretagne*' (as distinct from '*la Grande Bretagne*': Great Britain) and this later became simply Bretagne (Brittany). Christianity came fairly late to the Bretons, but they then espoused it with a passion they have not entirely lost; their army of local saints, their curious religious sculptures and festivals, still have real meaning for many country people. Brittany was not annexed to the French Crown until 1532, and today most of its people still feel some sense of Breton nationhood. Very few of them want outright independence: but they do seek more autonomy, and they are eagerly keeping alive their own Breton culture.

Like most seafarers, they are a hardy people; stockily built, often with fair complexions and eyes blue or grey. Like most Celts they are eloquent and poetic, by turns passionate and dour. For centuries many of them lived by fishing; and their long struggle with the treacherous seas, costing so many lives, has given them a keen sense of life's tragedy and has sharpened their religious spirit. Today, with Europe's fishing industries in decline, Brittany has a mere 10,000 or so fishermen (though much of France's navy and merchant fleet is still manned by Bretons). Farming remains a major activity: this is the foremost region of France for agricultural output.

Even more than elsewhere in France, the farming world has changed radically since the war, and mostly for the better. In pre-war days there was stark poverty, even

Brittany

in the fertile coastal areas. A family might live six to a room on a mud floor with no plumbing or electricity, maybe sharing their living quarters with their animals. But the modernization of the farms has changed all that. Many hundreds of thousands have left for jobs in the cities; and the new generation of farmers who have remained on the land have dynamically transformed their profession and lifestyle. They travel abroad, they have smart cars and stylish, modern clothes, their leisure habits are much like those of city folk. The price paid has been a steady decline of the old picturesque peasant culture which was bred of isolation, superstition and poverty. The Bretons are aware of this loss; and today, maybe a little self-consciously, they are trying to revive this old culture as best they can. Significantly, though, the impetus has come more from city-dwellers and intellectuals than from what is left of the peasantry. As the traditional *coiffes* die out in the villages, so the Breton literary clubs

begin to burgeon in the towns.

The bid to revive the Breton language is one crucial issue. This Celtic tongue, rather similar to Welsh, used to be a *lingua franca* in the western part of the province, '*la Bretagne bretonnante*', though never in the east around Rennes where French always predominated. Until 20 or so years ago, French governments waged a campaign to stamp out Breton in the supposed interests of French national unity. Pupils who spoke Breton in school would be punished or mercilessly teased by state teachers; one woman today remembers as a child being locked up all night in the school basement.

This kind of action bore results, for it terrorized many Breton peasants and induced a sense of inferiority: young men joining Army units found themselves despised and insulted if they spoke Breton or could not manage proper French. So, almost to this day, peasants who spoke Breton among themselves would actually try

(Right and below) The Breton language is still spoken daily by some older people, especially those in remote villages where the lifestyle – like the advertisements – retains a pre-war flavour.

to prevent their own children from learning it to protect them from what they felt would be a handicap! Today these attitudes are changed, for Paris has stopped its campaign. But the legacy of the long attrition is that Breton has been steadily dying out as a daily language; and the rural exodus has hastened the process as the once-isolated peasants have moved to the towns. Today Breton is spoken only among older people who know each other well, in families or between friends, and is no more a *lingua franca*. The number of Breton speakers is thought to have fallen since 1930 from 1.2 million to 600,000 (Brittany's population is 2.5 million) and it is still falling as the older peasants die.

Some effort to reverse this continuing trend has now begun to come from younger Bretons. Now that the Government has changed its policy, Breton can be taught in state *lycées*; and some 2,000 pupils a year take it as an option in the *baccalauréat* (secondary school examina-tions). These young idealists, however, are motivated more by local patriotism and by a desire to discover and affirm their Breton identity, than by any need to use the language as a living, daily tool. Among themselves they continue to speak French: Breton they use for talking maybe to grandparents, or for reading the many books published in Breton, or for singing the old Breton hymns and folksongs at festivals. As a practical second language to French, however, they in fact find English infinitely more useful. Indeed, even the keenest Breton nationalists doubt that there is much future for the language as a vehicle of daily speech. One obstacle to its survival is that it has no inherent overall unity, but many variants, and a Breton speaker from Vannes in the south can hard-ly understand another from, say, Brest. Breton seems fated to die out from country areas, and to become in-stead a museum-language, the preserve of a few thousand students and other town-dwellers.

The city of Quimper, on the river Odet, still has many fine fifteenth-century buildings.

Brittany/Folk Traditions

In Brittany, the recent folk-culture revival may be more important than the linguistic one; and this too has come mainly from the young, in search of their Breton roots. In the villages, it takes the form of singing and dancing. Recent years have seen the formation of scores of local *cercles celtiques* (folk-dance groups) and *bagads* (a Breton word meaning a group of musicians), especially in western Brittany where traditions are strongest. These amateur groups tour the villages, playing at the local fêtes to which they have lent a new lease of life. Hands linked together, often forming a circle, the troupe will perform the stately slow-swaying Breton dances. The *bagads* accompany them, and also play on their own or with a singer, usually a man with a growling bass voice, typically Breton. The Breton instruments are the *bombarde*, a kind of oboe, and the *biniou*, which is rather like Scottish bagpipes save that it has only one pipe, not three. The local manufacture of these instruments had been dying out, but has now been modestly revived by the *bagads'* own renaissance.

A local fête is a *fest-noz* ('festive night') and these are much in vogue. After the costumed folk-groups and *bagads* have given their display, then it is the turn of the villagers in their ordinary clothes to dance the night away to Breton rhythms. To some people's regret, Breton music has become a victim of its own popularity: it has been commercialized, so that there is now Breton pop,

even Breton rock. But the Breton-ness remains. At one village near Vannes the annual fête is organized by the *curé*, a connoisseur of malt whisky, who himself has trained the dancers and musicians. The afternoon is a five-hour festival of song and dance, together with the popular sport of Breton wrestling (similar to Cornish). Then follows a big open-air supper of tripe. Then comes the *fest-noz*, and by three o'clock in the morning many revellers have to be carried home to bed.

The folk-groups and the *bagads* wear the lovely old Breton costumes – the men in embroidered waistcoats and felt hats, the girls in black dresses with coloured velvet borders and brightly coloured aprons with lace linings. Today, these costumes have died out of daily use, and are seldom seen in the streets. Nor, except rarely, does one see any more the famous Breton *coiffes* (white lace head-dresses) that vary in style from area to area; best known is the high, narrow *coiffe* of the Bigouden country, west of Quimper. These *coiffes* with their elaborate hairstyles take at least 30 minutes to iron and put on – too long for a modern generation in a hurry. Nor are they very practical: occasionally one sees a woman in a Bigouden *coiffe* in a car, her head tilted over sideways – a comic sight. However, just a few *coiffes* and costumes are still being made in the villages today, to meet the needs of the folk-group revival. Many families still own beautiful costumes handed down from past

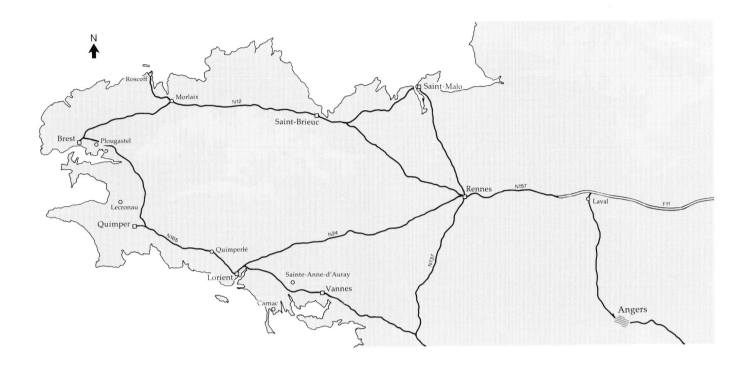

(Left) A procession during the pardon *festival at* Sainte-Anne-la-Palud.

(Below) The traditional Breton coiffe – the high head-dress – is part of the costume still worn by some older people at a pardon.

generations. These they will take out of their cupboards to wear on a special occasion – such as a fête, or a *pardon*.

The *pardon* is a Christian festival special to Brittany, when the people of a town or village gather to pay homage to their local saint, to pray for forgiveness or make a vow. Costumed villagers parade through the streets, carrying banners, candles and statues of saints, while clergy and pilgrims chant prayers and hymns. The largest and most spectacular *pardons* are at Sainte-Anne-la-Palud on the last Sunday in August, and on 26 July at Sainte-Anne-d'Auray, Brittany's main religious centre. At Locronan there are what are called *tromenies*; here the *pardon* takes the form of a long procession over the hills surrounding this very picturesque village.

Pardons today attract many tourists; but they remain basically an expression of Breton piety. In early Christian times this people created hundreds of their own saints, many never officially recognized by Rome. Then, in the sixteenth century, they began building calvaries and ossuaries, with elaborate stone carvings that depicted saints, the life of Christ and the Passion. Many still exist in cemeteries, or sometimes alone by the sea where drowned sailors are commemorated. Today Bretons are losing some of their old piety, while the clergy is facing a severe lack of young recruits. Weekly attendance at Mass in a Breton village, around 25 to 30 per cent, however, remains about twice the French average.

Brittany/The New Brittany

The post-war transformation of Brittany's farming has been a great saga. The region has long possessed a big agricultural potential, notably in livestock, dairy products, poultry and vegetables. Until 30 or so years ago, it was much under-utilized. The farms were too small and ill-equipped, the farmers too backward to cope with modern production methods and marketing. Rural over-population meant that there might be ten mouths to feed on one 20-acre smallholding. Since the war, modernization has followed much the same pattern as elsewhere in France, though in Brittany the changes have been even more striking. Three-quarters of the farm population has left the land, either for Paris or the Breton cities.

In the 1950s and 1960s, however, a dynamic new generation of farmers arose, led by the hard-headed idealists of the Jeunesse Agricole Chrétienne, and in one haul they have taken Breton farming from the Middle Ages into the late twentieth century. They have grouped together in big cooperatives; they have enlarged their farms, invested in modern equipment, taken training courses (as their parents never did), and have even travelled abroad to study the latest techniques. They have also learned the techniques of modern marketing, so that today they sell a large part of their produce to the rest of France and the Common Market. The statistics are striking. Since 1970, Brittany's production of milk, beef and pork has doubled; that of eggs and poultry has quadrupled. With five per cent of France's population, Brittany accounts for 21 per cent of French milk output, 40 per cent of pigs and of eggs and poultry, 64 per cent of artichokes and cauliflowers. And 66 per cent of all French exports of eggs and poultry come from Brittany.

One or two examples may illustrate the changes. On the plain near Brest, one farmer in his mid-thirties told his story: 'We grew up in utter poverty. My father had only 27 acres, eleven cows, some cauliflowers – and six children. In 1960, we still had no running water, no heating save a wood stove, no television or even radio, no car, just an old horse-cart. But in 1969 we persuaded my father to retire and let us modernize the farm. We've enlarged it to 60 acres, and now we have a big modern piggery with 320 sows. My wife and I have a new Peugeot 504, and a colour television. The first holiday of my life was in 1975, but now we go to the Côte d'Azur.' In this, as in other cases, the key issue has been the change of generations. One elderly farmer, in a poor part of Brittany in the 1960s, rather than spend money on mending the broken gaps in his hedges, made his wife and children stand guard in turns all day, to stop the cattle from straying. By 1975 he had died, and his son had done the mending.

The most important story is that of Alexis Gourvennec, a farmer on the rich plain around Morlaix, where cauliflowers, artichokes and potatoes are grown. In 1961, aged only 24, he led a spectacular revolt: he and his colleagues invaded and seized the sub-prefecture in Morlaix in protest against their exploitation by middlemen who were manipulating the market and not giving them a fair price for their produce. The Gaullist government quickly responded to Gourvennec's demands by passing a law

making it easier for farmers to organize their own marketing. This led him to set up a sales cooperative that today is the most famous and powerful in France, with 4,000 members. It has succeeded in imposing its prices on the middlemen, by withholding its produce if they threaten to drop too low in a glut period. Thus, Breton farmers have learned at last to control the market, and no longer be the pawns of the middlemen.

In the 1970s, Gourvennec and his friends started a shipping company, Brittany Ferries, with the aim above all of selling their produce to Britain, which had just joined the Common Market. This has been a success: the company's Roscoff-Plymouth and Saint-Malo-Portsmouth services do a roaring trade not only with tourism but also with Breton farm exports. This is believed to be the only example in Europe of farmers creating their own shipping line and taking the lead in regional economic expansion. Gourvennec today is a rich and powerful man, a key Breton figure. His dynamism is typical of the new modern Brittany.

Although most Breton farming has become more sophisticated, some small farmers still use traditional methods, such as horses for ploughing.

(Below left and right) Two typical Breton landscapes. All over the province, old farmhouses stand beside pasturelands, for livestock breeding and dairy farming are major activities.

Brittany/The New Brittany

Farmhouses old and new are built in a simple style with stone walls and grey tiled roofs.

(Opposite above) Life has become easier for the majority of Breton farmers thanks to modern equipment and techniques.

(Opposite centre) Artichokes are one of the main vegetable crops which grow well in the rich soil of north-west Brittany.

(Opposite below) Some farmers grow maize as fodder for their livestock. It is dried and stored in racks.

Not all the region, however, has been as successful as this. There are still upland areas where smallholders scrape a living from inefficient mixed farming. Even on the coastal plains, change may not have been solely for the better. A dairy farmer near Vannes said: 'Of course we have far more modern comforts and gadgets than my parents did, and we eat much better, too – we have meat far more often. But I reckon I work as hard as my father did, though admittedly there is less manual drudgery involved, now that we have machines.' Above all, it is the women who are not always sure how far their lot has really improved. A farmer's wife on the north coast said: 'Yes, in my youth, life was tough. We had no plumbing, and every day we had to carry water 400 yards up a steep hill from the well. Every day, too, there was the chore of milking the cows and cleaning out the pigsty, without machines. Modern equipment has improved all that – but it's the men who benefit most. The husband sits comfortably on his tractor, but it's the wife who's expected to dig and weed the corners that the tractor can't reach. And the wife does all the accounts, too: that's her accepted job – and today's paperwork is fearsome. I reck-

on that I work nearly twice as hard as my husband.'

Despite this, girls from towns are now far readier to marry farmers. But farmers' daughters still tend to leave the farm and seek a job in town, in an office or in industry – when they can. But Brittany is still seriously under-industrialized, and even in the boom years of the 1960s and early 1970s, not nearly enough new jobs were created to meet the needs of the mass exodus from the land. One of the few success stories has been in food-processing, which has expanded fast, enabling Brittany to derive industrial profit, and new jobs, from its own farm produce. For example, 37 per cent of all French deep-freezing of vegetables is now done in Brittany.

There have also been some attempts to bring new small factories to the villages and little towns, so that the rural emigrants need not leave home in search of a job. In the village of Landaul near Lorient, one industrialist was initially seduced by the lure of Paris and went to seek his career there: but then he decided to devote himself to his homeland, so he came back, and in 1965 set up a small plant in Landaul, making metal frames. Today this employs 180 people, mostly local villagers. It has done much

to reanimate Landaul, whose population has been actually rising, unlike that of most Breton villages. The *patron* is admired as a local benefactor. But examples of this kind are not common, especially in today's harder times.

In this land of granite, the rural architecture has a simple and austere dignity. Farmsteads and village houses are plain grey stone buildings, sometimes with whitewashed plaster façades. Everywhere there are modern villas too, especially in holiday areas near the coast; but, happily, these have been built to harmonize with the local style. They have white walls and steep tiled roofs, and look neat and prosperous.

In modernizing their homes, many farmers have moved over to a dull and even tasteless post-war style of furniture and decor. However, in some manors and farmsteads it is still possible to find examples of the traditional Breton furniture, which is as elaborate as the buildings are simple – heavy cupboards, chests and dressers made of dark oak, with ornately carved surfaces. There are even still a few of the curious old box-beds, virtual sleeping-cupboards, more picturesque than practical. Until about 20 years ago this old-style furniture was steadily disappearing: but now it is back in fashion with today's nostalgia-minded age, and the period pieces are eagerly bought up not only by the Parisian middle-class to furnish its *résidences secondaires*, but also by Breton country folk themselves. One Breton has suggested: 'In the 1950s and 1960s, when we were modernizing so keenly, many peasants came to think of their old furniture and folk costumes as inferior and unworthy, and in some cases they would even burn them. They might also abandon their graceful old farmsteads and build modern villas beside them. But now the pendulum has swung back, and the old is in vogue once more.' It is the same story as in some other traditionalist areas, such as Auvergne.

Bretons have remained more consistently faithful to their cuisine, which is, of course, closely related to local produce. This is one of the major regions of France for fish and shellfish: oysters, mussels, shrimps, prawns and scallops are plentiful, and on and near the coast one finds various fish specialities. Among them, *cotriade* (a rich fish stew), *palourdes farcies* (clams baked with garlic and herbs) and *lotte* (monkfish) or lobster *à l'armoricaine* (a rich, possibly over-rich, brown sauce of tomatoes, shallots, garlic and brandy, sometimes wrongly called *américaine*). Inland, the cuisine leans towards meat and poultry. Gastronomically, this is not one of the most distinguished of French regions. The country people, however, have their own simple, tasty dishes, such as *potée bretonne* (a *pot-au-feu* of beef with carrots and other vegetables), *gigot* of salt-pasture lamb with *haricots blancs*, and various forms of *charcuterie*, using local pig meat. Desserts include the rather stodgy *far breton*, a wheatmeal pudding stuffed with dried plums; more delectable, in season, are the strawberries of Plougastel. And everywhere there are *crêperies*, cheap restaurants or little stalls, serving thin pancakes filled maybe with ham or cheese, Breton honey or jam. The Bretons frequently accompany these with local cider, a popular drink in a region that produces no wine of its own.

NORMANDY

Springtime blossom in the apple-orchards, plump brindled dairy cows in the lush meadows, half-timbered cottages, neat hedgerows and copses, piles of creamy cheeses – this is the usual picture-postcard image of Normandy, and it is fully authentic. Few other French provinces have so strong a rural personality, or so gloriously live up to their reputation. It is a sleek, self-confident region, in some ways more similar to the pastoral south of England – say, parts of Sussex or South Devon – than it is to much of the rest of France.

Maybe this is not so surprising, seeing how close Normandy lies across the Channel, and how much its history has been intertwined with that of England since 1066 and even earlier. The Normans are among the least Latin of French peoples. Their land was heavily colonized by Scandinavians in the tenth century ('Norman' derives from 'Northman'); and this has left its imprint even today, in the looks and temperament of a people who tend to be taller than most Frenchmen, more frequently blue-eyed and fair-haired, and decidedly more stolid and phlegmatic. You could say they were not unlike the English. The weather, too, which is damp and changeable, has an English quality to it, as does the scenery. No wonder the English often feel more at home here than anywhere else in France.

The province today consists of two official regions: Upper Normandy to the east, and Lower Normandy to the west. The former, with Rouen as its capital, lies astride the Seine valley: it is an area of big towns and modern industries, an area turned towards nearby Paris, and also towards the outside world via its great port of Le Havre. But it is rich farming country, too. Wheat, sugar-beet and flax grow on the fertile chalky plateaux of the Caux district, between Rouen and the coast.

Lower Normandy stretches as far west as the great sea-girt abbey of Mont-Saint-Michel on the confines of Brittany. The Cotentin peninsula, with Cherbourg at its tip, is a giant block of granite bordered by rocky headlands. East of here, around Caen, the regional capital, is what most people would regard as quintessential Normandy – the luscious and smiling Pays d'Auge, land of cheeses, cream and cider, and the wooded *bocage* country where hedges break the gentle hills into a patchwork of small fields. Everywhere the pastures are as brilliant a green as in Ireland and more fertile. The region is of great scenic variety, too: for example, vast beech forests on the borders of Maine; and, south of Caen, the curious hilly area known, with a touch of hyperbole, as 'Norman Switzerland', where the river Orne winds between rocky escarpments. Well, not exactly the Matterhorn, but certainly picturesque in its own way.

Much of Lower Normandy was badly scarred in the epic battles of 1944. Over 200,000 buildings were destroyed and whole towns and villages wiped out. They were hurriedly rebuilt after the war, some in attractive local style, some in ugly concrete. Fortunately, plenty of the old rural architecture *has* survived, or been expertly restored – and it is among the finest and most distinctive in France. To the west, in the granite land of the Manche *département*, the houses are of local grey-pink stone. Here are hundreds of handsome manors and small châteaux, with steep gabled roofs and little pinnacled turrets. Some have a round exterior tower: this was built to contain a spiral staircase, though it gives the building the air of some feudal fortress. The Manche is the poorest part of Normandy, yet its rural housing has a remarkably stately quality; many farmhouses look quite manorial.

Further east, around Caen and Rouen, there was no

33

Normandy

local stone for building: so the traditional houses tend to be half-timbered, with cob walls, their criss-cross beams painted attractive pastel shades. As in Alsace, where there is also no stone but plenty of wood, this half-timbering was done not for aesthetic effect but out of necessity, and at the time was considered rather inferior. Only modern taste finds this building style so picturesque. It should be added that Normandy contains some of the finest and grandest abbeys and monastic buildings in France, such as the half-ruined eleventh-century abbey of Jumièges, set in a wooded loop of the Seine; and the graceful abbey of Le Bec-Hellouin, part twelfth-century, part seventeenth.

Agriculturally, Normandy is one of the richest and most varied of French provinces. Apple orchards abound, mainly in the Pays d'Auge east of Caen and in the *bocage* to its south-west: these small bitter apples are not for eating, but for making cider and Calvados. Corn is grown on the eastern plains, and vegetables (carrots and cabbages) in the Cotentin. Horses are bred in the Saint-Lô area and in the Orne. But the greatest glory of Normandy is its cattle, reared partly for slaughter but above all for the famous dairy products: over a quarter of all French beef, milk and butter comes from a province with a bare 6 per cent of France's total population.

The humid climate and the rich clayey soil make for grassy pastures of special succulence, highly suited to dairy cattle. Many country towns have a weekly cattle market, where the black-smocked farmers arrive with their staves for marshalling their beasts, and when business is over they repair to the nearest café for a glass or three of *'calva'*. Of Normandy's one million dairy cows, some 20 per cent are Friesians, but the rest are the race known as 'Norman' – smaller but sturdy creatures with sleek coats of white and brindled brown or black. Their heads are white, with black or brown patches round the eyes like spectacles. They give a creamy milk high in fat content, ideally suited for making butter and fatty cheeses such as Camembert.

Normandy milk has a wide range of outlets. It is sold fresh, mainly by big cooperatives; it goes to make yoghurt, or the delicious slightly salty Normandy butter, regarded by some as the world's finest; and it provides the fresh cream that is used so liberally in the local cuisine. But its noblest use is for Normandy's famous cheeses, notably Pont l'Evêque, Livarot, and the ubiquitous Camembert. Of these, the first two date from the thirteenth century or before: the Plantagenets used to stock them in the cellars of their castles both in Normandy and England, and Livarot is even mentioned in the *Roman de la Rose*. Pont l'Evêque, square-shaped, a creamy cheese rather milder than Camembert, is made in the Pays d'Auge and named after a town there. Livarot, called after a village south of Lisieux, is an astonishing

Half-timbered houses, like this one in the Pays d'Auge, are characteristic of central and eastern Normandy.

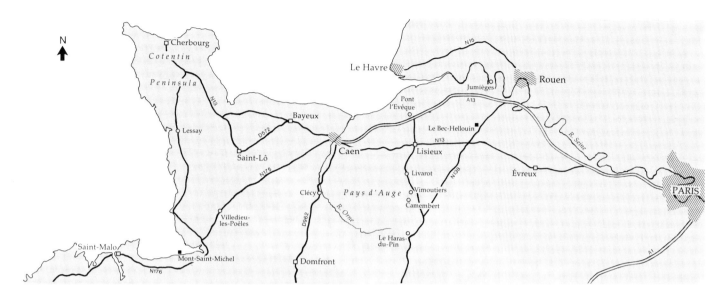

cheese, orange-coloured, pungent and aromatic. Its potent smell and flavour make it something of an acquired taste, and it is not exported much, though the Normans are very fond of it. However, Livarot today is actually less pungent than in the old days, due to a shift in public taste towards milder cheeses. Is this decadence? Maybe not, for one factor is that most people in pre-war days were too poor to eat much meat, so Livarot was often a main course: now that meat is the main dish, there is less demand for a strong cheese to give a meal weight. An intriguing footnote for the sociologists of cheese.

The parvenu Camembert was allegedly created in the late eighteenth century by a farmer's wife in the village of that name south of Vimoutiers (Pays d'Auge) where a

Pont l'Evêque is a soft cheese with a creamy texture which is made in a square shape.

Normandy

statue of her now stands. Legend has it that a priest she was hiding during the Revolution gave her the recipe. Today, Camembert accounts for half of Normandy's cheese output. It comes mainly from the Pays d'Auge and from the south of the Orne *département*, where Domfront houses the world's largest cheese factory (so it is claimed), fully automated, turning out 350,000 Camemberts a day. A visit to any Camembert factory is hard on the nostrils, for there is a stench of ammonia; and the Normans who work here all day in the warm humidity of a Turkish bath, constantly churning, ladling, shoving, packaging, have what seems a tougher job than a worker in a noisy modern car plant. As with Roquefort, the crucial ingredient for the Camembert is penicillin, without which it would remain just any mild cream cheese, lacking that unique ripe odour which the poet Léon-Paul Lafargue compared to 'the feet of the Lord' (*'les pieds de Dieu'*). Well, unwashed feet, anyway, divine or not.

Like Burgundy-type wines, Camemberts are made all over the world. But *le véritable* Camembert comes only from Normandy; and finally in 1982 the Normans won the legal right to an *appellation contrôlée* guarantee for their product that now enables them to sue any impostor, French or foreign, who tries to pass off as 'Norman' a Camembert-type cheese made elsewhere.

Camemberts are of two basic kinds: 'fresh milk', and 'pasteurized milk'. The former is much preferred by connoisseurs, for it has a stronger, earthier taste. But it varies from month to month, with the cow's milk, according to the weather and the health of the herd. The connoisseur must therefore follow these vagaries much more closely than with vintage wines, for a Camembert's life is a mere

(Above) The most famous of French cheeses, Camembert, was invented in Normandy where the 'true Camembert' is made.

(Right) An omelette Mère Poulard being prepared to the special recipe at the famous restaurant in Mont-Saint-Michel.

three weeks (freezing ruins the taste): he must be aware, for example, that this month's Camembert is an amusing but second-rate little *cru*, so better wait for next month. This does not please modern sales executives one bit.

Pasteurized milk irons out these inconsistencies, producing a blander, unvarying, predictable cheese. It is much easier to make in large quantities with modern techniques in a big factory; it is cheaper; it meets the new taste for milder cheeses; it can be exported to countries such as the United States and the United Kingdom which refuse non-pasteurized products; and it is easier to market. So no wonder that 90 per cent of Camemberts are now 'pasteurized'. The 'fresh milk' kind is made only in smaller factories, or on the farm – and, sadly, it is slowly dying out. Camembert today is a mass modern industry, and the big firms are steadily squeezing out the smaller ones and the farmer's artisanal product.

Cheese is not the only food that Normans care about. Theirs is a lavish and varied cuisine, where local cream plays a major role. Mussels, sole and other fish are stewed in cream; *escalope normande* is served in a cream-and-mushroom sauce; *poulet Vallée d'Auge* too has a sauce of cream and tiny onions; hot apple tart comes flamed in *calvados* with a jug of fresh cream to pour over it. Other specialities enjoyed by rural folk include *tripe à la mode de Caen* (cooked in cider or Calvados, with calf's foot and onions); Rouen duckling (prepared in a variety of ways, sometimes with cherries or *à l'orange*); *andouilles* (chitterlings) from Vire; and omelettes of all kinds, sometimes served sweet and *flambées* for dessert, as at the famous Mère Poulard restaurant in Mont-Saint-Michel. A copious Norman banquet will include pauses between courses when glasses of Calvados are drunk (*le trou normand*) to aid the digestion.

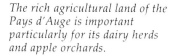

The rich agricultural land of the Pays d'Auge is important particularly for its dairy herds and apple orchards.

Normandy

In the Calvados département, *many farmhouses look more like small châteaux, with their typical pointed turrets.*

Most of Normandy today is modern, well organized, confident and (despite recent recession) very prosperous. However, the Manche *département* in the west is poorer than the rest of the province and suffers from its relative isolation. It is sometimes called 'Breton Normandy', for the scenery – notably the rocky granite coast – is more Breton than Norman. But the farming people lack the new-found dynamism of their Breton neighbours. The land here is fertile, but the livestock farms are mostly still too small to be properly viable. Farmers still endure the drudgery of having to milk and tend their cows every day of the year: generally they are too individualistic to group together and share these chores on a rota. This is a relatively backward area, suspicious, lethargic, more than a little feudal, and less influenced than most by the great modern changes of post-war rural France. It is not typical of the rest of Normandy.

In the province as a whole, country people are hard-working and hard-headed, but kindly, with a reputation for extreme prudence. They will not commit themselves easily. *'Une réponse de Norman'* is a reply that says neither 'yes' nor 'no' to a straight question. Ask a Norman if it's a fine day, and he'll say, 'Well, it could be better, but it could be worse' (or so other Frenchmen suppose). In short, the Norman shares the British penchant for under-statement, and is a very different creature from his romantic, eloquent, whimsical Celtic neighbour, the Breton. Unlike Bretons, the Normans have little surviv-ing folk culture; nor is there as much of a local dialect as in many parts of France. 'The country people don't dance and sing here, as they do in Auvergne or the Midi', com-plained one immigrant, 'they're a dour lot.' This can be explained partly by the phlegmatic Norman tempera-ment. But the lack of folk tradition may have another explanation too. In France as elsewhere, areas with a strong surviving folk-culture tend to be those which over the centuries have been colonized, or have felt them-selves 'colonized', and have thus kept up their own culture as a means of preserving their identity.

This is as true of Bretons, Basques, Alsatians, as of, say, Irish or Slovenes. But the proud Normans have never been colonized (at least, not since the tenth century when the Northern invaders were quickly assimilated). On the contrary, they have long been a race of colonizers and traders, focused on the big world outside. So they have felt less need to preserve their own culture.

However, there do still exist a few old Norman folk-songs and costumes; and today a younger generation, mostly city students as usual, are attempting to revive them. In this milieu, *'le bal-folk'* (with traditional music and dresses) is becoming popular. Some old handicrafts are also being kept alive, such as copper-work at Ville-dieu-les-Poêles. This town's name (*poêle* means 'stove') indicates its history as a centre of kitchen copperware; and today it has a museum devoted to this. Clécy, south of Caen, contains a small museum of Norman folklore. All over Normandy there are country fairs in summer – notably the Foire de Sainte-Croix at Lessay (Manche) in September – where the farmers buy and sell their horses, sheep and cattle, followed by much eating and drinking. But these fairs have a solid practical basis; this is not a province of riotous carnival for its own sake.

Horses and Horse-breeding

Normandy is well placed to profit from the recent boom in horse-riding sports in France, for since the eighteenth century this has been the principal French breeding-ground for horses, due to the richness of its grazing pastures. One-third of all French horses are born in Lower Normandy. The breeding is done by small private owners, but is closely supervised by the state *haras* (stud-farms) which belong to the Ministry of Agriculture. These own and loan out the stallions and strictly control the genetic quality of all breeding: any foal born without their seal of approval is virtually worthless. It is a typical example of French *étatisme* (state ubiquity).

The *haras* were set up under Louis XIV, mainly to meet the needs of the Army's cavalry. Today, virtually the only horses they supply direct to the state are those for the 450-strong troupe of the ceremonial Garde Républicaine. But there are still 23 state *haras* across France; and two of the biggest are in Lower Normandy, at Saint-Lô and Le Haras-du-Pin. They are palatial establishments, with château-like stables set around a wide *cour d'honneur*. In fact, Le Haras-du-Pin is known as 'the horses' Versailles', for it was grandly designed by Louis XIV's architect, Mansart. Here the daily ritual of exercising the 100 or so stallions is an impressive sight, which visitors can watch. At Saint-Lô in summer there are weekly riding and driving displays, also open to the public.

Le Pin's speciality is English-style racing thoroughbreds (*les pur-sang anglais*). Saint-Lô's 150 stallions are more varied: some *pur-sang*, but also trotters, saddle-horses and ponies for riding clubs, and farm and cart-horses. Normandy horses are reputed for their gracefulness, longevity and toughness: the mares sleep out at night even in winter. February to July is the mating season, when the *haras'* stallions go the rounds of the local breeders (1,800 of them in the Saint-Lô area, most with just two or three mares). Each stallion will 'cover' up to 60 mares annually but the rest of the year he spends alone tethered in his stall at Saint-Lô, and is given little exercise.

After the war, horses appeared to be a dying species in France, as they were no longer needed by the Army, nor by the farms which were then rapidly mechanizing. The horse population, down to 80,000 in 1960, has since risen to 350,000. This has been due above all to the new French passion for sporting activities, notably those of a back-to-nature kind: the numbers of people who belong to riding-clubs or join riding excursions have risen tenfold since 1972, to 300,000.

The famous stud-farm of Le Haras-du-Pin is one of the largest in France.

Normandy/The Apple Industry

Cider and Calvados in Normandy are made from smallish, bitter apples, green, yellow and red, which are not very suitable for eating.

According to Dr Raymond Dumay, in his excellent book *Guide des Alcools* (Stock, 1973), Calvados owes everything to wartime, including even its name.

It seems that the monks from Ireland were the first to plant apple trees in Normandy in the sixth century, while they were creating the famous abbeys and religious orders such as Caen, Bayeux and Rouen. By the time of Charlemagne (A.D. 800), the growing of apples and the production of cider had become so important that certain controls were imposed on pruning, grafting and cider-pressing. Following the conquest of England by William the Conqueror in the middle of the eleventh century, Normandy eventually passed under English tutelage, and while the production of cider continued, it was not until 1553 that mention is made of an *eau-de-vie de cidre*. This received its name from the *département* of Calvados, so called after one of the ships from Spain's Invincible Armada (*El Calvador*), which went down off the Normandy coast in 1558.

It was not, however, until the First World War that Calvados became a part of French life: the troops from Normandy and Brittany arrived at the trenches with their flasks filled with the local *eau-de-vie*, and assured for Calvados a recognition that it had never acquired in the restaurants and dining rooms of France. Later, the exodus from the countryside to Paris in the 1920s and 1930s

caused the *café-calva* (black coffee brightened up with a good measure of young Calvados, designed to get one, or keep one, going in the morning) to become *de rigueur* in certain sections of the city. Finally, the advent of World War II gave both the Germans and the Allies a taste for the cider-based *eau-de-vie*, thereby creating an export market for the future.

The centre of production of quality Calvados is to be found in the Pays d'Auge, stretching across three *départements*: Calvados, Orne and Eure. This is also the countryside well known for its Normandy butter and the famous cheeses Livarot, Pont l'Evêque and Camembert. Apple orchards and grazing cattle are the most common sights in Normandy.

Calvados is made from the distillation of cider, made from apples, and in rare cases *poiré* made from pears. The fruit is crushed and pressed, and the juice extracted must ferment for at least a month to produce a cider or perry of at least 4° alcohol. Then comes the distillation into *eau-de-vie* which is generally better the longer it takes. Calvados du Pays d'Auge (the only Calvados to have an *appellation contrôlée*, the other regions being simply *appellations reglementées*) has to use an alambic of the Cognac type, whereby distillation takes place in two stages, permitting the 'heads and tails' of the first distillation to be removed before the final distillation of the *coeur* (heart) of the *eau-de-vie*. The ten other *appellations reglementées* Calvados, of which the best is the Calvados du Domfrontais, may use a continuous still, although to make a finer quality, they are encouraged to use the two-stage alambics.

The majority of Calvados is drunk young, and in Paris or locally this means in the twelve months after it has been distilled. However, as the image of Calvados has improved from something used for *flambé*-ing to that of an after-dinner *digestif*, demand is on the increase for aged Calvados of superior quality. Ageing generally takes place in very large casks, often holding several thousand litres, and sometimes in smaller barrels of 250-600 litres. The longer the time it is left in cask, the more colour the Calvados will take on and the more alcohol it will lose. Thus, a genuine 50-year-old *eau-de-vie* will be darker in colour and softer on the palate than one of ten years. Young Calvados almost always have colouring agents and distilled water added to them to achieve the same effect.

Very few Calvados carry the date of the year the apples were picked. The government has passed a law that forbids the vintaging of Cognac, leaving Armagnac and Calvados the only *eaux-de-vie* that may carry a date. The farmers in the *départements* of the south-west where Armagnac is produced have for many years kept a part of their harvest separate, to be sold as an unblended vintage. Stocks of vintage Armagnac are rare and command a considerable price, to the extent that a *vigneron*'s daughter is judged as much on the years of *eau-de-vie* in the family cellar as on her looks! The demand for vintage Calvados being relatively recent, there are very few old vintages. Often, the exact age of the barrels will have been lost, the blends being described as 'Réserve Ancestrale' or 'Vieille Réserve', and if there is an age mentioned, it is usually rounded off to fifteen, twenty-five or fifty years, to indicate the approximate age.

The Normandy cuisine being very rich, based as it is on the local butter and cream, Calvados is often proposed in the middle of a lengthy meal. This is known as *le trou Normand*, a shot of not-too-young Calvados, served in between the two meat courses, and drunk straight to clean and refresh the system. Many Paris restaurants have copied this idea, replacing the *eau-de-vie* with a sorbet. A good Normand would not approve.

Calvados is uniquely Normand, and has not been copied. This is because it comes exclusively from cider apples or pears that flourish in a soil too rich, and a climate too northerly, for the vine. Young and fruity, old and subtle, Calvados should always keep the distinctive flavour of the fruit from which it comes.

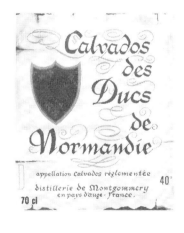

Apple trees are a familiar and pleasing feature of the Normandy landscape.

PICARDY

Prosperous Picardy is a region of large grain and sugar-beet farms, stretching for miles across gently rolling plains between the Paris basin to the south and the Lille industrial area to the north. The long straight roads are lined with poplars, planted originally to give shade to horsemen and infantry. But the landscape is not monotonous, for Picardy is also a land of forest and waterway. The plains are intersected by fertile valleys – notably the Somme, Oise and Aisne – where the winding rivers abound in fish and are bordered with market gardens. The numerous forests of beech and oak (Compiègne is the best known) were formerly royal hunting preserves; today they belong to the French state and are open to the public. Here the visitor can hire a horse or bicycle, or even a horse-drawn carriage, and go for long rides along the well-tended woodland tracks. To the west, astride the Somme estuary, Picardy's coastline is short, flat and not especially scenic, but does offer some surprises: at the Marquenterre bird sanctuary, France's largest outside the Camargue, over 300 species live amid the sand dunes and the reedy lagoons.

The Picardy farmer is at the opposite extreme from the cliché stereotype of the backward French peasant smallholder. Mechanization – the replacement of horses and handploughs by tractors and harvesters – began here earlier than in other parts of France, long before World War II; and today some farms are of over 1,000 acres, huge by French standards. Mostly they are very efficient, with wheat, maize, barley, sugar-beet and potatoes as their main produce. Much of the barley goes to supply the big breweries of the nearby Nord; the sugar-beet is sold to Picardy's numerous sugar-mills; and many of the potatoes are processed into starch in local factories. There is even a plant making potato crisps. In short, modern food-processing techniques using local produce are more highly developed here than in most parts of France; and a farmer can generally earn more money from these outlets than from selling his produce on the market for fresh consumption.

Yet Picardy farming is not all large-scale crop-growing.

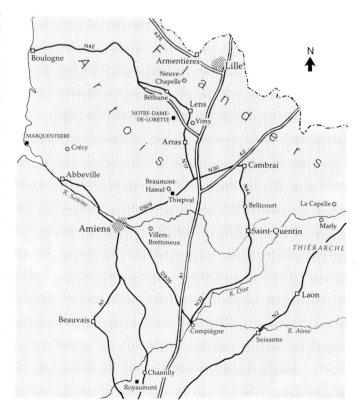

Picardy

The river Marne winding through a landscape of low wooded hills and pastures in the south-eastern corner of Picardy.

In the west, around Abbeville, the low hilly *bocage* country with its little dairy farms and apple-orchards resembles adjacent Normandy. And beside the Somme in the eastern suburbs of Amiens are the curious *hortillonnages*, a network of little canals enclosing market gardens of vegetables, flowers and herbs. Until recently this was a real market-on-the-water, where the growers sold their produce from small barges, as in Bangkok. A few of these boat-shops survive, as a tourist attraction: but they have largely been replaced by big vans on dry ground, less picturesque but more practical.

For a region so rich in agriculture, Picardy has remarkably little gastronomic tradition, apart from a few delicacies such as tripe soup, duck *pâtés*, and *ficelle picards* (a crêpe with ham and a mushroom sauce). Like many northerners, the Picard country people are hard-working, practical, reserved, a bit dour: but their latent *joie-de-vivre* does come alive at carnival times. The most colourful summer carnivals are those in the towns, such as Amiens, Beauvais, Saint-Quentin. But some villages too retain their costumed fêtes: for example, the annual cheese fair at La Capelle.

In the west of the region, much of the rural architecture consists of small half-timbered houses with cob walls, enlivened maybe with flowers and creepers – again, rather Norman. To the south, within the orbit of Paris, is a forested land dotted with grand châteaux and abbeys bearing famous names – Compiègne, Chantilly, Royaumont. In the north-east, towards the Belgian frontier, the hilly zone of the Thiérarche has verdant pastures and apple orchards used for cider, and is known above all for its unusual fortified churches, some 60 in all. From the twelfth to the seventeenth century, invading and marauding armies repeatedly passed this way; so, for protection, the villagers turned their handsome turretted red-brick churches virtually into fortresses – and a remarkable sight they are.

On the fertile plain of northern Picardy, between Amiens and Saint-Quentin, the larger farms are handsome brick buildings, each set around a wide courtyard. But this was an area that suffered terribly in the Somme battles of World War I. A few farms managed to survive, others were carefully restored in local style. But the villages, many of them totally destroyed, were hastily rebuilt in the early 1920s in an ugly utilitarian style and have lost their true Picard character. Across the centuries, in fact, Picardy has seen more than its share of wars and invasions. For example, at Crécy near Abbeville a memorial records the battle where England defeated France in 1346. And in the forest of Compiègne is the famous clearing where the Armistice of November 1918 was signed in a railway carriage.

War Graves

Today, the fields of Picardy, Artois and Flanders are smiling and peaceful; the grain grows high, the poppies bloom. Yet it is hard to escape constant reminders of the insane horror of World War I, for every two or three miles in this corner of France the visitor will come across some neatly-tended cemetery of Allied or German war dead, and here and there a soaring hilltop memorial. Of the Commonwealth War Graves Commission's 2,900 cemeteries in France, containing the graves or memorials of 575,000 dead, the vast majority are north of the Somme between Amiens and Cambrai, and further north around Arras, Béthune and Armentières, while 205,000 others lie buried across the Belgian border around Ypres. A visit to these cemeteries and memorials is a sobering experience.

In that long and cruel war of the trenches, much of the worst fighting took place on the rolling high ground north of the Somme, where British and Empire troops attacked *en masse* in July 1916 and lost thousands of dead for every hundred yards they pushed back the German line. Here on a hilltop at Thiepval there now stands the largest British memorial, designed by Sir Edwin Lutyens and unveiled in 1932: set on 16 masonry piers, it is a massive red-brick arch rising 150 feet skywards. The site of Thiepval was chosen mainly because this hill was the strongest and most obstinately defended of all the German positions in the Somme area, and the battles here were among the bloodiest. Engraved on the memorial are the names of 73,000 British troops who fell in the area but have no known graves.

Three miles to the north is the Newfoundland Regiment's memorial park at Beaumont-Hamel, watched over by a statue of a caribou. Here many of the original trenches have been preserved; also the twisted skeleton of the so-called 'Danger Tree', isolated on a slope where German shrapnel was especially deadly.

On 1 July 1916, the German trenches were attacked by 801 Newfoundlanders; by the next day, all but 68 of them were dead or wounded. The attack failed, under withering German fire. 'It was a magnificent display of trained valour', wrote a senior officer afterwards, 'its assault failed because dead men can advance no further.'

Of the Allied dead with no known graves, Australian soldiers have a memorial at Villers-Bretonneux east of Amiens; Indians are commemorated at Neuve-Chapelle and New Zealanders at Longueval, while at Bellincourt, beside the Cambrai-Saint-Quentin road, is a cenotaph paying tribute to the United States Army's attack on the Hindenburg Line in 1918. But the most majestic, and possibly the most moving, of all the Allied memorials in the region is the famous Canadian one at Vimy Ridge, on a hill above the coal-mining basin north of Arras. Three Canadian divisions seized this ridge, at terrible cost, in April 1917. The memorial consists of 16,500 tonnes of stone and concrete, and was unveiled in 1936 by King Edward VIII. Its two towering stelae of white stone, 'erected by the people of Canada, in memory of its 60,000 dead', are flanked by sculptures of weeping, pensive women, including the figure of Canada brooding over the graves of her brave dead. Other sculptures are of guns shrouded in olive and laurel. Close by, the Canadian dug-outs and trenches have been carefully preserved, and can be visited.

Just to the north is the French military mausoleum of Notre-Dame-de-Lorette. Nearby, beside the Arras-Béthune road, is a huge German cemetery with neat rows of little black crosses; Allied cemeteries, in contrast, tend to have white tombstones. Well over 60 years later, these thousands of cemeteries are still kept in beautiful condition, thanks to the patient work of the various national war graves commissions. Many graves bear wreaths and flowers, and are still visited by the families of the fallen.

(Above) The British war memorial at Thiepval.

(Right) The cemetery at Delville Wood near Longueval.

ILE-DE-FRANCE

In the early Middle Ages the heartland of royal France was the area bounded by the rivers Marne, Seine and Oise, which thus came to be known as the 'Isle' of France, for people in those days regarded anywhere girt by water as an island. Today, the Ile-de-France 'region' covers eight *départements*, running from west of Versailles to south of Fontainebleau, and eastwards into the lush Brie country. The Ile-de-France, with Paris at its centre, is a shallow limestone basin ringed with big forests of oak and beech – 'the lungs of Paris' they are sometimes called, for they help to purify the air of this heavily industrial area.

Most of the region is flat and unattractive. The Paris conurbation of ten million people has spread itself across the plain in ever-widening rings – first the inter-war rash of unplanned *pavillons*, little ugly bungalows with untidy gardens in what are now the inner suburbs; then the post-war developments, the vast high-rise dormitories of cheap 'social' housing, and the smarter estates of California-style villas and flats with their private tennis courts and swimming pools. New motorways and ring-roads cut through the cornfields, and the air hums with jets to-ing and fro-ing from the Orly and Roissy/Charles-de-Gaulle airports. But the Ile-de-France has not lost all of its picturesque charm. Here, ancient half-ruined abbeys such as Royaumont stand beside quiet-flowing streams, and majestic châteaux overlook ornate parks – Versailles, Fontainebleau and many lesser ones, too. It is a region of prettily wooded valleys, such as the Chevreuse, where Parisians on summer Sundays go out for picnics and fishing and boating expeditions – albeit that today they go bumper-to-tail in their cohorts of Renaults and Peugeots, rather than on bicycles as in the romantic age

typified by Jean Renoir's film *Partie de campagne*.

The great forests used to be royal hunting grounds, full of deer. Today, the largest are in State hands, open to the public, and are finely maintained. Much of the wood is used for furniture. Fontainebleau (see pp. 52–3) and Rambouillet are two of the main forests, together with Compiègne which lies just across the region's border in Picardy. Agriculture is still important in the Ile-de-France, despite the urban sprawl. The south-west of the region includes part of the rich wheat-plain of the Beauce, round Chartres. Nearer Paris there is much market gardening – watercress, asparagus, cauliflowers and white beans. Even within the Paris urban belt, mushrooms are cultivated, and cut flowers such as orchids, while the eastern part of the region produces one of France's noblest cheeses, Brie. There are even just a few vineyards, too, at Suresnes and Argenteuil in the north-west suburbs, yielding some unremarkable white and rosé wines for local consumption. The Ile-de-France no longer has gastronomic specialities of its own, but the restaurants of greater Paris offer a dazzling range of dishes from all over the world.

Local cuisine may have little tradition here, but the same is certainly not true of another art at which the French have long excelled: painting. While some of France's great artists have opted for sunny Provence, many others have spent at least part of their lives in the Paris region, attracted by its subtleties of light and its pastoral landscapes. Since Corot's day, the village of Barbizon in the forest of Fontainebleau has been an important centre for painters. In the 1870s, many leading Impressionists and post-Impressionists who had first lived in Paris began to move out to work in the nearby

Ile-de-France

countryside. Pissarro and Cézanne went to Pontoise. Renoir and Monet preferred Bougival, a pretty village on the Seine just west of Paris, where they produced some of their most evocative paintings of boating parties and outdoor riverside cafés full of pretty girls. Renoir also painted further upstream at Argenteuil, but he would not recognize that place today. Sisley, the English Impressionist, spent the last part of his life at Moret on the river Loing, near Fontainebleau: here he painted some of his best-known landscapes, and here he died in poverty in 1899. A sense of tragedy also haunts Auvers-sur-Oise, north-west of Paris, for here the deranged Van Gogh spent his final months, before shooting himself in 1890. He died in the inn now called the 'Van Gogh' and is buried in the cemetery nearby.

Since the war, the population of greater Paris has risen from five to ten million, and new suburbs have spread on every side. Some villages have become totally engulfed and have lost their old rural character: in such places, glossy blocks of flats and modern shopping centres stand on what was farmland only twenty years ago, and the old village with its little shops is almost forgotten. Some local mayors welcome this new urbanization for the extra trade and prosperity it brings, but others try to resist it. Crespières, for instance, north-west of Versailles, has managed to retain its village ambiance, but some commuters have come in, too, so it is the kind of place – typical of many such – where two very different lifestyles coexist. The mayor, Jean Perrochon, is a prosperous local wheat farmer. He says: 'Some places round here have been ruined by hasty, ill-planned growth, but here we decided to prevent this. True, our population has risen since 1945 from 600 to 1,500, but we allow no new buildings of more than two storeys. Lots of engineers, executives and others have built villas here, and they commute to their jobs in the modern businesses of western Paris. These newcomers get on easily with the old villagers, and we're a small enough community to have kept much of the old rural warmth. But, of course, some things have changed. There's a big new supermarket nearby, so most of our little local groceries and other local shops have closed. Also we now have only three cafés, compared with seven in 1950. People are losing the café-going habit. They'd rather stay at home and watch television.'

Despite the urban sprawl there are still many charming places to visit. Maisons-Laffitte, north of Saint-Germain, contains the leading horse-racing and training stables in France, housed in the outbuildings of a classic seventeenth-century château. Enghien-les-Bains, in the messy north-west suburbs, has the only casino in the Paris region, standing beside a lake. By French law casinos are allowed only in spa towns or resorts, so it is not surprising that this one has a bigger turnover than almost any other in France. Nearby Sannois, a conical hill with fine views over the north Paris plain, is a proletarian excursion centre where, as Michelin quaintly puts it, *"les couples joyeux assiègent les dancings et les guingettes"*.

Out to the west, near Meulan, the safari park at Thoiry claims to be the first imitator of Whipsnade or Longleat on the Continent. Much odder still is the Vallée des Peaux-Rouges (Redskin valley) at Fleurines, near Senlis, where the French act out cowboy-and-indian fantasies as an escape from the strains of city living. Two local men took over a dusty little gorge and deserted quarry that could just about pass for Nebraska, filled the hollow with wigwams, rodeo bulls and bison imported from the United States, then on the upper ridge built a mock-Western 'Fleurines City' complete with le saloon, le trading-post and le sherriff office (sic). It is a kind of

The château of Vaux-le-Vicomte, south-east of Paris, was the model for Versailles.

49

Ile-de-France

funfair open to the public, where the staff wear stetsons but – alas – are more likely to be drinking Pernod than moonshine. Here, members of Le Paris Western Club will sometimes provide dramatic entertainment, re-enacting the sagas of Doc Miller and Buffalo Bill. You may even be lucky to find a troupe including a Citroën car-worker doing a spirited Sioux dance in full war-paint, and you might meet the club's oddest member, a Parisienne ex-concierge who has literally turned herself into a Sioux, living most of the year in her Sioux wigwam and eating boiled maize with her fingers: 'When I wear European clothes, I feel in disguise.'

Leaving such frivolities aside, the main appeal of the Ile-de-France to many visitors resides in its many majestic châteaux and abbeys. Versailles and Fontaine-bleau are too well-known to call for further description; and anyway they are both on the edge of big towns, so can hardly be said to belong to 'rural France'. Among other châteaux, pride of place should go to Vaux-le-Vicomte, near Melun, built in 1660 by Fouquet, a Superintendent of Finance under Louis XIV. Its most notable feature is the garden, designed by Le Nôtre, the man who invented the formal style of French garden that later found its highest expression at Versailles. Here at Vaux the garden consists of a classic geometry of lawns, avenues, statues, fountains and rectangular pools. Le Nôtre also laid out the formal park at Sceaux, just south of Paris, where the château now contains an interesting museum of the folk-culture of the Ile-de-France.

The château of Rambouillet, between Versailles and Chartres, has been the President of the Republic's official summer residence since 1897, and is open to the public when he is absent. It is an imposing building with pinnacled towers, set in a formal park, in one corner of which is a national sheep-rearing farm. Parts of the château date from the fourteenth century. East of here, the

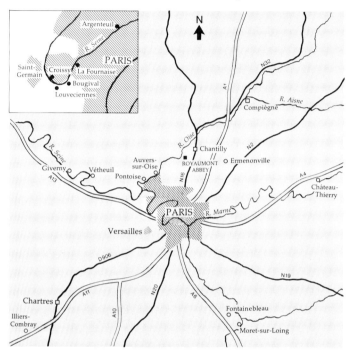

Sunset over the little town of Pierrefonds, on the edge of the Forest of Compiègne.

(Opposite) The church of Longvilliers near Rochefort-en-Yvelines.

sixteenth-century château of Dampierre stands in a tranquil setting of lakes and woodlands, and is surrounded by a moat of running water; here again the garden is by Le Nôtre. Pierrefonds, over to the north-east of Paris, towards Compiègne, is a vast medieval structure, heavily restored by Viollet-le-Duc in the nineteenth century.

Of the abbeys of the Paris region, probably the most celebrated historically is – or was – Port-Royal, in the Chevreuse valley, first founded as a Cistercian convent in 1204. In the seventeenth century it became famous as the headquarters of the Jansenist religious community. Today little is left of the abbey but a few ruins, amid a lovely sylvan setting. North-east of Paris, Chaâlis is a thirteenth-century Cistercian abbey, also largely ruined, but beautifully set beside a lake in a forest. Close by is a desert area known as the 'sea of sand', now turned into an amusement park with a small zoo. It was here in the forest of Ermenonville that a Turkish airliner crashed in 1974, killing over 300 people – the worst air disaster in post-war France. The eighteenth-century château of Ermenonville is associated with the philosopher Jean-Jacques Rousseau, who died here in 1778 and was buried on the small 'island of poplars' in a corner of the park; later his remains were moved to the Panthéon in Paris.

Lastly, the distinguished Cistercian abbey of Royaumont lies in pretty country by a stream, west of Chantilly. This fine Gothic structure was built in the thirteenth century by Louis IX, later canonized as Saint Louis, and was a major religious and cultural community through the Middle Ages and until the Revolution. Then it suffered badly and parts of it were used as a cotton factory. The abbey itself is partly in ruins, but its adjacent monastery, now in private hands, has been carefully restored and is the home of one of Europe's leading cultural centres – a kind of country club for artists, scholars and scientists. The place is so idyllic that it is worth recommending to any organization wanting a venue near Paris for a conference; or, if you are engaged in creative or academic work, you can stay as an individual. Royaumont is also open to visits by tourists.

Ile-de-France/Fontainebleau

Favourite hunting ground of French rulers from Saint Louis to Napoleon III, the forest of Fontainebleau is for over eight million hikers, rock climbers and strollers who visit it each year, one of the lungs of Paris. Like Paris, too, it has its Grands Boulevards, Avenues and cross-roads, many of them straight as a ruler and all identified, like city streets, with metal name-plaques nailed to the trees. Some were created long ago, like the Route Ronde which Henri IV traced in a great semi-circle around the château of Fontainebleau itself. But many are nineteenth-century creations, the work of Claude-François Denecourt (1788-1875). Denecourt devoted a lifetime to studying the forest and making it easier to explore; between 1844 and his death he created 169 kilometres of signposted trails. The work was continued by his successor Colinet, who added 100 more kilometres, and today the whole vast network is maintained by voluntary associations and the Office National des Forêts.

The forest is immense, stretching 20 kilometres north-south from Melun to Nemours, 25 kilometres east-west from Moret to Milly-la-Forêt. Apart from the trees, mainly oak, beech and pine, its attraction lies in long broken chains of curiously shaped sandstone rocks which run roughly from east to west and are much used as a training ground by rock-climbers. By the time Denecourt began to explore the forest, its beauties were already known to many painters, and the tradition linking it to French artistic life had begun.

Then in the 1830s a group of neo-classical painters began to frequent the *pension* kept by Monsieur Ganne in the forest hamlet of Barbizon. By 1835 they had been followed by the two painters who were to immortalize the Barbizon school, Théodore Rousseau (1812-67) and Jean-François Millet (1815-75). Both of them are buried in the cemetery of the village of Chailly-en-Bière, outside which Millet painted his *Angelus* in 1857. Their houses, like the *pension* of *Le père Ganne*, can still be seen.

Ganne offered simple fare and lodgings. At first his inn had only two upstairs rooms, later there were quarters beside the garden. Ganne had only limited confidence in his customers' solvency and obliged them to hand over their money on arrival. The fastidious Goncourt brothers were not impressed by conditions *chez Ganne* and complained of 'the monotony of the omelettes, the stains on the tablecloth, and the tin fork that soils the hands'. They lived a simple, rigorous life, rising at dawn and setting off into the forest to sketch (they were not 'open-air painters'; they made sketches and drawings which were later 'arranged' in the studio). They dined early and by nine everyone was asleep. Their poverty was such that the sculptor Carpeaux, who wore ostentatious rings, was taken for a police informer when he arrived on a visit to Rousseau. Millet kept a garden to help feed his wife and nine children. A notable exception was Rosa Bonheur (1822-99) who bought a château near the forest at Le By where, in order to study animals from nature, she kept dogs, cats, cows, and sheep, as well as a yak, a gazelle, monkeys, an eagle, and a lion.

In spring 1863 a new generation of young painters appeared in the forest with the first visit of Monet, Renoir and Frédéric Bazille. They disliked Millet and never stayed at Barbizon, preferring the slightly more comfortable conditions at the *Cheval Blanc* or the *Lion d'Or* at Chailly. They returned several times in the 1860s. Renoir was in the habit of walking the 60 kilometres from Paris in two stages, dossing down overnight in a stable or haystack. It was in the forest of Fontainebleau that he exclaimed, referring to the new practice of painting landscape out of doors, 'Landscape painting is a sport!' Certainly his own life at Fontainebleau was adventurous enough. One time he saved from arrest an opposition

(Left) The château of Fontainebleau.

(Right) August Renoir, Portrait du peintre Bazille.

(Far right) Frédéric Bazille, Portrait de Renoir.

journalist, Raoul Rigaut, who was being hunted by the Imperial police. Later Rigaut repaid the debt during the Commune when Renoir, painting by the Seine, was himself arrested on suspicion of spying on the defences of Paris. It was at Chailly that Bazille painted his *Ambulance Improvisée* in which Monet, who had injured his leg, is seen recumbent in a sickbay rigged up for him by the former medical student Bazille. Monet's final stay at Chailly ended when, not for the first time, he did a moonlight flit from a hotel. Among the works he left behind was the incomplete *Déjeuner sur l'herbe*, the most ambitious undertaking of his early period. Years later, eaten away by mildew, it was rediscovered by the painter who cut out and preserved the intact parts, one of which would eventually find its way to the Louvre.

After 1865, the painters who had not yet been labelled 'Impressionists' abandoned Chailly and stayed at Marlotte, further south. Renoir commemorated one of their stays in this small village in his painting *Le Cabaret de la Mère Anthony,* which shows Sisley, Pissarro, Bazille, Cézanne, *la mère Anthony,* and Nana the maid. By the early 1870s they had turned their attention to the north-western outskirts of Paris, except for Sisley, the only Impressionist who did not achieve recognition in his lifetime. He lived in poverty at Moret after the Franco-Prussian War brought ruin to the family business which had provided him with the means and leisure to paint.

Nevertheless, the forest continued to attract painters.

In 1872, out of the 300 inhabitants of Barbizon, 100 were artists. Robert Louis Stevenson, who first visited Barbizon early in 1875, later described the painters' communities there and in the surrounding area. 'Palizzi bore rule at Grez,' he wrote, and Cernay had 'the admirable, placid Pelouse'; only Barbizon, since the recent death of Millet, was a 'headless commonwealth'.

The forest's links with the arts continued after the decline of the Barbizon school. For 25 years the poet Stéphane Mallarmé spent his holidays near the Pont de Valvins where he died in 1898. Katherine Mansfield, in search of a doctor who 'could dominate and discipline her will' in 1922 joined the community founded at La Prieuré in Fontainebleau by the magnetic Gurdjieff. After enduring spartan conditions, she died of tuberculosis on 9 January 1923. Other twentieth-century artists associated with the forest include Jean Cocteau, who lived at Milly-la-Forêt, and the gypsy guitar king Django Reinhardt, who died at Samois in 1953. The area forms a vivid background setting to Patricia Highsmith's novel *Ripley's Game.*

But for the crowds of walkers who every Saturday and Sunday morning in the year pour from the train at Bois-le-Roi and Fontainebleau, the last word lies with Stevenson: 'Our society . . . was full of high spirits, of laughter, and of the initiative of youth. . . . We returned from long stations in the fortifying air, our spirits refreshed by the silence of the forest.'

Ile-de-France/Writers and Artists

Impressionism was born in the western and north-western suburbs of Paris at the time when the city was beginning to spill out into the surrounding villages from the walls and *faubourgs* which had long contained it. Both in their movements and in their paintings, the Impressionists recorded this westward expansion in the late nineteenth century. After returning from England where he had fled the Franco-Prussian War, Monet settled at Argenteuil, then further west at Vétheuil. In 1888 he found the farmhouse at Giverny near the confluence of the little river Epte and the Seine where he lived until his death in 1926. Pissarro, the 'wise old man' of Impressionism, worked at Louveciennes near Versailles. When he returned from England in 1871 he found that his studio had been pillaged by Prussian soldiers and many of his canvases destroyed. From there he moved out to Pontoise where he spent the next ten years. It was cheaper than living in Paris, but even so he gardened and raised chickens and rabbits to help support his family of seven children. Sisley painted at Marly before moving out definitively to Moret-sur-Loing.

By the late 1860s and early 1870s, Argenteuil, Bougival, Croissy and other villages and islands in the Seine valley had become a playground for the Parisians – bathing, sculling, picnicking and roistering. This part of the countryside was accessible to the crowds because it was served by the Paris-Saint-Germain railway. *Guinguettes,* riverside cabaret-bars, flourished. Two of them in particular are remembered. La Grenouillère was a floating café on a pontoon moored to the bank in a backwater of the Seine at the island of Croissy. Here Monet and Renoir set up their easels side by side in the late 1860s, taking rapid notes of the strollers and reflections in the water. La Fournaise, 2 kilometres upstream, was much frequented by Renoir in the late 1870s, and provided the setting for his scene of scullers enjoying the pleasures of outdoor life, *Le Déjeuner des canotiers.*

Argenteuil, when Monet settled there around 1872, was a village of 8,000 people. It had been recommended to him by the well-to-do Manet, whose family had an estate across the Seine at Gennevilliers. Monet rented a riverside house from the widow of a Paris notary, and there painted his home and his family, the village, the river, and the joys of life on it and its banks. One day in 1874 Manet painted him in the little boat he had fitted out as a studio on the Seine; the riverbank in the foreground is verdant, but beyond, on the far side of the river, factory chimneys can be seen belching smoke.

In 1890, at Giverny, Monet bought a strip of marshland across the road from his house, and in the following year, diverting the stream which flowed through it, began to create a water garden, starting with a little pond. Soon weeping willows, iris and bamboo were growing round the pool, clusters of lilies floated in it, and a Japanese bridge crossed it. 'I took time in understanding my water-lilies . . . I planted them for pleasure, I cultivated them without thinking of painting them . . . And then suddenly I had the revelation of the delights of my pond.

Camille Pissarro, Femme dans un enclos.

(Opposite) Monet's house at Giverny.

I took my palette . . . Since then I have scarcely had any other model.' This lotus land which Monet painted for over twenty years became the *Nymphéas,* the huge murals which can be seen today in two oval rooms of the Orangerie of the Tuileries and which have earned the museum the name 'the Sistine Chapel of Impressionism'.

Not only painters found the upper Seine valley a cheaper, less distracting workplace than the capital. In the late 1870s Zola bought a cottage at Médan and used it as his principal residence for the rest of his life, although he kept up his contacts in the city and confessed that he missed its tittle-tattle.

A few kilometres away at Pontoise, Cézanne spent the winter of 1872 painting with Pissarro, then moved upstream to Auvers-sur-Oise. Here was the weekend house of Doctor Gachet, an artist himself and friend and host of the Impressionists. Pissarro introduced Van Gogh to Gachet, and it was at Gachet's house that Van Gogh shot himself in a fit of despair on 27 July 1890, while the doctor was absent. He died two days later in a room of the café Ravoux, and is buried in the village cemetery.

Ermenonville, north of Paris, is noted for its associations with Jean-Jacques Rousseau, who arrived at the château in May 1778 at the invitation of the Marquis de Girardin, who admired his work. In a transport of delight Rousseau assured his host that this was where he wished to stay until the end of his days. His wish was granted, for on 2 July he died, apparently of an apoplectic stroke. He was buried at Ermenonville, but sixteen years later, during the Revolution, his remains were removed to the Pantheon in Paris and placed with those of Voltaire.

On the other side of Paris lies Château-Thierry on the Marne, where Lafontaine was born, and beyond is Illiers, south-west of Chartres, a little market town where a draper named Jules Amiot lived and prospered over a century ago. In the late 1870s he and his wife were visited by his brother-in-law with *his* wife and their two sons. For one of the sons, Marcel Proust, boyhood memories of life at Illiers would be stored away for many years before being transmuted into the great novel *À la recherche du temps perdu.* Illiers became the Combray of the book, and the accidental tasting of tea and a small cake, a *madeleine,* is the act through which the narrator summons up the times of childhood there. Today Illiers has become in its turn 'Illiers-Combray', and the making of *madeleines* a minor local industry.

THE LOIRE

The Loire area of France consists of two modern regions: the Pays de la Loire, astride the lower Loire valley around Nantes and Angers; and the region so poetically named 'Centre', with Orléans as its capital, on the river's middle stretch. Here, around Tours, is the old province of Touraine, known as 'the garden of France' because of the fertile abundance of its flowers, fruit and vegetables. It is also the most historic sector of the Loire, for here stand many of the famous châteaux where the kings of France held court and amused themselves.

The Loire is France's longest river, running for 600 miles from the Massif Central to the sea at Nantes. One of its many tributaries confusingly bears almost the same name as itself: the Loir. The wide lands on either side of the Loire valley are not scenically dramatic, but they contain much that is varied and unusual. To the east, the wheat plains of the Beauce, around Chartres, and the sombre heathland of the Sologne, south of Orléans. To the north, the serene oak-forests of Maine. And seawards, the quiet lagoons and marshes of the Brière and the Vendée plains, with their memories of the bloody Royalist uprising of 1793.

Each area has its own style of farming and its own rural life. The Beauce is a low limestone plateau with flat horizons, where the red clayey topsoil is ideal for wheat, barley and maize. Productivity here is among the world's highest: 150 hundredweight of corn per acre in an average year, twice the yield of most parts of North America. Farms are not so large as the biggest in Picardy, but many exceed 300 acres, and the farmers are prosperous and sophisticated, far removed from the old-style French peasant. The farmhouses themselves are imposing stone buildings, each set around a wide courtyard where the former stables and granaries now house combine harves-

ters and other machinery. And yet, despite this air of opulence, the suicide rate in the Beauce is the highest in France; bachelor farmers are the worst afflicted. It is thought to be something to do with the melancholy and monotony of this flat, unbroken plain.

Melancholy is also a keynote of the Sologne, another wide flat region, covered with forests of birch and pine, heathland, and reedy lakes (see picture on left). The simple farm cottages are long and low, either half-timbered or made of brick, often with thatched roofs. The Sologne is not very fertile, but it is excellent game country – alike for the well-off Parisians who have weekend homes here, and for poachers. Sometimes professional poachers will come from Paris for the day to take their bag. Prosecution is not easy, even if they are caught, for in France it is not illegal to trespass on unfenced property, and few of the big estates have fences.

Touraine is very different: a smiling land astride the Loire, where the well-organized farms grow everything in plenty – apples, strawberries, apricots, melons, vegetables such as asparagus and artichokes, and vines too. This is the home of the William pear, and of the Reine-Claude plum, named after François I's wife. Many meadows are dotted with walnut trees.

To the west, the former kingdom of Anjou (capital Angers) is also renowned for its fruit and vegetables and for horticulture, which was introduced here in the fifteenth century by 'Good King René', a lover of flowers. Anjou's more distinctive speciality is button mushrooms (*champignons de Paris*) which are cultivated on a massive scale in caves in the tufa rocks around Saumur. This town even has a mushroom museum. Of the thousands of caves all over this area, many have served also as dwellings since medieval days. A few decades ago, a generation wanting

The Loire

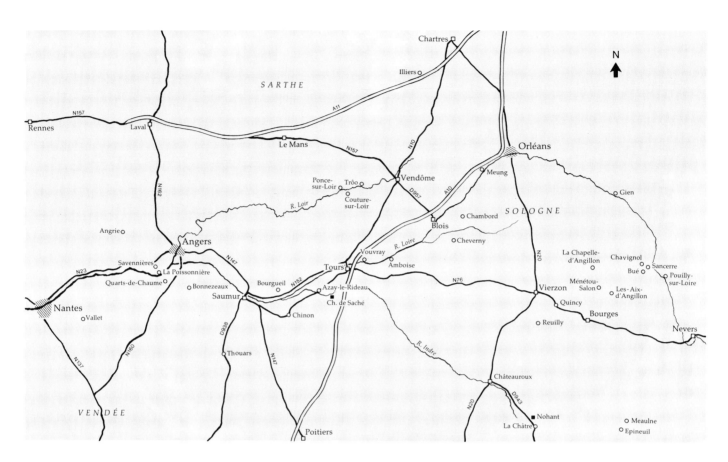

modern comforts began to abandon them. But in today's ecological age the caves are again becoming inhabited by back-to-nature pioneers. One such troglodyte couple is the English poet and critic Geoffrey Grigson and his wife Jane, the cookery writer, who for years have lived in a cave at Troo, on the Loir, to the north. These cave-dwellings, usually semi-modernized, are cool in summer and snug in winter, and their white façades are often gaily decorated with flowers or vine-creepers. Some are open to visitors on payment of a modest fee. Many very pretty above-ground rural houses are also made of the local white tufa stone.

The Loire's food-processing industries, too, have more than a touch of the bizarre. Here you will find two big egg-smashing factories, used for biscuit making; a plant making concentrated mushroom juice for flavouring ice-cream; and a couscous factory doing a substantial export trade to Egypt. Even more curious, in this area rich in cattle and poultry, five slaughterhouses today specialize in selling frozen chicken, beef and mincemeat to the richer Middle East countries. The only condition is that the slaughter must take place according to Islamic rules: that is, the butcher must be a Muslim, and the animal's head must be turned to Mecca at the moment of its death. These conditions are not hard to fulfil, and all exports are guaranteed as such.

The traditional cuisine of the Loire benefits from the quality and range of local produce. Starting downstream, we find first the tender ducklings of Nantes served with tiny green peas; eels or bass cooked in white wine; *poc-*

house, a rich fish stew; and the famous *beurre blanc* sauce that goes with many fish dishes. Further east, Touraine and Anjou specialize in *coq au vin* and pork with prunes, while in the Sologne game reigns supreme – quail *pâté*, pheasant casserole, venison with black cherry sauce, and much else. The fruit of the Loire makes for a fine array of desserts (notably, *tarte tatin*, a caramelized hot apple tart), while walnuts are used both in salads and cakes. As in some other areas, a high gastronomic moment of the small farmer's year is the killing of a pig, when family, friends and local notables are invited to a series of banquets to savour its delicacies – from fresh roast pork to the most complex *charcuteries*.

(Far left) The château of
Montreuil-Bellay.

(Above) The château of
Chenonceaux.

(Left) The keep at Loches.

(Opposite) The château of
Azay-le-Rideau on the river
Indre.

Folk traditions, in the form of song and dance and costumed fêtes, have never flourished strongly in the Loire, maybe for the same reasons discussed in the Normandy chapter. However, Maine and Anjou have long been noted for their rural handicrafts, and today attempts are being made to preserve and even revive them. Ponce-sur-Loir has a recently created craft centre that groups some 30 artisans doing pottery, weaving, ironwork and glass-blowing; elsewhere in the Sarthe you can find wood-gilding, tapestry-weaving, cask-making. Saint-Laurent de la Plaine, west of Angers, has a museum of old crafts.

Angrie, to the north, is one of several villages that stage a haymaking festival in August. All the villagers gather, including ex-inhabitants who now work in the towns; traditional costumes are worn by those who still have any; and everyone spends one whole day doing the crop-harvesting and haymaking, followed by much merriment. The older inhabitants stage a display of some of the local crafts (woodcutting, stonemasonry, etc.) that have died out in the villages under the impact of modern industry. The event is typical of the current nostalgic search for a renewal of links with tradition.

The tourist can share in some of these activities. A few places hold courses in weaving and pottery. In the Sarthe in summer there are guided tours of local farms and craft centres where the visitor can study the breeding of goats, poultry, mushrooms. There is also fishing or the possibility of hiring a cabin cruiser for a river holiday. Some of the more curious rural corners of the region reward exploration. To the west, near the coast at La Baule, the marshland of the Grande Brière is today a national park and bird sanctuary, where the old thatched cottages beside the lagoons have been restored to their original nineteenth-century state, forming an outdoor museum.

South of the Loire from Nantes, one can visit the region known as the 'Vendée militaire', where in 1793 Royalists and Catholics rose in bitter rebellion against Paris after the execution of Louis XVI. The guide gives a candidly partisan account of the Government army's 'atrocities' when the rebellion was put down: Vendée, still the most Catholic part of France, has neither forgotten nor forgiven. Here at the château of Le Puy-du-Fou, still half-ruined after being sacked in the fighting, a grand nocturnal pageant is staged all through the summer, telling the saga of the Vendée wars, with 600 costumed performers and 30 horses. It is most spectacular, and worth a visit. Or if you prefer the well-worn tourist beaten track, there is always François I's former hunting-lodge near Blois, the 440-room château of Chambord.

The Loire/Writers

Across the centuries, no other region of France has inspired more great writers than the country of the middle Loire. Many were born and lived here; others came to settle here, in this pleasing countryside within easy reach of Paris.

Honoré de Balzac was born at Tours in 1799, then went to school at Vendôme where he seems to have been a lazy and undisciplined pupil. Part of his later life he spent at the Château de Saché, south-west of Tours, where he wrote several of his novels including *Le Père Goriot*. The château is now a small Balzac museum, and his bedroom has been kept as it was in his day. In an earlier age, François Rabelais (1494-1553) was born and brought up in a manor-house outside Chinon, and later used the surrounding countryside as setting for parts of *Pantagruel* and *Gargantua*. The manor, La Devinière, now houses a Rabelais museum. The poet François Villon had a more tenuous and unhappy connection with the region, for he was twice exiled there from Paris and spent some time in prison at Orléans and Meung.

Above all, literary pilgrims today can be rewarded by following the traces of Ronsard, George Sand, Alain-Fournier and Proust, all of whom were passionately attached to some corner or other of this region.

Pierre de Ronsard, the great lyric poet of the Renaissance, is associated with the verdant country of the Loir valley west of Vendôme, and many of his poems evoke this landscape of orchards and vineyards bordered with willows and poplars. He was born here in the graceful manor of La Poissonnière, and it was by the cascading water of the Loir that he first fell in love. In the church of Couture-sur-Loir, the reclining statues in the nave are of his well-to-do parents. In his mature years Ronsard devoted himself to the Church and was put in charge of three priories in the area. He continued to write love-poems, chastely celebrating his idealized love for beautiful women he had known, notably Cassandre, the daughter of a Florentine banker, and Hélène de Surgères, a maid of honour of Cathérine de Medicis. At his priory of Croixval he consecrated a fountain to Hélène, who inspired his most famous sonnet, '*Quand vous serez bien vieille, au soir, à la chandelle. . .*' Racked with gout, Ronsard died and was buried in 1585 in his priory of Saint-Cosme, near Tours.

Much further south, in the Berry, near La Châtre, the lovely eighteenth-century château of Nohant was the family home of the Baroness Dudevant, who wrote under the name George Sand. Here she spent her youth; and many of her novels describe the village and château life of the area. After her tempestuous years in Paris, she retired to Nohant as *châtelaine* where she kept open house to many of the 'great' of her day, such as Liszt, Flaubert, Balzac, and of course her lover Chopin. Today the château is a Sand museum, with her bedroom, study and dining-room preserved as they were in her time.

Henri Fournier also used a *nom-de-plume*, Alain-Fournier. Son of a village schoolmaster, he was born in 1886 at La Chapelle-d'Angillon on the edge of the wild Sologne, north of Bourges. Then, at the age of five he moved with his parents to the village school at Epineuil-

Les Oeuvres de M. F. Rabelais D. en Medecine
ou est contenue l'histoire des faicts heroïques de
Gargantua et de son fils Pantagruel

(Above) François Rabelais.

(Left) Rabelais' house, La Devinière.

(Above) Honoré de Balzac.

(Opposite above) Pierre Ronsard.

(Opposite below) George Sand.

le-Fleuriel, 40 miles south of Bourges, far from the Sologne. *Le Grand Meaulnes,* his classic dream-like novel of adolescence, is in many ways autobiographical, and reflects his romantic love for the rural world of his childhood. Critics' attempts to identify the novel's topography have often led to confusion, for it is a synthesis of two separate areas. Sainte-Agathe, the village in the book, is based on Epineuil (there is in fact a real village called Meaulne nearby); today the village school contains a small Alain-Fournier museum, and the classroom benches remain as they were when he was a pupil there. But the mysterious forest where Meaulnes finds his enchanted manor is clearly the Sologne (to which Fournier would often return from Epineuil); and the manor itself is probably an amalgam of the château of Loroy, near La Chapelle, and of another château near Epineuil, and quite possibly of others too. At all events, lovers of the novel will find a visit to the strange Sologne landscape a memorable and moving experience.

North of the Loire, on the plain south-west of Chartres, the gloomy little town of Illiers was the setting and inspiration for parts of the greatest autobiographical novel in world literature, *À la recherche du temps perdu.* Marcel Proust's forebears were petit-bourgeois small traders in Illiers; but his father became a famous doctor who married a rich Jewess and lived in Paris, where Proust was born in 1871. As a child he would go to spend holidays in his aunt's rather pokey little half-timbered house in the centre of Illiers, which in the novel became '*la maison de Tante Léonie*', just as Illiers became 'Combray'. Like Four-

nier and many other writers, Proust changed and transposed reality a good deal, but many of his real childhood memories survive intact in the novel, described with 'Proustian' vividness.

The house is now a museum, run by Les Amis de Marcel Proust, and is reconstituted as it was in his day, in all its Victorian taste: sombre wood panelling and windows with small tinted panes. Here is Proust's little room with its alcove bed, the famous magic lantern, the view over the small garden, the wardrobe for the *mouchoirs* that his asthma demanded so often. Here is his aunt's room, where preserved under a glass cover is an actual *madeleine* sponge-cake, not Proust's actual original, but still (*madeleines* are shell-shaped because Illiers was formerly on the route to Santiago-de-Compostela, and the cake took its shape from the shells pilgrims wore in their hats). Here, too, is the kitchen of the servant 'Françoise', and the garden gate with the famous jangling bell that Proust remembered so poignantly. On the edge of the town the visitor today can still take the two walks that Proust took so often and were then to play such key roles in his book: Swann's Way and Guermantes' Way (although those two wealthy families in the novel were not themselves based on any Illiers originals). The town of Illiers today, with its tall church, its market-place, its little shops, has not greatly changed in appearance and character since Proust's day. As Proust's English biographer, George Painter, has pointed out, the real landscape of Illiers does indeed closely resemble the created, mythical landscape of Combray.

(Left) Illiers, the 'Combray' in Proust's novel, A la recherche du temps perdu.

(Above) Marcel Proust.

The Loire/Local Wines

The wines of the Loire valley are as varied as the river is long. Virtually every style of wine is to be found, from the driest whites perfect for an aperitif, to the rich full whites for dessert, from the light, fruity Gamay reds to the serious, slightly rustic Cabernets, the complete range of rosés, and the second most famous sparkling wine in France. And while the individual vineyards have little in common, the Loire river itself lends them a family air of purity and grace.

These are the perfect 'local' wines, simply delicious on the spot, giving one no wish to drink anything else. The impression they leave is so pleasant that many of them, particularly Muscadet, Vouvray and Sancerre, have become popular the world over.

The Loire rises in the Auvergne, where the best known wine is Saint-Pourçain, but it is not until it passes through Nevers that the wines become more typical. From the Nivernais comes the dry, fruity Sancerre, grown around the villages of Sancerre, Chavignol and Bué and, from the other side of the river, the slightly more elegant Pouilly-Fumé. A little red and rosé is made in Sancerre from the Pinot Noir, showing that it is not

that far from Burgundy. Wines similar to Sancerre are made from the Sauvignon grape at Ménétou-Salon, Quincy and Reuilly. Very little wine is now made around Gien, where a hundred years ago there were 800 vine-growers. Even the Vins de L'Orléanais, while enjoying a slight upsurge in popularity, are being engulfed by the city of Orléans itself.

It is really not until the château country – Blois, Cheverny, Chambord – that the vines begin in earnest, being planted without a break right up to the mouth of the Loire at Nantes. Going westwards, the Sauvignon whites, Pineau d'Aunis rosés and Gamay reds lead into the historic wines of Touraine. As is general for the Loire valley, they are mostly white: the splendid Vouvrays, dry, even slightly tart in cool years, lusciously honeyed from finer summers; the aromatic but lighter Montlouis, Vouvray's younger brother; the almost austere Jasnières, once the favourite wine of the kings of France, now virtually extinct. All these are made from the Chenin Blanc, known locally as the Pineau de la Loire. At Amboise, the city joins its name to Touraine to produce red, rosé and white wines under the appellation Touraine-Amboise.

(Left) The vineyard Clos de l'Echo near Chinon.

(Right) The château of Saumur from across the Loire.

Other towns less grand than Amboise, Mesland and Azay-le-Rideau, do the same. Between Tours and Saumur, maturing in caves carved out from the limestone tufa subsoil of the region, are found the finest red wines of the Loire valley. Once the most sought-after wines of France, at the time when the Loire valley and Champagne had the Paris market to themselves, Chinon and Bourgueil now sell for little more than a Beaujolais-Villages. However, while they may be drunk young and at cellar temperature (like a Beaujolais), in taste they have more in common with the wines of the Médoc. They are among the truest wines of France, and are acquiring a justifiably good reputation.

At Saumur, we enter the region of Anjou, where the white wines are incomparably better, and better known, than the reds. Saumur-Champigny is the name of an attractive, fruity red wine, like a rather more rustic Bourgueil, while Saumur itself is famous for its 'méthode Champenoise' sparkling wine. As the river moves westwards, we encounter the finest sweet white wines of the Loire valley: Bonnezeaux, Coteaux du Layon and Quarts-de-Chaume. Current fashion and economic reality have seen the quantity of sweet wine diminish in favour of a drier white, picked early, some pleasant reds and the still popular Cabernet d'Anjou rosés, but the quality remains with the luscious dessert wines. One of the best dry whites comes from Savennières, on the right bank.

The fourth distinctive change comes as the Loire enters the Pays Nantais. Here, passing through the pleasant everyday wines from the Coteaux d'Ancenis, the style becomes very dry and almost exclusively white. The most famous wine is Muscadet. Little known outside the region in the 1930s, this pale, almost cracklingly crisp wine later conquered Paris, France and the entire world. Unlike many of the very local Loire wines, Muscadet travels well, but it is still at its best 'sur place' with a plate of shellfish. The best wines come from the *département* of the Sèvre-et-Maine, around the town of Vallet. Even drier than Muscadet, and often too green for most tastes, is the Gros Plant du Pays Nantais.

To many travellers, the Loire valley is the heart of France, the purest expression of what France has to offer. The variety of country wines of the region is yet another aspect of that richness.

CHAMPAGNE

The province of Champagne consists of a wide-rolling chalky plain, stretching from the mountainous Ardennes in the north to Burgundy in the south. Its name comes from the Latin *campania*, meaning 'flat country'; and in turn it has bestowed its name on the world's most famous wine, produced on the slopes south of Reims. In French, this wine is masculine with a small 'c' – *le champagne* – while the province is feminine: la Champagne.

Rather like Picardy, Champagne is fertile agricultural country with big prosperous farms producing grain and sugar-beet (the sugar-mill at Connantre in the Marne is claimed to be the world's largest). There are great forests, where wild game is hunted in winter. And here and there are ranges of hills, such as the Argonne, scene of some of the bloodiest battles of World War I. To the north is the vast plateau of the Ardennes, most of it in Belgium but some in France; here, winters are harsh and wet, but in summer tourists come in thousands to admire the grandiose scenery – for example, the rocky escarpments of the winding Meuse valley north of Charleville.

If the grapes for champagne are the province's greatest source of wealth, its major under-used asset is its forest land. There are 2,600 square miles of forest, mostly oak, beech and poplar, but most of it is divided between 120,000 private smallholders, and they have not grouped together to create an efficient modern wood industry. The felled trees are carted off to other parts of France, or more often abroad, to be converted into furniture or wood pulp. Moreover, there has been no proper policy of re-afforestation, so that Champagne is gradually losing her forests; and this is a threat to the environment. Landowners find there is far more money to be made from crops than from wood, so they have been uprooting their woodlands and turning the land over to sugar-beet or grain. In many places this has been leading to soil erosion, and to a decline in local animal and plant life. Happily, the French government in the 1970s at last became alert to these dangers, and a recent law now forbids the uprooting of trees without special permission.

Soil is Champagne's most precious possession. It is the special chalky soil of the vineyard region that lends such quality to its wines. To the south-east, between Troyes and Saint-Dizier, the area known as 'la Champagne humide' has damp clayey soil, unusually fertile, where dairy cows and other livestock grow fat. In between, around Châlons-sur-Marne, is a district which used to be known contemptuously as 'la Champagne pouilleuse' ('wretchedly poor'); its soil was dry and thin, and in the eighteenth century the writer Michelet described it as 'an expanse of white chalk, dirty, poor'. But then the planting of trees made the soil richer, and today this is a prosperous wheat plain. It is sad that the recent uprooting of trees may have begun to reverse the process.

The people of Champagne, the Champenois, are hardworking, serious, reserved with strangers, and without the extrovert jollity often associated with wine-producing areas. But, as much as other Frenchmen, they know how to eat well. Many dishes are cooked in champagne – kidneys, chicken, stuffed trout, crayfish, snails. One speciality is the grilled pigs' trotters of Sainte-Ménéhould in the Argonne, simmered in wine and coated in breadcrumbs. Troyes is famous for its *andouillettes*. Brillat-Savarin and Maroilles are two succulent cheeses, while western Champagne overlaps into the country of Brie, with its huge, round soft cheeses.

Rural architecture is of interesting variety. In 'la Champagne humide' and around Troyes, many houses are half-timbered, with gently sloping tiled roofs. Further

Champagne

north, in the area that today prefers to be known as 'dry' rather than 'wretched' Champagne, the houses have chalk walls and steep roofs.

Central Champagne from Reims to the Argonne was in the front line during most of World War I and many villages were destroyed. But then the region tenaciously and industriously rebuilt itself; little factories, most of them making textiles, were soon booming in the villages around Reims. However, since the mid-1970s, crisis has hit the textile industry, here as elsewhere in Europe, and many factories have closed. These villages today wear a down-at-heel air. The stormclouds of war may have blown away, but today there are grey economic clouds over the rolling chalky plains.

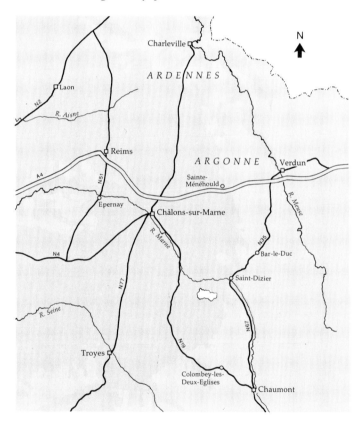

The wide valley of the Marne is fertile agricultural land, much of it given over to grain and sugar-beet.

Colombey-les-Deux-Eglises

Colombey-les-Deux-Eglises, on the main road west of Chaumont in the Haute-Marne, is one of the most famous of French villages simply because it was the country home of General de Gaulle. In 1934 he bought La Boisserie, a handsome nineteenth-century creeper-covered mansion on a wooded hill, with sweeping views over the rolling cornfields and forests below – a landscape that he described in his memoirs as 'all impregnated with calm, vast, blurred and mournful horizons'.

De Gaulle loved this view, and the house. He spent his years of political retirement here in 1946-58, and again in 1969-70. Veneration for de Gaulle is still very strong in France, notably among older people; and thousands come to visit this house which is filled with mementoes. In the foyer, *inter alia*, is a fifteenth-century Virgin given to the General by Chancellor Adenauer; in the dining-room, a porcelain mosaic cock, gift of the former King of Afghanistan. The library, where the great man died so suddenly and peacefully on 9 November 1970, is lined with signed photographs of Churchill, Roosevelt and others. Adjacent to the library is the little alcove study where he wrote his memoirs.

Nearby, the small village cemetery contains the grave of de Gaulle, his wife Yvonne, and their handicapped daughter Anne, so deeply loved, who died aged twenty. There is just a plain tombstone, and beside it a crucifix statue adorned with wreaths laid mostly by regiments of the Free French forces. It is all very simple, dignified, tasteful – which is more than can be said of the numerous souvenir shops in the village, selling de Gaulle candlesticks, walking-sticks, ashtrays, key-rings, frying-pans, and other examples of kitsch.

On a hilltop a mile away, visible far across the plain, stands the great memorial in granite and concrete, 145 feet high, in the form of a Cross of Lorraine, erected by the Gaullist faithful in 1972. Next to it is a small museum of Gaulliana, including the black Citroën 15CV that he drove in 1955-8. And inscribed on the base of the memorial is a typical de Gaulle quotation which just about sums up all that people have so often found most inspiring, and infuriating, about him: 'There exists a pact twenty centuries old between the grandeur of La France and the freedom of the world.'

In his memoirs de Gaulle wrote of La Boisserie: 'Silence fills my house . . . From a high point in the garden, my eye takes in the wild hollows where the forest envelops the site as the sea beats against a headland. I see the night cover the landscape. Then, gazing at the stars, I become imbued with the insignificance of things.'

Champagne/The Champagne Industry

The most important town in Champagne is Reims, and this has been so for 2000 years. At the time of the Roman invasion Reims (at that time known as Durocortorum) was the supply centre for the Roman armies on their conquest of Europe. The wine that was so essential to the legionnaires came from Greece or Sicily and was shipped to Reims in amphoras, to be redistributed among the camps. After the conquest, around 50 B.C., the Gallo-Romans planted vines throughout the region, and ceased to rely on imports from the Mediterranean countries. The vines flourished, villas and estates grew up around Reims and what is now Épernay, and a prosperous wine trade became established. The Barbarian invasions, however, destroyed everything. The Gallo-Roman civilization was broken, people fled the country to the towns, and the vines disappeared completely.

What the Barbarians had ruined was re-established by the Christians. The rise of the monasteries is an integral part of the replanting of the vine in France. Abbeys were founded in Champagne (Hautvillers in around 650, Saint-Basle, Saint-Thierry), and these communities brought life back to the region. As the vines produced, commerce began again and wines from Champagne were exported by river to Paris, and overland to the North and East. For many centuries, viticulture was the monopoly of the monasteries, but the fame of the wine spread, and little by little nobles and landed families laid out their own vineyards. Even up to the 1660s, the wine produced was mostly red, although there were a few off-coloured white wines that showed an annoying tendency to sparkle. By the end of the sevententh century the fashion had turned towards these white wines, but it was not until the discovery of the 'sparkle' by Dom Pérignon (cellar-master at the Abbaye de Hautvillers from 1688 to 1715) that the beginnings of a true Champagne appear. To be truly sparkling, rather than merely 'lively', a proper

The Champagne wine harvest in the Marne valley.

(Opposite above) Grapes being emptied into a press at the start of the Champagne-making process.

(Opposite below) A wine cellar in Champagne.

bottle had to be stoppered by a proper cork, and these were not seen together until the early years of the eighteenth century. Once this desirable wine was produced, a commercial network was needed to sell it. These *négociants*, names that are still famous today, were based in Reims: first Ruinart in 1729, then Clicquot, Heidsieck, and in Épernay, Claude Moët. The chalk pits, from which chalk had been extracted in Roman times to build the city, were opened up to be used as cellars and, as business expanded, further excavation took place to leave Reims a rabbit-warren of underground cellars. Épernay, on the river Marne, soon became a centre of commerce, followed by the small village of Aÿ.

Yet even at the beginning of the nineteenth century, Champagne had hardly begun its conquest of the world. Previously limited to the Royal Court and to the nobles of Paris and the Ile-de-France, Champagne began to be exported in earnest after the fall of Napoleon in 1815. Invading armies had formed a taste for the sparkling wine of Champagne, and it was only with the onset of peace that the men could return to the vineyards, and production could rise. Reims quickly asserted its predominance in the production and sale of Champagne. New businesses were founded with such un-French names as Krug, Taittinger, Roederer, Piper, while at Aÿ, Bollinger and Deutz et Geldermann began trading. These 'foreign' companies brought with them a clientele from all over Europe, particularly the North and East. The Industrial Revolution and the spread of capitalism fuelled

the success of Champagne, which began to be exported all over the world. In 1848 the railway connection was opened between Épernay and Paris, and Moët, Pol Roger, Perrier-Jouet, Ayala and Mercier took full advantage of this new access to their best market.

By the 1870s, the pattern of the Champagne trade as we know it today had emerged. A relatively small number of *négociants*, known as 'les Grandes Marques', with vast cellars, large stocks of wine and energetic salesmen, opened up and then controlled the market. Methods of cultivation were improved and especially strong bottles used to diminish the heavy percentage of breakages. In France as well as abroad, Champagne had become a way of life that neither of the two World Wars, which inflicted terrible disaster on the region, could alter.

Yet for almost 250 years after the 'discovery' of Champagne by Dom Pérignon, the main factor in the equation of production was largely ignored. The *vignerons,* or growers, who owned the vines from which came 85 per cent of the grapes to make Champagne (the 'Grandes Marques' owning the rest), were treated almost feudally by the grand houses of Reims, Épernay and Aÿ. In 1910–11 the *vignerons* took to the streets to fight for their rights and to prevent the importation into Champagne of lesser wines from more southern vineyards. The Champagne Riots resulted in great loss of life (and of Champagne) and several Champagne houses, particularly in Aÿ, were burnt to the ground. From this emerged the 'contract' between growers and *négociants* that exists in much the same form to this day, whereby a price is arrived at for the kilo of grapes that is in the best interests of both parties. The *vignerons,* however, are not obliged to sell to the *négociants,* even though there are contracts that have been respected through several generations. Many smallholders, unwilling to sell their grapes in what was usually a buyer's market, but with no capital or insufficient production to make their own Champagne, grouped together to form cooperatives. Since the 1950s this has intensified, and with the larger *propriétaires* making the wine themselves, over half the crop in Champagne is currently exploited directly by the growers.

But while *négociants* and growers compete with each other for sales, there remains a very close cooperation between the different parts of the Champagne trade. The Comité Interprofessionel du Vin de Champagne (C.I.V.C.) collects taxes that finance control of abuses of the name of Champagne and a successful advertising programme. The 'Grandes Marques' and the family *vignerons* keep their cellars open for the public to see the Champagne-making process and taste the result. The region has been admirably signposted for the motorist, with three specific routes to follow: the Blue Route, which starts from Reims and concentrates on the Montagne de Reims; the Red Route, centred on Épernay and Aÿ, with discursions down the Marne valley; and the Green Route, to the south of Épernay in the heart of the Côte-de-Blancs. But perhaps the most lasting publicity are the people of Champagne themselves, who love their unique product, and who like nothing better than the (subdued) pop of a Champagne cork.

ALSACE-LORRAINE

Against a backdrop of conflict, Alsace-Lorraine finally emerged as a union of two profoundly different provinces. On the one hand Lorraine, tugged this way and that over the centuries between the Holy Roman Empire and the Kingdom of France; on the other, Alsace, divided into a host of principalities. A union with a distinctly Germanic flavour as reflected in its free towns, its multiple domains and manors and its complex networks of serfdom. At the Treaty of Westphalia in 1648 France received all the Imperial Habsburg rights to Alsace, while at the same time being granted rights to its portion of Lorraine, including Metz, Toul and Verdun. This was the first real union and marked the beginning of a slow process of absorption into France. The provinces played a major role in the Revolution, then, in 1871, France was forced to give up Alsace and parts of Lorraine, including the Moselle and Metz. Alsace-Lorraine proper was created. The annexation of the provinces by Germany caused many of their population to migrate into the heart of France itself and its colonies. Then came the war in 1914 and Alsace-Lorraine was once again part of France, which it has continued to be to this day, apart from an 'interlude' during World War II.

Though united in their historical vicissitudes, the two provinces are totally different from each other in landscape, tongue, customs, architecture and, of course, people. Alsace has a pronounced personality, its area split into three main zones: the Vosges, that imposing barrier and ubiquitous horizon with its massy peaks, then gentle hills that recline against the mountains, with their covering of vineyards, and finally the plain of Alsace, bounded by the Rhine. Lorraine is a contrast of vast, austere plateaux, precipitous hills and valleys that are warm and peaceful. It is by and large a rough

diamond, with reserved, even taciturn men who keep themselves to themselves. The people of Alsace are the 'Mediterraneans of the East'. They are talkative and love good living, festivals, flowers, indeed colour in general, which they apply with liberal enthusiasm to their houses, furniture and walls. While a typical Lorraine village ranges its grey farms along a rough road where heaps of timber and slurry were once piled high in front of the houses without any concession to appearance.

Alsace is a highly diversified region. In the Vosges there are extensive mountain pastures where farm animals graze free during the summer months. Dark pine forests trace the familiar bluish contour of the Vosges, while lower down the plains are rich in a mixture of tobacco, grain crops, vegetables and moors. It is a well-cultivated landscape but not at all monotonous. Along the smaller rivers, files of poplar trees form huge natural hedges of awesome perspective, while along the Rhine itself, the mysterious forests creak and whisper in their undergrowth of dark creepers and brushwood.

To the south the landscape is formed of valleys broken up into small parcels of orchards. The plains around Strasbourg are vast fields where wide tracts of hops spring up among the more familiar varieties of crop. In summer the countryside is covered with the green of aerial plants, while in winter the scene is dominated by pine forests. It is a rich region, with huge farms crouching amid generous villages. To the north again are more valleys, orchards and mixed farming. But whether the farms themselves are small or large, they share a clean-cut look.

At the foot of the Vosges, the vineyards are laid out irregularly on the often bleak slopes. Closer to the mountain's crest the layer of soil thins down to a bare

Alsace-Lorraine

Cobbled streets lined with
ancient half-timbered and
gabled buildings with steep
tiled roofs make up the charm
of the village of Riquewihr.

(Opposite) Riquewihr is a
'wine town' in the true sense: it
is a working village, dedicated
to the vine.

minimum over the rock. The land falls to the plain as its long folds widen into valley floors that crumple the surface of the earth. The countryside is studded with small- to medium-sized farms and far-flung allotments.

The vine-growers have a long tradition of development and expansion. Nearly one-third of them sell their wine themselves, thereby establishing a French and foreign clientele. Indeed the entire gamut of human contact is based upon a jovial cordiality much in evidence at wine tastings that feature the indigenous grape varieties: Gewürztraminer, Riesling, Tokay. Here it is the grape that counts, rather than the locality, although there are some celebrated estates that closely link the one with the other.

The vineyards form an especially agreeable interlude between the agricultural plains and the less welcoming uplands. The atmosphere is typified by the *cafés à vins* and by wine cellars where you tipple among the vats and casks. It is not uncommon to find vineyards right in the middle of a town or village. The vine also coexists happily with fruit trees, and all these contrasts impart to the villages a truly relaxed, unhurried feeling further enhanced by a bustling street life.

In the mountains, the harshness of the land has left its mark on the upland dwellers whose basic nature nevertheless remains kind and jovial, with a sociability born out of a long tradition of living and working together. It is a life that reflects close-woven human relationships in perfect harmony with deep-rooted individualism as characterized by the importance of a comfortable home and the way in which a house faces the inner courtyard rather than the road. There are many associations and an adherence to custom that defies the spread of organized education and the breaks with tradition which it entails. Saturday nights are devoted to the enjoyment of the *galette au jambon*, a sort of crisp ham pancake known locally, and rather inappropriately, as *tarte flambée*. A basic love of discussion, even of polemics, is tempered by sociability and good humour. This forms a seedbed for storytellers and folksingers and for a dramatic spirit which is at the root of village plays packed with up-to-the-minute local events. The religious cohesion is also stronger here than in the rest of France. The people have a deep attachment to their province and to its peculiarities. In Alsace, customs have been adapted to

modern life so that the maintenance of Alsatian identity, for instance, has become synonymous with the protection of the ecology.

This sense of identity is particularly pronounced in the architecture. Imagine leaving Lorraine and crossing into Alsace at the Col du Bonhomme: you have been travelling through long, strung-out villages with their severe rows of undecorated terraced houses, then suddenly the scene changes to the *style alsacien* which, while basically Germanic, is neverthless inimitable in its originality. The people of Alsace take pride in maintaining and ornamenting their houses; flowers abound in summer to form a perfect complement to the half-timbered houses. Here again there is great diversity: in southern Alsace, in the 'sundgau', the dwellings are constructed entirely on a timber framework, while the houses of the Vosges are built of the mountain sandstone with timbers in the ceilings and on the walls clad in beech or pine. The villages of the Alsatian plains are extensive, with narrow terraced streets. The market towns are especially proud of their long main streets that constitute a main axis bounded on either side by orchards and meadows.

The love of ornamentation is reflected in the painted furniture, in the carving of certain beams and even in the casks of the richer cellars. The churches, too, are heavily decorated, and the baroque is not merely religious, but also secular: witness the porches on the older houses of southern Alsace. There is a wealth of colour and a richness of design found typically in the chintzes of Mulhouse. The same stylistic tendencies are to be found in the rejuvenated trades and crafts such as pottery and earthenware from Soufflenheim and Betschdorf, with their brightly coloured kitchen pots and more elaborate vases. Then there are the makers of stoves and ranges with their hand-made tiles, while weavers in the villages on the plain make traditional linen fabrics.

This caring, skilful artistry is found yet again in the cuisine. In Alsace they adore fruit tarts of many colours, light for mirabelle, dark for plums. There is much stress on culinary presentation, too: trout in Riesling, game in rich wine sauces with a myriad of flavour nuances. Then there is *foie gras*, rich in spices and herbs. As a rural region, Alsace retains its more rustic flavours, and there is nothing to compare with its sauerkraut and smoked sausages. Everywhere there is a sense of well-being and a true appreciation of things simple yet robust.

Nor is Lorraine devoid of a love of 'good things', but the Alsatians are not so afraid of showing their love of comfort, of uncomplicated good living. In Lorraine, feelings are more restrained, more internalized, and a perhaps exaggerated discretion might be mistaken for a cold remoteness. Friendships are long in the forging and cordiality only triumphs over reserve after a sort of trial period. The simple farmers in particular have a fear and distrust of display of any kind, preferring qualities of strength, solidity and realism before ease and comfort. Nevertheless, the sensitivity is there beneath the surface, and is a constituent part of an otherwise somewhat brusque nature.

Alsace-Lorraine/Festivals

In Alsace, festivals are a way of life. The Alsatians love entertainment, especially when they make it themselves, a feature that makes their festivals so authentic. One such occasion commemorates the multiple marriages of 'friend Fritz', a character that runs through much of the popular literature of the region. The festival reflects the jolly, friendly atmosphere of weddings in the good old days, complete with coach and horses and costumes of yesteryear. But amid all this folklore, there is a population that believes in it enough to overcome the more artificial aspect: it is simply the people at play.

Every year brings its own historical festivals, like those at Ribeauvillé, their origins rooted in medieval legend. The lord of Ribeaupierre, master of the entire area, once came upon a travelling musician and his family, all in great distress by the roadside as the musician had broken his fife and had thus lost his means of support. Moved by this story, Ribeaupierre gave the man his purse, and in his gratitude the player frequently came to his benefactor's castle, bringing his fellow itinerant players with him. They pronounced the lord 'king of the strolling players', and for this honour he and his descendants protected them down the centuries. Today, the festival faithfully revives the medieval scene, with lords and ladies on horseback and their men-at-arms. Then the play begins in earnest, with simulated bear-baiting, knights battling in full armour and colourful processions round the town. French and German visitors from far afield come to applaud the amateur actors playing out their own history, and the 'props' and scenery are the real thing – luxurious vineyards, the town with its ramparts, ruined castles and medieval houses.

Festivals like this are to be found in many a small town and village throughout Alsace. Others spring from old customs, the heritage of pagan times, plucked from the old Germanic or Celtic cultures and 'adapted' to suit Christian tastes. Some villages are famous for their votive festivals, and those devoted to the vine are perhaps the more famous. There are also smaller local festivals when old games are revived.

At the annual feast day in
Ribeauvillé, the traditional
kugelhopf cakes are paraded
round the village.

(Opposite) Festivals play an
integral part in Alsatian life
and traditional costumes are
still worn with pride.

Alsace-Lorraine/Wines

The wines of Alsace come from one of the prettiest wine-growing regions in the world. Flanked by the Vosges mountains on one side and the Rhine valley on the other, the vineyards surround the villages along the Route des Vins on a 70-mile stretch from Strasbourg in the north to Mulhouse in the south. It is astonishing to see how many streets full of medieval buildings have survived the many wars, and how much the cheerful, solid Alsatian character prevails in a country that has been bounced back and forth between France and Germany for so long.

The Vosges mountains shelter the Alsatian vineyards from the wind and rain coming from the west, leaving Colmar the second driest town in France after Perpignan. A cold winter gives the vines a late start and the grapes ripen slowly through the hot, dry summer to be picked in mid-October or even later, making this one of the last vineyards in France to be harvested.

The resulting wines are very aromatic, clean, fruity even spicy in the mouth and generally have a dry finish. They all have a certain family resemblance, 'le style Alsace', and in fact all sell under one *appellation* – Alsace – with the different types of wine being sold under the name of the grapes from which they are made. Thus, a plain 'vin blanc d'Alsace' will come from the less fine varieties such as the Chasselas and the Knipperlé, while wines made from the noble grape varieties – Sylvaner, Pinot Blanc or Klevener, Pinot Gris or Tokay d'Alsace, Traminer, Gewürztraminer, Riesling and Muscat – will be named as such. These are all white wines. There is a little Pinot Noir grown, which makes a rosé, and an increasing quantity of Crémant d'Alsace, a sparkling wine made in the Champagne manner.

While the Alsatians still tend to drink beer with their meals and wine as an aperitif or on any other occasion, their wines go very well with food. The Chasselas or the Zwicker are light, cheerful, quaffing wines. Sylvaner or Edelzwicker (a blend of two or more 'cepages nobles') are fruity, fresh and elegant with first courses. Pinot Blanc, a cousin of the Chardonnay from Burgundy, has more personality and goes well with fish and light meats. Riesling with its classy lemony bouquet and long, firm finish is perfect with oysters, smoked salmon, all fish and any dish cooked in Riesling. Traminer and the extra-spicy Gewürztraminer go with the game that abounds in Alsace (although many Alsatian growers admit a fondness for Claret), while the rather richer Tokay seems equally happy with *foie gras* or dessert. Only the Muscat should be drunk on its own, preferably as an aperitif.

The Alsatians are most hospitable and are rightly proud of their Route des Vins that passes through such picturesque villages as Mittelbergheim, Kaysersberg and especially Riquewihr. Most villages have a local cooperative, and there are few vine-growers who will not welcome you in for a tasting. The centre of the wine business is Colmar, where there is a wine museum, as well as the spectacular fine arts museum.

(Opposite) The famous wine village of Riquewihr.

(Above left) Ammerschwir on the Route des Vins.

(Above right) Much of the picturesque village of Riquewihr has been preserved as it must have been in the sixteenth and seventeenth centuries.

(Right) The fortified church at Hunawihr.

Alsace-Lorraine/The Vosges Mountains

The Vosges are unique mountains that look like no other; their 'balloon' shape reveals a wealth of individual features. Walls tower skyward culminating in the peaks of the High Vosges, where mountain pastures dominate the treeline. The lower forests are more mysterious and darker, with horizons that are dictated by the very existence of the wood which protects and shelters but also conceals. The impression of being enclosed in the heart of the forest is overcome when one finally breaches the treeline to emerge on the summit and look back down on vast open spaces where herds of cattle graze the summer away. Up here there was once a long tradition of cheesemaking, mainly Munster, a task undertaken by mountain cowherds. Today, the dairy farmers often consign their milk to processers who have cool cellars hewn into the solid rock. Nevertheless, in certain areas the herds still ascend to the high pastures in spring, and the cowherds still burn sheaves of grass in their mountain huts as their forefathers once did as both a ritual of protection and sort of disinfection.

The Vosges is also a world of water within the forests, with a constant sound of running water from springs and waterfalls. Mountain lakes shine brightly beneath the highland sunshine, then turn almost black as a cloud obscures the sun. These forests are the workplace of the traditional woodcutter, and the felled logs were once carried on huge sleds with timber runners, while the logman straddled the timber to hold it in place. The paths they followed can still be seen.

In the foothills of the Vosges, medieval man constructed a long line of castles reminiscent of the robber fortresses perched above the Rhine. Near Colmar, the towers of Eguisheim in their red sandstone rear up in massive square keeps that date from the eleventh century. Here, too, are the three castles of Ribeauvillé,

fiefs of the Ribeaupierre family. Sometimes, when perched upon a rock, the feudal castles of La Hardt to the north of Saverne present the visitor with a real puzzle, and he will be hard pressed to tell where man's work ends and that of Nature begins. The castles have been hewn into the living rock, and since many of the original fortifications have now been dismantled, one is left with the ghost of a castle that seems to grow from the rock and form part of its own relief. In Lorraine as well as in Alsace, these edifices impart a very special dimension to the landscape, imbuing it with added power and mystery, constant reminders of the ancient lords of the land who once ruled both forest and rock of the Vosges.

Steel-blue fir-trees clothe the slopes of the Vosges mountains.

*(Above and left) To the west,
the Vosges descend gently to
the Lorraine plateau.*

JURA

The Jura massif rises abruptly from the rich farmland of the Bresse plain and the valley of the Sâone, becoming a series of plateaux which rise like a staircase to the 'mountains' on the Swiss border. Lengthwise the massif forms a north-south crescent which in France extends through the *départements* of the Doubs, the Jura and the Ain, most of the ancient province of Franche-Comté.

Independence, realism, toughness, frugality and caution are the qualities of the traditional Jura countryman. His temperament has been shaped by extremes of climate and above all by the rigours of winter; the high Jura, known as 'the Jurassian Siberia', is one of the coldest parts of France.

Even on the hottest day of summer the villager on the high plateau cannot shake off thoughts of the coming winter; the size of the woodpile beside his vast, squat, low-roofed house and in his loft is a measure of his foresight. In the past, most householders in those villages fortunate enough to own woodland 'did their wood' and this habit, which almost died out with the coming of cheap and convenient fuel oil, is now on the way back, an instance of the way rocketing energy costs are bringing back old traditions.

On the plain as well as in the hills the seasons are unequal in length: hard winters dominated by the bitter east wind known as the *Bise* or 'Kiss'; a spring often so short as to be scarcely noticeable; hot summers punctuated by epic storms; long, golden autumns fading gently into winter. High up there are only two seasons: a summer lasting four months and a winter lasting eight, with snow lying on the ground until April.

Yet at the same time the Jura countryside is a region of plenty: wine grown on the Revermont, the slope of the first plateau; salt made at Salins-les-Bains, now rather down-at-heel, an immensely wealthy centre in medieval times as well as occasioning the region's most extraordinary architectural curio, the royal salt works built by Ledoux at Arc-et-Senans; wood for heating and building – over 40 per cent of Franche-Comté is wooded; abundant fish in the lakes and rushing torrents; milk and cheese aplenty; mushrooms from the forests. But much physical effort and ingenuity is required to wrest this bounty from a pitiless nature.

The cuisine is based on the presence of a fairly limited range of superb natural produce: trout from the streams which provide some of France's best fishing; game on hand from nearby Bresse, cooked in local wine and accompanied with ceps, morels and chanterelles; mountain-cured hams and sausages such as the famous Jésu of Morteau. All this has been made known, but not too well known, by M. André Jeunet, the genial giant who keeps the Hôtel de Paris in Arbois. Cheese is either Comté ('French gruyère'), preferably without too many holes and probably made in one of the 400-odd village farm cooperatives whose existence was first mentioned as early as the thirteenth century, and which are a distinctive feature of the Jura, or else the smooth Morbier, or from higher up near the Swiss border the Vacherin or Mont d'Or, so creamy that it can be eaten with a spoon.

Until the nineteenth century the Jura vineyard, confined to the narrow escarpment joining the plain to the first plateau, was one of the most important in France. Then it was ravaged by the phylloxera disease, and languished barely productive for many years. For the proprietors it was more immediately profitable to use their land for farming than to invest in new vines which would not produce for five years. It was not until after World War II that the vineyard was put back on the map

Jura

by a dynamic grower and businessman, Henri Maire of Arbois. Centres of production of this highly distinctive wine which has many admirers include L'Etoile, Château-Chalon (which has no château but is famed for its *vin jaune*); and Arbois's neighbouring village of Pupillin which traditionally stands up to its nearby Goliath with the taunting rhyme which runs: 'Arbois le nom, Pupillin le bon.'

Absinthe was produced on a large scale in the Jura at Pontarlier until the fiery liquor was outlawed by the Government on the outbreak of World War I. Thereby hangs a tale which shows alcohol in the service of science. On 11 August 1901, the Pernod distillery was struck by lightning and a devastating fire broke out. A workman opened the taps of the absinthe vats to avoid an explosion and a million litres flowed into the water of the river Doubs. The courageous firemen, refreshing themselves with water from the heavily dosed river, became euphoric and waves of laughter and singing swept over the tragic scene as they stumbled about their work. Two days later, the nostrils of villagers living near the source of the Franche-Comté's other great river, the Loue, were tickled by a strong odour of absinthe. They hastened to the source where they noted that 'the water was foaming in white soapy flakes in the eddies of enormous masses of dirty green scum'. The mystery of the origin of the Loue, which had long preoccupied geologists, had at last been solved.

The spirit distilled from the macerated roots of the gentian plant of the second plateau of the Jura is considered by those fortunate enough to obtain it as the best *digestif* in the world.

Extremes of climate have also governed the evolution of rural architecture. Like most things in the Jura the massive, foursquare farmhouses, often built in a terrace row along the village street, are strictly functional. The living quarters, on one or at most two floors represent only a small fraction of the space beneath those astonishing expanses of tiled roof. The rest is a loft of cathedral-like proportions, the roof supported by intricate systems of wooden pillars which are hidden masterpieces produced in the past by anonymous craftsmen whose descendants, happily, still maintain this great tradition. Forage is traditionally stored in the loft, and spectacular fires are not uncommon when lightning strikes during summer storms; the farmhouses are then replaced by new, unmemorable, fireproof structures. But the loft also contains within its envelope a cushion of air which superbly moderates summer heat and winter cold. Like the domestic buildings the village churches, with their distinctive belfry tops wearing a cap of tiles like Marianne's, are solid rather than elegant.

The long winters on the high plateaux fostered the development of the precision cottage industries which are another marked feature of the rural Jura: watchmaking in the Haut Doubs; diamond cutting, the optical industry and woodcarving in the Haut Jura. The optics industry began in the eighteenth century when a farmer had the bright idea of using fencing wire to make rims for his spectacles. Today the industry is centred on the little town of Morez, but the villages of the canton of Saint-Claude in which Morez lies are given over almost entirely to small-scale industrial enterprises. Already in 1958 agriculture only constituted 8.5 per cent and industry 58 per cent of economic activity in the canton, and since then the agricultural share of the economy has dropped even further.

Another, newer rural industry has suddenly come to the Jura countryside in recent years. With its vast forests of conifers and broadleaved trees, its lakes, rivers and spectacular panoramas, the region has always been ideal for decentralized, off-the-beaten-track tourism, the pillar

of which is the village hotel to which the same visitors return year after year. (Attempts to promote large-scale tourist facilities in recent years have not on the whole been fortunate.) But in the early 1970s the new boom in cross-country skiing brought a big change in the pattern of tourism.

Many villages, most notably the tiny hamlet of La Chapelle des Bois on the border of the Doubs and the Jura, have set out to promote this sport which requires inexpensive equipment, minimal specialized training (along with maximum caution where weather conditions are concerned), and for which the Jura with its thousands of kilometres of forest paths is an ideal setting. A Grande Traversée du Jura, stretching from the Ain to Mouthe, has been established. Each village which is situated on the route has a primitive refuge for the skiers and many of them have trained monitors. The Transjurassienne has rapidly become France's biggest cross-country skiing race and annually attracts more than 3,500 competitors of all ages.

The writers and artists of the Jura have reflected not only the austerity and hardness of the region but also a vein of wild fantasy and excess which, although easily ignored on superficial acquaintance, is an integral part of the character of Jura country people.

Anyone who wishes to get the feel of the Jura countryside from afar could do no better than look carefully at Courbet's paintings of the region which formed him. He immortalized his birthplace, Ornans in the Doubs, with the great *Burial at Ornans* in the Louvre, but also captured many other scenes of life in the region – the return from market, the poacher in a snowy landscape (no one ever painted snow better), the hunter, the rocky waterfalls, the lonely farmhouse – and looking at them is to become aware of how little the aspect of the people and places has changed since then.

Gruyère, known locally as Comté, is the most important, and most famous, of the region's cheeses.

Jura

If Courbet is the painter of the Jura, its poet is harder to find, although Rouget de Lisle, who wrote *La Marseillaise*, came from Lons le Saunier. But there is no lack of regional novelists with plenty of poetry in them.

Louis Pergaud (1882-1915) won the Goncourt Prize in 1910 with a collection of animal tales entitled *De Goupil à Margot*. But his lasting achievement is *La Guerre des Boutons*, 'novel of my twelfth year', still in print and casting its spell on children and adults after seventy years. This story of Homeric combats between the children of two villages in the Doubs evokes unforgettably the brooding harshness of the region, and the traps of climate, poverty, family, and growing up. Pergaud was tragically killed in World War I as he was reaching the height of his literary powers.

Marcel Aymé (1902-67) is a Jura writer whose true genius was slow to be recognized. His blending of the real, barnyard world with extravagant creatures of fantasy presents country life as Aymé saw it in the Jura early in the century after a surrealist wand has been waved over it. His masterpiece, *La Jument verte* (1933; *The Green Mare*, 1938) could perhaps best be described as *Cold Comfort Farm*, French-style.

Another Jura writer, now largely forgotten, was Auguste Bailly, who wrote a number of earthy novels in the 1920s about life on the high Jura plateau around

Saint-Laurent-en-Grandvaux. The men of Grandvaux, the 'Grandvalliers', in the not-too-distant past were famed for their epic journeys through Europe peddling wood and cheese. Each driver leading six robust carts each drawn by a single horse, they followed an astonishing itinerary: Paris, Lyons, Bordeaux, Marseilles, Le Havre, Vienna, Milan, Madrid. The historian Lucien Fèbvre wrote of them: '. . . they bought on the spot whatever could fill the gaps in their carts bought and sold, bought, bartered and exchanged their merchandise twenty times.' In spring, they were back in their villages with groceries, seeds, sugar and coffee, ready to become once more farmers, woodcutters and cheesemakers.

A final anecdote about the rugged people of this high plateau illustrates their unshakable independence as well as a sly humour, which may be more Anglo-Saxon than Gallic! On 9 May 1800, Napoleon, then First Consul, stopped at Les Rousses on his way to his second Italian campaign. Les Rousses was a poor village and the commissaries seeking food for the army had little luck. As a joke a shopkeeper offered to sell potatoes at one *écu* each. He was dragged before Bonaparte for insolence. 'How dare you ask such an exorbitant price?' cried the First Consul. 'Are potatoes so rare in this part of the world?' Unperturbed, the shopkeeper replied, 'No, your excellency, potatoes are not rare . . . but First Consuls are!'

(Left) The Jura massif forms the boundary between France and northern Switzerland. This mountainous region provides excellent sporting and skiing.

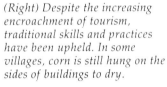

(Right) Despite the increasing encroachment of tourism, traditional skills and practices have been upheld. In some villages, corn is still hung on the sides of buildings to dry.

Rocks and waterfall at Baumes-les-messieurs.

BURGUNDY

Burgundy for some people typifies much that is best about rural France – a land of wine and song, joviality and hearty living. This image is only partly true, for the famous vineyards cover only a small sector of this large and diverse region where the people for the most part are not especially bibulous or jolly. They are proud, however, of belonging to one of the most historic of French provinces, where the past has everywhere left its imprint. The solitary rock of Solutré, rising from the plain west of Mâcon, bears remains of a Stone Age settlement dating from 12,000 to 15,000 B.C. Alésia, northwest of Dijon, was a hilltop capital of the Gauls where Vercingétorix made his final doomed stand against Julius Caesar. Much later, Burgundy became a focal centre of Christianity, as witness the great abbey of Cluny. In the fourteenth and fifteenth centuries it was an independent dukedom, its domains stretching from the Low Countries to the borders of Provence. Today, as in the past, it lies astride one of Europe's major through-routes: the big motorway junction near Beaune unites holiday traffic pouring south from many parts of northern Europe.

Though nowhere mountainous, Burgundy is a conglomerate of wooded hills intersected by broad valleys where three main rivers flow: the Saône, the Yonne and the upper Seine. The east-facing vine-slopes of the Côte d'Or and the Mâconnais are backed by forested limestone plateaux. Elsewhere, the scenery is more gentle and pastoral, as cattle graze in the water-meadows and corn grows on the rolling plains. It is a fertile land, blessed by nature. But it contains also one wilder zone, unlike the rest: the Morvan. This is a rocky granite massif of great beauty, with fast-flowing streams and waterfalls, hillsides bright with wild flowers, and clear blue lakes bordered by forests of oak and beech.

And the Burgundians? They tend to be burly, with large round smiling faces. Robert Speaight, actor and writer, has described them as 'earthy and realistic, generally balanced, physically tough, argumentative, eloquent, and slightly mischievous' (*The Companion Guide to Burgundy*, Collins, 1975). This is probably truest of the vine-growing regions: elsewhere, in Bresse and the Auxois, for instance, people are more reserved. And even the farmer of the Côte d'Or vineyards is no mere bundle of ingenuous jollity. He can also be wary: he will not make new friends easily, though once a friendship is formed, he will be doggedly loyal. Equally he has a keen sense of commerce and public relations, knowing well that those lusty songs he sings at the big touristy wine festivals are good for Burgundy's image, hence for trade. Yet he is no hypocrite. He *is* genuinely gregarious, enjoying banquets and wine-parties where the famous local drinking-songs are belted out in chorus – 'Joyeux Enfants de la Bourgogne' and 'Chevaliers de la Table Ronde'.

Some of the old customs connected with banquets and drinking have recently been revived: for example, the *cousinerie*, when the people of a village all welcome each other as 'cousins' over extensive drinking in a wine-cellar. At a wedding, the bridal couple are given a special wine-cup made of tin, pewter or silver (depending on the families' wealth); they drink together, plighting their troth, and must keep the cup for ever.

'Je suis fier d'être bourguignon' is perhaps the most typical of local drinking-songs. Regional patriotism here is expansive and self-confident, and the Burgundian will seldom emigrate unless he must. Emigration has been mainly from the Morvan, traditionally a poor area like the Auvergne. The Morvandiaux, as the inhabitants are called, used to live remote, isolated lives in dingy thatch-

Burgundy

ed cottages in their forests, wary of change and progress. Today they are more prosperous and open. But this lovely area is still the most backward in Burgundy.

In the hillier parts of the province, many villages are built round a well. The traditional vinegrower's house is a curious edifice, for the cellar is its centrepiece. This was built first, at just below ground level, and then the living rooms were put on top of it. First-floor rooms are often connected by an open corridor, a kind of verandah. And the cellar is still in a sense the main room, for this is where the banquets and parties are held. In the Côte d'Or, the roofs of patterned coloured tiles that are so striking a feature of many grand buildings (the Hôtel-Dieu at Beaune, for example) can be found also in small villages on a few leading buildings, such as the church, the *mairie*, or a manor. Elsewhere in Burgundy, and not-

ably in the Auxois, one finds a few fortified medieval hilltop villages, such as Flavigny and Châteauneuf. It is a province of architectural diversity, stretching as it does from the confines of the Ile-de-France, at Sens, down to Bresse where the roofs of red curved tiles have the look of buildings of the Midi.

In many parts of Burgundy, and not only the vine-growing areas, the local people have been keeping alive their festivals and folk traditions. Semur-en-Auxois is the scene of the oldest horse-race in France, dating from 1649: the Course à la Bague. It is held every May, and the winner gets a gold ring which he keeps till the next year. On the river Yonne in summer there are nautical jousts: teams of people aboard rival boats do battle with long wooden lances, and the aim is to topple the other boat over. Dijon has a major international folklore festival in

Burgundy is a region of rolling wooded hills cut by wide river-valleys. Vines clothe the slopes of the Côte d'Or and the Mâconnais in the east.

(Above) Festivals are held in many parts of Burgundy, in both towns and villages, where old costumes and folk traditions are kept alive.

(Opposite) Place François Rude, Dijon. The city is the historic capital of Burgundy and today is an important centre of industry and commerce.

September, while at Châteauneuf-en-Auxois on Christmas Eve there is a medieval midnight mass, as in Provence. Museums depicting aspects of traditional life include a costume and folk museum at Château-Chinon, a timber-floating museum at Clamecy and a crafts museum at Romanèche-Thorins.

Besides visiting such places, the enterprising tourist can also, if he wishes, share more directly in country life. Various centres hold courses on rural crafts. At Ratilly (Yonne) you can stay in a château and be taught pottery. Other châteaux will teach you how to weave the local way. At Nuits-Saint-Georges, the Countess de Loisy welcomes paying guests to her family home and lectures them on Burgundy wines and culture. And, especially popular with English and Americans, at Pailly (Yonne) there are residential courses on French cookery, which are held in an eighteenth-century farmhouse. This is where to learn how to manage that subtle *beurre blanc* for your *turbot poché*.

The grape may be Burgundy's most renowned agricultural product, but it is by no means the only one. In fact, even in the Côte d'Or *département*, vines cover only 2.8 per cent of the farming land, most of which is given over to cereals, vegetables and livestock. Mixed farming is common. A farmer lucky enough to have a large number of acres – say, more than 150 – will probably devote himself to cereals, which provide a secure and steady income since the prices are fixed by the Common Market. Pig-breeding requires less land but is a more chancy business, as prices fluctuate.

After the vine, the principal glory of Burgundy farming is cattle and notably the famous Charolais beef which is produced mainly on the fertile pastures around Charolles, west of the Mâcon hills. Here a visit to a cattle market is quite an experience, notably the big one held every Thursday at Saint-Christophe-en-Brionnais where the farmers and dealers stand around in their hundreds. The cattle are not weighed: the parties to a deal estimate an animal's weight simply by looking at it.

Charolais beef in a wine sauce (*entrecôte marchand de vin*) is just one of many celebrated local dishes of a province that has been a gastronomic centre since Gallo-Roman days – and not surprisingly, for good wine habitually brings good cooking in its wake. Dijon, well known for its aromatic mustards, today has a big gastronomic fair every November; and it is probably true to say that the country people of Burgundy eat as well as any in France. A banquet might begin with parsleyed ham baked in white wine and marinated in vinegar (*jambon persillé*) or a simpler leek-and-potato soup (*potée*). Then might come snails or crayfish, or even frogs; then one of the dark wine stews so popular locally, such as *coq au vin* or *boeuf bourguignonne*. This is not a great region for cheeses: but the pungent, creamy Epoisses, made in the town of that name, rivals any Norman product, though strangely it is little known outside Burgundy.

Burgundy/Wines

The wine industry of Burgundy is a fascinating but complicated subject. Although there are only two main grape varieties, Pinot Noir for the reds and Chardonnay for the whites, and a well-defined vineyard area producing a handful of famous wines such as Chablis, Nuits-Saint-Georges, Pommard and Beaujolais, this apparent simplicity only serves in fact to hide a situation of extraordinary complexity.

Burgundy is divided into five major wine regions: Chablis (Yonne), Côte de Nuits and Côte de Beaune (Côte d'Or), Côte Chalonnaise (Saône-et-Loire), Mâconnais (Saône-et-Loire) and Beaujolais (Saône-et-Loire and

Rhône). Of these, the finest wines come from the historical Duchy of Burgundy and are mostly to be found on the west of the Route Nationale 74, travelling south from Dijon to Chagny. They are generally named after the village around which the vines grow; names like Gevrey-Chambertin, Vosne-Romanée, Beaune, Meursault, Volnay are known to every wine-lover. These are the Appellations Communales, the finer wines from each village carrying the name of the particular vineyard, Gevrey-Chambertin les Combettes for example, or if it happens to be a blend of more than one superior vineyard, Gevrey-Chambertin Premier Cru. The Grands

(Above) The Burgundian wine industry is complex and idiosyncratic, as are the wines themselves. Each appellation has its own particular character.

(Left) A vineyard at Gevrey-Chambertin, one of the villages to the south of Dijon where many of the finest wines of the region are produced.

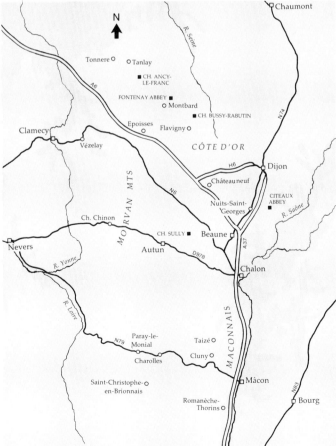

Crus, the very finest wines, do not use the village name, but only that of their vineyard: Chambertin, Musigny, Corton, Montrachet.

Each appellation has its distinct character, being lighter, richer, quicker maturing or harder than its neighbour, and in each village the vines are separated into pocket-handkerchief-sized plots, often only a few rows of vines, which distinguish differences in quality and in ownership. A few acres of a climat may be owned by more than a dozen proprietors. This parcelling is what produces the kaleidoscopic range of styles in the wines of Burgundy and provides the basis for the intricate and intertwined system of commerce.

This system is made up of the people who tend the vines, the people who make the wines and the people who sell it. Sometimes they are all the same person; more often they are not. The *vigneron* or vine-grower generally looks after his own vines and, if he is an absentee landlord, the vines are farmed under contract to another vine-grower, who usually receives half the crop in return. At the vintage, the grower makes his own wine and sometimes that of his landlord. In Burgundy it is very rare, except in plentiful years like 1982, for the *vigneron* to sell his grapes to a *négociant*, very different from the situation in Champagne.

Once the wine has finished fermenting, it becomes a commercial proposition. In some cases, the grower will keep all the wine, age it in the barrel and bottle it to sell under his own label. In most cases he will sell a portion of the wine to a *négociant*, keeping back the rest to bottle himself for his private clients, and in some cases he will sell the lot in bulk, bottling nothing.

The middleman in these sales between the vineyard and the *négociant* is the *courtier*, or broker. His job is to keep the flow of trade moving between the sellers and the buyers in the interests of both. Brokers are not allowed to hold stock, or to buy wine on their own account, in case they might be tempted to speculate. Theirs is an honourable and indispensable profession. The role of the *négociant-éleveur* is clear from the word: to purchase wines from the growers, to bring them up from an unfinished state and to re-sell them, in most cases, in the bottle. Such *négociants*, with vast cellars in and around Nuits-Saint-Georges and Beaune, have been responsible for the world marketing of Burgundy, and to a great extent for the prosperity of the region.

However, the classic equation where the *vigneron* farms the land and makes the wine, the *courtier* brokes it and the *négociant* bottles and sells it, has completely changed in the last two decades. Bottling at the *domaine* was virtually unknown until the 1920s, when the Marquis d'Angerville, Henri Gouges, Armand Rousseau and a few other like-minded growers began to fight against fraud in Burgundy, bottling wines in their own cellars to give a guarantee of authenticity. Even in 1969, only one-quarter of the wines from the Côte d'Or were bottled at the property. By 1978, this had risen to over one-half, although it fell back a little with the very large crop of 1979. The successful selling of Burgundy by the *négociants* had persuaded the growers that the future lay in

Burgundy/Wines

Vines being harvested at the village of Corton.

In Burgundy, each vigneron *makes his own wine. After fermentation a proportion of the wine is usually sold to a* négociant, *while the grower keeps the rest, ages it in the barrel, and then bottles it.*

bottling their own wine. Many of the great *négociants*, Bouchard Père et Fils, Drouhin, Faiveley, Jadot, Latour and others own considerable vineyard holdings, but they no longer rule the market. Today, the vine-grower is of equal importance in the Burgundy wine trade.

Burgundy in the 1930s, however, presented a far less healthy picture: the economic slump and a series of bad vintages had brought the wine trade to its knees, and the Appellation Contrôlée system was not yet in operation. It was in response to the falling sales and prestige that the Confrérie des Chavaliers de Tastevin was founded. Based on the idea of the medieval orders of chivalry, the Confrérie was to promote the wines of Burgundy through a series of banquets and festivities. The Château Clos de Vougeot, a magnificent Cistercian building set in

dor. The *négociants* make a point of inviting their most important clients for the weekend, and buyers and journalists fill every hotel room for miles around.

The main reason for this concentration of Burgundy lovers is the auction at the Hôtel Dieu on Sunday afternoon. The Hôtel Dieu, known generally as the Hospices de Beaune, was founded in 1443 by Nicolas Rolin, Chancellor of Burgundy. He and his wife, Guigone de Salins, endowed the Hospices (a hospital caring for the old and infirm) with their own vineyards, a tradition that still exists. To the long list of famous *cuvées* – the Beaune of les Dames Hospitalières, the Corton of Dr Peste, the Volnay of Général Muteau – have been added the Corton-Vergennes of Paul Chanson in 1975 and the Mazis-Chambertin of Madeleine Collignon in 1977. The auction of these wines is the high point of the Burgundy calendar, and has made the Hospices de Beaune the largest charity in the world. The prices paid are partly an indication of the quality of the vintage, as far as it can be judged from wines that are scarcely six weeks old, and rather more so of its commercial standing. The prestige of acquiring a *cuvée* is such that the wines of the Hospices vineyards are more expensive than similar appellations from even the best growers.

The weekend of the Trois Glorieuses has the atmosphere of a carnival, although sometimes a snow-covered one. The *négociants* throw open their cellars for tastings, shops are decorated with streamers and banners, and there are many parades. On the Saturday (for professionals only) and on Sunday there is a tasting at the Hôtel de Ville with examples of virtually every wine made that year from Chablis to Beaujolais. Everyone complains that the wines are too young to taste, but all the wine-makers are there, and it is a fascinating experience.

Those committed Burgundy lovers who were at the Chevaliers de Tastevin dinner the evening before and who sat through the auction on Sunday afternoon, will surely be found at the 'Dîner aux Candelles' that same evening. This is a more elegant, less boisterous affair than the Tastevin, and is organized by the *négociants*. It is held in the candlelit surroundings of one of bastions of the city walls, or in the crypt of one of the churches in Beaune. The food is just as Burgundian but less Rabelaisian, and the wines are donated by the *négociants* concerned, each one offering his *cuvées de prestige*. It is impossible to taste everything, and it is no surprise that one is more easily served the wines of one's host than those of his colleagues.

The third banquet of the Trois Glorieuses is a lunch at Meursault. This event is called 'La Paulée de Meursault', after the word for the rest taken at midday by the vineyard workers. It is really a fête for the local growers and merchants, and it is certainly more amusing and probably more difficult to get invited to than the two grander banquets. The Comte Lafon presents a prize of 100 bottles of his Meursault for the best literary work on Burgundy that year, the lunch lasts all afternoon and in the evening the *vignerons* of Meursault keep their cellars open for those needing further refreshment after such an arduous three days.

its own vineyards, was acquired, and the entertaining and promotion begun that has resulted in the Confrérie being copied by almost every wine region in France, and itself opening sub-chapters all over the world.

The most famous banquet of all is held on the third Saturday in November. It is the opening event of Les Trois Glorieuses, a three-day event to celebrate and sell the latest vintage. While the style of the Confrérie dinners varies little, always a truly Burgundian six-course meal with wines to match (all specially 'Tasteviné', the accolade that the Confrérie gives to wines that do well in their regular tastings), the dinner before the Hospices de Beaune is the most prestigious event of their year. Dress is formal, a trifle unusual for some *vignerons,* and the dinner is presided over by minor royalty or an ambassa-

Burgundy/Abbeys and Châteaux

In few regions of France does the countryside contain a richer array of great buildings: ancient abbeys and churches, witnesses to Burgundy's key role in medieval Christendom, and châteaux dating from the days of its prowess as a dukedom. In the little town of Cluny, near Mâcon, the great Romanesque abbey was *the* most influential religious and intellectual centre in Europe, in the hundred years or so that followed its creation in the early twelfth century. Its church was also the largest in Christendom until Saint Peter's, Rome, was built 500 years later. Alas, the abbey and its church were pillaged during the Wars of Religion, and they suffered again and worse at the Revolution. Today only parts of the vast complex of buildings survive, but enough for the visitor to gain some idea of their past glory. Cluny influenced the style of many other Romanesque churches in the region, and happily some of these have remained more or less intact: for example, the great Basilica of the Sacré-Coeur at Paray-le-Monial, west of Cluny.

The Cistercians built in a more simple and austere style than the luxury-loving monks of Cluny. The great abbey of Cîteaux, south of Dijon, was the *maison mère* of their Order, founded in 1098. Today, almost nothing of this building remains. But the twelfth-century Cistercian abbey of Fontenay, near Montbard, has been restored to something like its original state (after having been made into a paper-factory at the Revolution) and is an impressive example of the harmonious Cistercian style. The cloisters, the vaulted chapter-house, and the timberwork of the dormitory are all beautiful; and so is the quiet parkland setting. To the west, beyond the Yonne valley, the marvellous Basilica of Vézelay stands majestically on its hilltop with a medieval village nestling at its foot. Vézelay was originally built by Benedictine monks in the ninth century, then rebuilt in the twelfth century after a terrible fire had ruined the church and killed a thousand pilgrims.

The modern church of Taizé, six miles north of Cluny, is famous in an entirely different manner. Founded in 1940 by a Swiss pastor, Taizé is Europe's leading oecumenical centre, where Catholics, Protestants and others, priests and laity alike, live, pray and work happily together. Taizé has fired the imagination of a young generation of post-war Christians, and sometimes up to 40,000 young pilgrims of all nations will be camping on its hillside. An Archbishop of Canterbury has been among the many visitors to this centre which has probably done as much as any other Christian movement to heal the breach between the different churches. Its Church of the Reconciliation, built of concrete in 1962, may not be beautiful: but it is a place of vibrant present-day spirituality.

Of the region's many fine châteaux, the best date from the Renaissance. Sully, near Autun, has been called 'the Fontainebleau of Burgundy'; it stands beside a small lake in a pretty park. Rather similar in style is Ancy-le-Franc, near Tonnerre, an imposing square mansion whose rooms contain fine frescoes and tapestries. Not far away, the Renaissance château of Tanlay is highly attractive, with its distinctive domed towers and its moat where water-lilies float. The stately château of Commarin, west of Dijon, also has round towers at the corners, but their roofs are pinnacled, not domed.

Epoisses, already noted for its cheeses, has a fine château with a curious history. A ducal building existed on this site in the sixth century when it was visited by Saint Columba. The present château, still lived in by its owners, has a double circuit of fortifications, the space between them filled with a garden designed by Le Nôtre. Finally, the most strange and interesting by far of Burgundy's châteaux is Bussy-Rabutin, near Montbard. In the seventeenth century it was the home of the splendidly outrageous Count Roger de Rabutin who was exiled there by Louis XIV for writing satirical stories and songs that lampooned court life. Undeterred, de Rabutin spent his time covering the walls of some rooms of his château with frescoes and verses that wickedly comment on life in the lascivious, bitchy world of the Sun King's court.

(Left) The Basilica of Vézelay.

The town of Vézelay in its hilltop setting.

(Right) The château of Rochepot.

SAVOY

Savoy lies between the upper valleys of the Rhône and the Isère, whose waters flow down from the mountains into the broad Rhône corridor and thence to the Mediterranean. It has been called the 'ceiling of Europe', with its snow-capped crown in the Massif du Blanc, a range of peaks over 4000 metres, some two miles, above sea level. These and the many other peaks of Savoy, some with sheer walls of granite rock, are skirted by forests of pine and larch, while tumbling streams irrigate the pastureland below before flowing into one of the region's lovely lakes – du Bourget, d'Annecy, Aigueblette and Montriand. It is a land of splendour and, for those who truly occupy it, the stubborn yet creative Savoyards, a land of generosity and danger.

Catholic and conservative, Savoyard families tended to be very large until this century, with several generations living under one roof. The old alpine chalets they occupied can still be seen: a ground floor of stone to house the animals, a first floor of wood traditionally surrounded by a balcony with numerous doors into the living quarters. A part of the first floor was used to store the drying hay, which would then be transferred into the massive loft. Because of the fire risk, most families also had a smaller barn which stood some distance from the main house, where grains, family heirlooms, Sunday clothes, hams and sausages, and the huge bells and leather harnesses of the cows were kept.

For half the year, snow covers the ground and the night temperatures are well below zero. In the old days, families would gather in the evenings on the ground floor of their house, among the animals for warmth, shelling nuts, spinning hemp which made them famous for their sacks and rope, and telling stories to the children. Towards the end of the last century these *veillées*

passed out of fashion, partly because the Church – a powerful force in this region – declared it improper for humans to bed down with animals!

In early summer, the women of the family left for the high pastures, where the cattle were put to graze on the rich young grass. They took with them their small children, their bedding, pots and pans, and bees. During the summer they lived in simple shelters, built from stone gathered from the mountain streams, milking the cows, making butter and cheese, collecting and bottling honey and tending to the children. Below in the valley, the men sowed wheat and rye, tended the tobacco and vines and visited their womenfolk each Sunday, taking provisions and no doubt news.

There were always those who found the life too arduous and unrewarding, often the younger sons, and these took to the road. In the early eighteenth century, in the reign of Louis XIV, the nomadic Savoyard pedlars were well known in the streets of Lyon and Dijon, selling local woollen cloth, hemp sacks and juniper berries, the 'tea' of Savoy, highly prized for its digestive properties. Others became stokers and sweeps, shoeshine boys and street-porters, walking as far as Paris, Marseilles and Nîmes to find employment. At home in the mountains, the Savoyards were known to travellers as reliable guides through the difficult terrain: in Paris they became cab drivers and today they are the single largest regional group of taxi drivers.

Though Savoy was always a thoroughfare for merchants on the road from Rome and Venice to Paris and Amsterdam, it was only in the eighteenth century that visitors began to linger among the awe-inspiring peaks. Two Englishmen, the student Wyndham and the seasoned traveller Pococke, are said to have started the trend

Savoy

in 1741 when they found their way through the strange, deep valleys of Haute-Savoie to Chamonix nestling beneath Mont Blanc. To their surprise and relief, they were welcomed by the local inhabitants who took them up to the Mer de Glace, a vast glacier that still edges its way slowly into the upper Rhône valley. In honour of the Englishmen, the first hotel in Chamonix, opened in 1770, was called 'Hôtel de Londres', and by the end of the century, the summer tourist trade was well established. Goethe, Victor Hugo, the Emperor Napoleon III, were among the early visitors.

By 1860, when Savoy joined the French Republic, the outside world had intruded irrevocably on the tranquillity and harmony of the region. The railway tracks already reached to Annecy and Chambéry, and were beginning to have that same devastating effect on local life as they did throughout Europe. Every year saw an increase in the number of tourists flocking to the mountains for their holidays, riding in style by the same trains that brought cheap foreign cloth and the downfall of the local cloth-making industry. At first the invasion was restricted to the summer – walking and climbing for those with stamina, a cure at the waters of Aix-les-Bains or Thonon for weaker souls – but by 1900, the winters also had their draw, for the world had discovered *le ski*.

At first the winter-sports of the city folk made little difference to the farmers. True, many villages that had once been quiet in the snow were now a beehive of activity throughout the year. New cafés and hotels were opened. On the farm, though, there was business as usual, feeding the livestock, repairing the house, the cart, the wine press. Only gradually did the winter landscape change. By 1923, however, when the winter Olympic games were held in Chamonix, the villages had begun to grow into towns and profound changes were taking place in the region.

Some of the loveliest villages were colonized by the tourists – Chamonix, Courcheval, Val d'Isère, Verbier, les Menuires – and when they and the slopes around them were full, purpose-built villages appeared, like Avorriaz, high above Morzine on the Swiss border. Connected to its mother town below by a steep, winding road and the *téléphérique*, Avorriaz emerged in the 1960s almost as a reproduction of fashionable Paris life, a stone and wooden honeycomb of shopping arcades, cafés and restaurants, a nightclub, a swimming pool, an ice-rink, and hundreds of studio flats each with a panoramic view of the Massif des Hautforts.

The twentieth century has also seen the industrial growth of Savoy, as her natural resources of wood, grains, tobacco and milk came to be fully exploited. The power came from Savoy's 'white coal', her snow and ice with its vast potential for hydro-electricity. High in the valleys of the Arc and Romanche, barrages were already

The Haute-Savoie contains some of the most spectacular mountain scenery in Europe. It is a landscape of richly contrasting colours and breath-taking vistas among high peaks, glaciers and lush alpine meadows.

producing electricity by 1900 for the rice-mills of Chambéry and the many wood mills and manufacturers of furniture and sledges. Gradually a major food processing industry also developed, making pasta from local wheat, canning local fruits, coating Savoyard almonds with sugar for the famous confectionery *dragées*.

Tobacco and alcohol also became major industries. The factory at le Petit Bugey provides the dark tobacco for France's most celebrated cigarette, *Gauloise*, while, thanks to selective vine breeding over the last 50 years,

the best of Savoy's wines – Apremont, Roussette, Mondeuse and Gamay – have now been elevated to '*crus réputés*'. Vermouth, a white wine flavoured with herbs and fortified with alcohol, said to have originated in Chambéry, is also a major export. The power for all these enterprises is still entirely locally supplied, for new dams have been built in all the higher valleys, notably at the extraordinary Barrage de Tignes, which still supplies most of the hydro-electric power for Grenoble.

The mountain cheeses, originally made in the high summer pastures to last the farmer's family through the winter, are now produced by ten large cooperatives and exported throughout the world. The most famous are the Gruyères of Comté, moist and crumbly with holes as big as nuts, and the smoother Beaufort which Brillat de Savarin, the *gastronome*, himself a son of Savoy, called the Prince of Cheeses (Brie being the King). But the tiny *tomme* cheeses, once ripened in caves, with their multi-coloured rind, and the smooth-textured Reblochon, are also well known.

Local beef and lamb, fish from the rivers and lakes, bread from the valley, wheat and cheese from the high pastures: these form the basis of the Savoyard cuisine. Vegetables grow well on the lower valley slops while fruits like apricots, cherries and peaches are abundant in early summer. Together with the excellent local honey they are used in tarts and other *pâtisserie*.

(Above) From Chamonix in its majestic valley setting a cable railway runs to within 1000 metres of the summit of Mont Blanc.

(Right) In the last twenty years Avorriaz has become a favoured, and fashionable, tourist centre for winter sports.

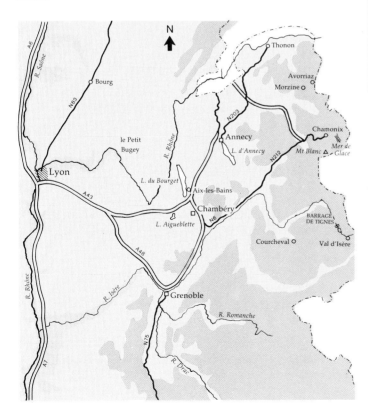

POITOU-CHARENTES

To the average foreign visitor Poitou-Charentes is less well known than many French regions and does not conjure up so sharp an image as, say, Burgundy or Normandy. Yet it is a region of great variety and interest, full of surprises, and it typifies much that is best about traditional rural France. It borders the middle part of the west coast, between the Loire estuary and Bordeaux; it comprises Poitou to the north, around its capital of Poitiers, and to the south the three ancient provinces of Aunis, Saintonge and Angoumois which today make up the *départements* of Charente and Charente-Maritime, known as 'les Charentes'. Here the river Charente winds its way from Angoulême through the vineyards of Cognac to reach the sea near the lovely old fortified seaport of La Rochelle.

Most of Poitou is a rolling plain where cattle, sheep and goats are bred on the fertile farmlands. The Charente district is part of the same plain: but here the scenery is more lush and pastoral, the light is brighter and the air milder, for sunny Charente seems to lie just south of that mysterious frontier separating northern from southern France. Everything, including the red-tiled roofs of the houses and the easy-going nature of the people, indicates that the Midi is close at hand.

The coast here is flat and marshy, with two big islands offshore (Ré and Oléron), whose splendid sandy beaches are crowded in summer. Some of the older peasant women in this area still wear a wide white traditional head-dress, the *quichenotte*, for protection against the sun. Legend has it that the word is a corruption of 'kiss not' and dates from the Hundred Years' War when women wore this coif as defence against too-amorous English soldiers.

Between Niort and the sea is the very curious area known as the Marais Poitevin ('marsh of Poitou'), a vast marshland with a society of its own. The Marais was created by an ingenious system of land reclamation begun in the thirteenth century and completed in the seventeenth. The seaward sector, the 'Marais Désseché' ('dried marsh') is a dullish open landscape criss-crossed by dykes and canals. Inland, nearer Niort, is the much more picturesque 'Marais Mouillé' ('wet marsh'), also known as 'La Venise Verte', an area of countless narrow canals that break the fields into tiny separate islands. The banks are lined with willows, elms and poplars. The peasants who live here in simple cabin-like houses have kept across the centuries their special way of life. For transport, these 'Maraîchins' (marsh-dwellers) have flat-bottomed boats which they push with poles, like punts, and they use them for carrying everything – the cows that graze in their fields, the weekly shopping, the children going to or from school, even parties of wedding guests. In summer the canals become cool tunnels of green, for the trees meet overhead. It is a strange, quiet, secluded world.

The country people of Poitou-Charentes are traditionalists, even more than most Frenchmen; sceptical, wary of change. In the north, towards the Vendée, many of them remain devoutly Catholic. But parts of Poitou and coastal Charente today remain strongholds of Protestantism, which took root more fervently here after the Reformation than in almost any other part of France. Many villages have a Protestant church. And isolated here and there in the countryside are small private Protestant cemeteries, enclosed by stone walls, sometimes with a cypress at each corner. Some of these cemeteries are still used for burials today. The region also abounds in Romanesque country churches, built in the days when

Poitou-Charentes

The canal at Coulin in the Marais Poitevin, a vast area of marshland cut by numerous canals and dykes.

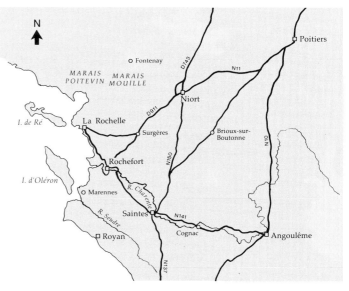

hordes of pilgrims passed this way on the routes to Santiago-de-Compostela. As opposed to the religious, the domestic architecture is unremarkable: but the white cottages of the Charente, built of local stone, do none the less have a certain charm.

This is a region where the old folk traditions are today being revived, as in many parts of France. Amateur groups have been formed with such names as 'Lo Gerbo Baudo': they perform the old dances and songs, and are much in demand for local festivals. It is a folk-culture marked by Occitan influences, with bright costumes and a lively style of dance. Some villages have also innovated *'gestes paysannes'*, illuminated pageants on summer evenings, when the villagers re-enact scenes from local history. The medieval town of Saintes has a major folklore festival in July. And in September at Brioux-sur-Boutonne, near Niort, there is an annual snail fair, the Foire aux Lumas (Latin for 'snail'), at which everyone devours the local speciality of snails-out-of-the-shell cooked in red wine and garlic.

All these activities are popular with local people, as well as with tourists. But for the latter, there is also plenty of organized rural tourism, such as holidays in a hired horse-drawn wagon. One special local feature is farming holidays for children, whereby a certain number of farmers receive six-to-thirteen-year-olds without their parents, give them board and lodging, and introduce them to farm life. They let them take part in feeding the animals, in doing the harvesting or tending the vines, and so on. This is proving popular with city children.

Agriculturally, this is a rich and diverse region, though individually the farms are not as large as on the northern French plains. Many smallholders still practise mixed farming, and many are still hampered by the parcellization of the fields which makes it hard for them to utilize fully their tractors and other machines. On the northern

plains, corn is produced and some sugar-beet. But above all this is an area of livestock, for meat and for dairy products. The local fawn-coated Parthenay cows are renowned, though today they are being replaced by the commoner Charolais breed. Together they produce milk for the prized butter of Charente, which vies with that of Normandy in quality. Its heartland is the Surgères area.

This is the leading French region for goat-breeding, with 400,000 of these animals, yielding half the total French production of goat's milk and cheese. Today the work is handled by big prosperous cooperatives. But originally the goat was the animal of the poor, a basic means of subsistence for the humble peasant. Each little farm might have three or four of them; and it would be the role of the wife, with her blue umbrella to protect her

from the sun, to take them out into the fields each day, to
supervise their feeding, to milk them and make the
cheese. Today, many farms have herds of 100 or more;
and in a *macho* spirit the men have now taken over the
task of dealing with the goats, which cannot be left to
mere women. A goat gives a very rich milk, full of pro-
teins, ideal for growing children. Its cheese is a mysterious and special recipe, since herbs and spices must
be added at just the right moment, to ensure the unique
tangy flavour. Poitou's most famous goat's cheese is the
small tower-shaped *chabichou*.

Market-gardening thrives in the coastal area, the marshes and the islands. Here onions, peas, artichokes, new
potatoes and the sweet pink Charentais melons all grow
abundantly, as do figs. On the Ile de Ré they cultivate
asparagus, while the marsh-dwellers have a special
succulent white bean, the *mojette*. The coastal strip is also
France's main breeding-ground for mussels and oysters:
in an average year, the Charente-Maritime produces over
50,000 tons of oysters, some 60 per cent of total French
output. The oysters come in several varieties, some flat,
others crinkly, like Portuguese. They are bred mainly on
the Ild d'Oléron, and in the estuary of the Seudre around
Marennes, in polders broken by dykes into thousands of
little watery rectangles.

On and near the coast, rural cuisine inclines towards
fish. *Mouclade* is a delicious stew of mussels in white
wine and cream with shallots; eels are cooked in wine
and garlic (*bouilliture d'anguilles*); *bar farci* is bass stuffed
with spinach, eggs and herbs. Inland, besides the local

Poitou-Charentes

snails in red wine, country dishes include goose stuffed with chestnuts, hare with sausages, duck liver with bilberries, and a variety of ways with eggs such as *oeufs à la tripe* (boiled eggs with tripe) and poached eggs with mussel sauce. In short, a highly gastronomic region, deserving to rank among the best in France.

A region, too, that supplies the world with one of the most prestigious and expensive of all drinks. Cognac (pop. 22,000), on the river Charente, is a one-industry town with a stately air. Almost every family earns its living, directly or indirectly, from the *eau-de-vie* made from the white grapes that grow on the chalky slopes all around. As well as the 218 brandy firms, there are other factories too: for example, a Saint-Gobain plant making cognac bottles; and so on. And it is a rich town, needless to say. In its main traffic-free shopping street, most of the shops not selling cognac are smart jewellers, their windows displaying cognac bottles wrapped in gold leaf.

Cognac was invented here almost by accident in the seventeenth century. The local people were having trouble with the exports of their rather dull white wine. So, to economize on sea transport costs, they began to distil it down to one-seventh of its volume. The customers, most of them in England or the Netherlands, were then supposed to drink it diluted with water: but they soon developed a taste for the brandy itself – happily for posterity. The Dutch dubbed it *brandewijn* (burnt wine), which the English corrupted into 'brandy'. The English have always been closely associated with the cognac business: several local firms are English in origin (e.g. Martell, founded 1715) or Irish (e.g. Hennessy).

Any distilled wine is a brandy. But 'cognac' is the *appellation contrôlée* name for brandies from grapes of the

(Above) One of the delicious local specialities of the region is goose stuffed with chestnuts.

(Left) Shrimps and crabs on sale at the market at Saintes, Charente-Maritime.

two Charentes, which are divided into six regions according to the quality of the soil: it is best where it is chalkiest. The superior regions are directly south of Cognac: Grande Champagne and, outside it, Petite Champagne. Then come the Borderies, then three outer regions known as 'Bois', yielding the more ordinary cognacs. Many cognacs are blended from grapes of different regions: the especially splendid ones called 'Fine Champagne' are a blend from the two Champagne areas (the word *champagne* means a hilly, chalky country, which here is much the same as in Champagne itself, near Reims, though the grapes are not the same).

The quality of a cognac depends partly on the soil, partly on the methods of distilling and ageing. And to enable these complex procedures to succeed, a special relationship has developed between the growers and the production firms. The grapes, mostly Ugni Blanc, are grown by 43,000 *viticulteurs*, who range from rich gentlemen-farmers in châteaux in the Grande Champagne to poor smallholders in the outer regions. Many growers do their own distilling: it is not unusual to find a farmer with 50 modest acres who has installed a modern alembic in his barn, costing some 300,000 francs. Once distilled, the crude *eau-de-vie* goes to the producers (some with famous names like Rémy Martin and Courvoisier) whose crucial job it is to age the liquid properly. This they do in special casks made of Limousin oak which give the colourless *eau-de-vie* its amber tint. Unlike wine, a cognac matures only in the cask, not in the bottle.

The price of a good cognac depends partly on its age. The cheaper 'XXX' are three to four years old. Then at five to six years come the VSOPs (more English influence – this stands for 'Very Superior Old Pale'). Older vintage cognacs are often 'Vieille Réserve'. Sometimes they are also called 'Napoléon', though strictly this should apply only to cognacs dating from the time of Napoleon III (and these hardly exist any more), before phylloxera destroyed the vineyards in 1872 and caused their replanting.

Growers, distillers and producers are closely associated in the Bureau National du Cognac which fixes each year's prices for the grapes and determines general policy. It is all a bit feudal, for within the BNC the pace tends to be set by the big producers, most of them old family firms – and very grand and proud they are too. They give instructions to the distillers, and supervise the growers' planting and tending of vines. Sometimes this paternalism is resented. But the growers accept that they could not manage without the producers, who handle all sales. Over 80 per cent of cognac is exported: the United States is the leading market, followed by Britain, with Japan fast becoming important. Rémy Martin holds the record among all French firms in all fields for the proportion of its output which goes for export: 96 per cent.

Sales rose steadily in the post-war boom decades, but have since levelled off in harder times. Today the cognac industry is also paying the price of its imprudent policy of over-planting of vines in the 1970s which has led to over-production and an expensive increase in stocks. After the bumper 1982 harvest, in order to avoid adding to these stocks, the decision was taken to destroy half the grapes – and the Common Market authorities paid out 300 million francs for having them made into industrial alcohol. The farmers, however, were paid only 7 per cent of what they would have earned if those grapes had been used for cognac. So they grumbled. Such are the vagaries of the European wine market today – even in Cognac.

(Above) Sea-food of all kinds plays an important part in the cuisine of the region.

(Right) After distillation, cognac is aged in Limousin oak which imparts both colour and flavour. Making the casks is in itself a craft which requires skill and experience.

DORDOGNE

The Dordogne, roughly equivalent to the region which the French call Périgord, is a region of great natural variety and splendour. Though part of Aquitaine, a separate chapter is devoted to it here, since this, of all French regions, has become the favourite haunt of visitors from northern Europe and the United States.

The variety of the area is indeed startling. To the east lies the Périgord Noir, with its forests of old oaks, broken by pine and chestnut woods, and bleak moorland. To the west around Bergerac lies a gentler land of vineyards, fruit orchards, strawberry and tobacco fields. To the north lie the forest of La Double and the Périgord Vert, with its meadows and woods. Few other areas of France can present such a panoply of changing scenery as that which lies between the river Lot to the south and the Vézère to the north.

The legacy of a long and tumultuous history is to be seen everywhere in the small towns, villages and countryside. Pre-Renaissance history and feudalism have left a particularly distinct mark in the form of castles, fortified manor houses and churches, tiny walled villages hiding in the shadow of towers high and low. During the Middle Ages, this was a frontier region between the English possession of Guyenne and the royal domain of the kings of France. The local nobility often found itself on one side or the other, according to the fortunes of war. Inevitably, the period left some striking examples of military architecture, such as the castles of Beynac, Castelnaud and Bonaguil. Half a dozen different architectural styles can often be observed in the same building, bearing witness in stone and mortar of continuity of habitation, of families which are deeply rooted in the life of the region.

Beron, in the south-west, is a particulary fine example of successive architectural transformations: a well-preserved keep, strong curtain walls, a Renaissance manor-house and a number of fine features dating from the eighteenth century. In the north of the region, well away from the towns, is the château of Hautefort, its imposing yet graceful outline dominating the countryside around. Apart from the major castles and fortified places, there are hundreds of smaller ones in the Dordogne, many of them built in the slightly ochre stone of the region, which looks yellowish in the summer evening sun. The sloping roofs of well-weathered tiles, pierced by dormer windows, are another distinctive feature of the manor houses and châteaux of the Dordogne.

The eventful history of the region during the Middle Ages also had its effect on the planning of towns and villages. Many of these, the *bastides*, were laid out to

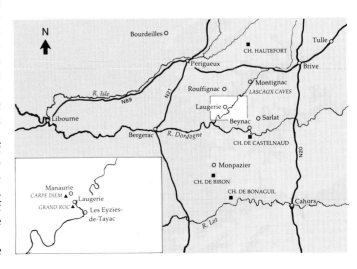

Dordogne

serve both military and civil purposes, their streets and alleyways all running at right-angles to each other. Typical of such towns is Monpazier, its main square surrounded by arcades, galleries and markets under oak-beamed roofs, still intact after 700 years.

The churches tend to be sober, four-square; towers are squat rather than soaring. Most of the smaller houses of the villages are built in the warm stone of the region. Here, as elsewhere in areas of rural France which have seen severe depopulation, many houses have been bought as second homes by French, English and Dutch city-dwellers. In most cases, though, this influx of a middle-class population from outside has ensured the preservation and eventual restoration of houses which would otherwise have fallen into ruin. And it is now a common event in the villages of the Dordogne to see, along with all the English and Dutch cars, façades stripped of the decorative accretions of later years and returned to their authentic, original stone. The villages themselves, such as Biron, Beynac and Bourdeilles, are often to be found clinging to the foot of some great castle or perched on the steeply sloping banks of one of the rivers of the region, the Dordogne or the Vézère, in an architectural jumble which freely mixes house, barn and stable. Although all the great historical styles can be traced in the succeeding generations of building, there remains the distinctive flavour of the Périgord, born of a self-sufficiency and a separateness from the rest of France. This individuality of a traditionally agricultural society is given marvellous expression in the simple strength of the most humble barns, low and long, or pigeon-lofts, formerly a sign of prosperity.

In spite of the flight from the land, exceptionally marked in the Dordogne, and the influx of a shifting population of secondary residence owners, the area still draws strongly on its agricultural and peasant past. The foreigners and the city-dwellers may have restored the houses, reassembled the ruins, but the indigenous traditional population has also ensured that the region has not simply become a desert of summer residences.

There is still a deep sense of family tradition and continuity in many of the agricultural areas of the region. Although holdings have got larger in the last two or three decades, there remain vestiges of subsistence farming. The family traditionally lived off the farm and sold the surplus, although individual members of the family would also carry out certain paid work, such as preparing stakes for the vines on the lower slopes or making charcoal. Now, the use of the farmland is more complex and sophisticated; maize and oats are grown as food for the cattle, kept both for milk and meat, and the poultry. The farmer may still sell wood, but he will also cultivate a more complex range of crops: tobacco, strawberries and a variety of vegetables. The farmer's wife will have her own particular responsibility, producing the wherewithal to pay the grocery bill: a few hens, geese, a pig or two and ducks for fattening.

The country around Bergerac is apparently an endless

The château of Monbazillac. The famous sweet white wine is produced in the locality.

Geese being force-fed to produce foie gras, *the speciality of the region.*

chequer-board of strawberries, asparagus, vines and orchards. In the Périgord Noir the forest brings a different, harsher aspect to cultivation. But this is also the country of the truffle, the 'black diamonds', which are the much sought-after quarry of pigs, dogs and poachers. In the farmyards are the flocks of geese, taking advantage of the open air and the greenery before undergoing the horrors of forced-feeding to produce the famous *foie gras* of the Périgord. Mixing with them will be the ducks, also about to be fattened for the table. Here, in the Périgord, there is a whole complex structure of rural activity based on the marvellous culinary traditions of this region, where eating is both an art and a passion.

Like most other aspects of life in the Dordogne, the cuisine has a deeply local flavour. And like the region's landscapes, it is a fascinating mixture of strength and *finesse*. The local stews and dishes with wine, needing long simmering, contrast with the perplexing variety of preserves, pâtés, sausages and hams. Cooking is done in lard or goose fat with lots of garlic. Morels, chanterelles and other edible mushrooms bring their own especial refinement to local dishes. Game is plentiful, as is fish, including river trout; and even the local trout farms usually keep their fish in running water. The great speciality of the region is, of course, its *foie gras*, which is prepared much more simply than that from Alsace; it is a great delicacy when eaten with the local black truffles, accompanied by the local sweet white wine, Monbazillac. The red wines of the Bergerac area, especially Pécharmant, make marvellous companions to meat dishes, while one of the region's plum brandies provides a satisfying *digestif* at the end of any meal in what is one of France's foremost gastronomic regions. Small restaurants can still be found in most villages where it is still possible to eat like a king for a very modest outlay.

The Dordogne is also a land of festivities and fêtes. One of the most famous of these is the festival of Sarlat.

Dordogne

For several days every summer the old city swarms with local visitors and tourists who come to see the plays performed in the open-air theatre located in a tiny square and surrounded by fine houses dating from the Middle Ages and the Renaissance. The foresters from the countryside around build their traditional huts, covered with foliage, in the streets. There are displays of work by the many craftsmen who have now come to work in the town and the surrounding villages: wrought-iron workers, making balconies in the old styles for the restoration of the historical houses, sculptors in wood, joiners and carpenters making traditional oak chests, dressers and huge cupboards. There are also antique fairs, where the tools and utensils of the past can be found: bellows, stoves, nut-crackers.

The revival of Occitan, the old language of the southwest, has recently gained new vigour here. Groups of actors now travel from village to village, giving performances in the traditional language, sometimes to the astonishment of the older inhabitants who now hear their *patois* revived. But the younger generations, especially of the educated middle-classes, are now deeply concerned that a sense of local history and tradition should survive. Even the traditional dances have found a new lease of life, in spite of the omnipresent disco.

The people of the Dordogne know how to live well but they are also very conscious of the cost of the good life. They are very strongly attached to their particular group and community, respecting its traditions, honouring its dead. Family disputes, inevitable in such long-lived communities, are rife; whole villages can be divided. Farms and hamlets have a solitary existence, minding their own business, yet everyone knows each other for 15 miles around, meeting at festivals, fairs, the market and the nearest town. Nowadays, there is more co-operation in the farming community, even extending to the purchase of jointly owned heavy machinery.

The measured and balanced quality of a regional civilization so deeply rooted in the traditional habits of rural life is a memorable aspect of this region. Even in the poorest lives, barely supported from the land, a nobility and dignity has always been strikingly evident; in the Dordogne the peasant has always been a lord.

Tobacco is one of the wide range of crops cultivated in the Dordogne.

Spring ploughing near the village of Saint-Avit-Sénieur, west of Bergerac.

Prehistoric Caves

South-West France can claim to be one of the most important continuously inhabited areas in the world. For 40,000 years *homo sapiens* has found a home in the land along the Dordogne and Vézère rivers and has left indelible traces of his passing. Deep in many of the caves or in shelters in the rockier parts of the region can be found the records of man's prehistoric development, records of man the hunter who was also frequently possessed of fine artistic skills.

The principal areas of prehistoric human habitation lie around the beautiful medieval town of Sarlat. Within fifteen miles of the town are Les Eyzies, Montignac and Lascaux. The Palaeolithic and Neolithic Periods are well represented throughout the area; almost all the Palaeolithic ages have left signs of their cultures: Chellean, Acheulean, Tayacian, Mousterian, Solutrian and Magdaleanian. The capital of this region of archaeological wealth is Les Eyzies-de-Tayac, located in a dramatic landscape of cliff and oxide-streaked rock. Through this countryside, where meadows and small woods nestle under dramatic rocky cliffs, runs the river Vézère along its canyon-like bed.

Going from Les Eyzies towards Sarlat are the caves of the Fond de Gaume and Les Combarelles. One of the more rewarding aspects of visiting the prehistoric caves is to delve into the ways in which the study of them during the nineteenth century led to the establishing of period classifications within the Stone Age. More generally, the location of the caves within dramatically varied countryside can suggest so well the world of thousands of years ago. Even though the climate and flora have changed, it is still easy to imagine primitive man eking out a precarious existence around the steep cliffs. Inside the caves were warmth and shelter, where we can now see abundant evidence of the development of primitive man as artists in the carved and painted animal forms he left behind.

Another important grouping of caves is at Montignac and Lascaux. The latter is one of the most important sites for the study of the prehistory. This was the temple where the hunters sought inspiration for success in the hunt, surrounded by the fine, multi-coloured frescoes representing their prey. Except in special circumstances, it is now unfortunately impossible to visit the caves of Lascaux, since it was discovered that the breathing of crowds of visitors was causing the paintings to deteriorate. However, the visitor can still see excellent reproductions at the site. In any case, the location of the Lascaux caves is well worth the visit, since they are set in an austere landscape of rare beauty.

Still taking Les Eyzies as the centre of exploration, the Vézère can be followed to the beautifully preserved sites of Langerie-Basse and Langerie-Haute. Close to Les Eyzies is the cave of Grand Roc, where the complex growths of stalactites and stalagmites resemble coral reefs below the ground. At the Carpe Diem cave, near the village of Manaurie, are more intricate stalactite displays. At Rouffignac is another fine cave with prehistoric paintings of mammoths, bison and rhinoceroses. To put all this in context, a visit to the museum of prehistory at Les Eyzies itself is advisable.

The sense of successive layers of human civilization and habitation is exceptionally strong throughout the region. Here, there is a feeling of continuous development and evolution over thousands of years, derived as much from the medieval ruins and modern vineyards as from the substantial vestiges of life before recorded history. In fact, if anyone were undertaking a living study of man's development, he could do much worse than concentrate his whole attention on the history of the Dordogne.

The cave paintings at Lascaux.

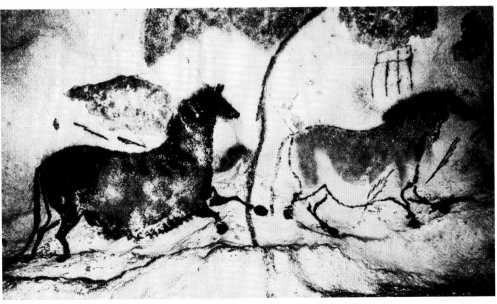

MASSIF CENTRAL

The Massif Central is a vast granite plateau that sprawls across the middle part of southern France. It is the highest region of the French interior (excluding the Alps and Pyrenees), though none of its peaks rises above 6,000 feet. Its heartland is the province of Auvergne; but it also spreads westward into the Limousin, and south into the *départements* of Aveyron and Lozère, with their bare limestone plateaux known as *les causses*, cut by deep canyons such as the lovely Gorges du Tarn. On its southern flank are the Cévennes mountains where Stevenson travelled with his donkey.

The massif is one of the strangest, wildest and least populated parts of France. Its spine is a high ridge of extinct volcanoes, which from a distance look stark and sinister, yet the valleys below them are lush and gentle. This is a land of gorgeous and varied scenery, with upland lakes full of trout and sweeping forests of pine, oak and chestnut; cattle graze on the green upland pastures, and the lower slopes are filled with orchards and fields of corn. Yet though summers are idyllic, winters can be long and hard, and the tortuous hilly roads are often snowbound. Before the coming of modern transport, this was an isolated region where man fought an unending battle against nature – and this has left tribal memories. For example, the true story of the 'Beast of the Gévaudan': a large wolf, or some think it was a bear, roamed the hills of the Lozère in the 1760s devouring some 70 people including children and shepherdesses.

The country people of the massif are a tough and resilient breed, hardened by the climate and by past centuries of poverty. The Auvergnat has often been regarded as the archetypal French peasant – stocky, dour, suspicious of strangers, and none too hygienic. But modern life has been changing him. Auvergne today is more open to the

world, and is now a tourist region with some good roads. This seems to have made the Auvergnat a little more open and friendly too, though his nature is still reserved and taciturn. He is hard-working, and exceptionally thrifty – the butt, in fact, of endless French jokes about his alleged penny-pinching, just like Scots and Swabians ('You don't use sausages for a dog-leash' is one local phrase). Auvergnats have some Celtic blood (the area's onetime Celtic inhabitants have left many traces), while the whole southern part of the massif is strongly impregnated with the medieval Occitan culture. Many older peasants still speak an Occitan *patois*, though it is now dying out.

This fairly poor region, with little traditional employment save in farming and handicrafts, has long obliged Auvergnats to emigrate in search of a living. Since the last century they have moved mainly to Paris which is sometimes called 'the largest city of Auvergne', for it contains more of them than the region's own capital, Clermont-Ferrand (pop. 160,000). Auvergnats in Paris would often start up little family businesses known as *bougnats* selling coal and firewood and combine this with running a modest café or bistrot on the same spot. Few *bougnats* survive today. But Auvergnats remain astonishingly successful in the café and restaurant trade: they own or run an estimated 60 per cent of all Paris cafés!

Rather like the Irish in the United States, many Auvergnats achieve far more success as emigrants than ever they would if they had stayed at home, and their flair and tenacity have carried some of them to top posts in France. Of modern politicians, Giscard d'Estaing, Jacques Chirac and the late Georges Pompidou all had rural roots in the Massif Central. Pompidou was born in the village of Montboudif in the Cantal, and often revisited it: canny,

113

Massif Central

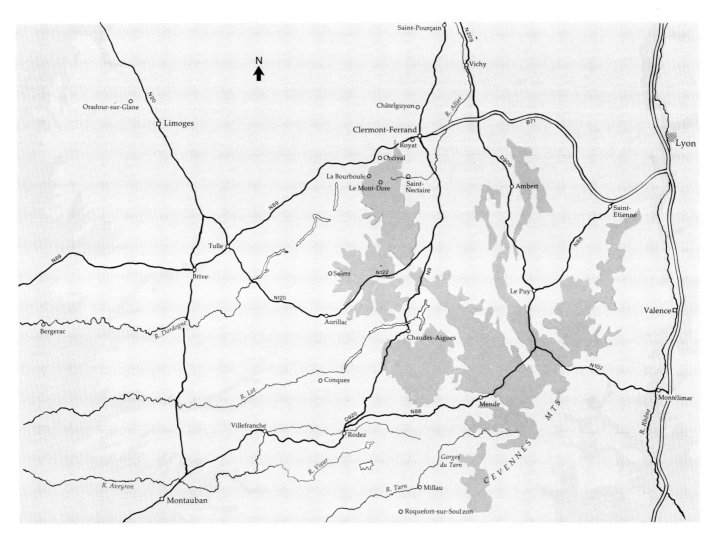

earthy, conservative, he seemed to many French to epito-mize Auvergnat rural qualities.

Auvergnats in Paris stick together in a tight colony, lending each other money, often inter-marrying. They have Auvergnat folk-dance clubs there, and a big annual ball. And they preserve an intense loyalty to the home-land they have left. Often in old age they go back there to retire, to die and be buried in the village of their birth. All this is equally true of their neighbours, the Aveyron-nais, who are more numerous in Paris than in the entire Aveyron (pop. 280,000). Today some of the younger ones soon tire of the Paris rat-race, and will go back home if they can find suitable work – like one young technician, son of poor emigré peasants, who returned to the Rodez of his childhood and succeeded in setting up a machine workshop there.

This intense nostalgia is for a region that has just a few really splendid buildings – notably, the Romanesque churches of Conques and Orcival, and the old hill village of Salers with its turreted Renaissance mansions – but where the farms are mostly poor-looking and ill-kempt and the domestic architecture is mediocre. The squat houses are built of local granite or basalt, with roofs of dark slate, sloping steeply to avoid damage from heavy

snowfalls. The Auvergnats despise exterior display, and will seldom prettify their austere house fronts, even with the odd pot of flowers. 'These severely practical people', said one newcomer, 'judge you more by the size of your vegetable garden than by the flowers you grow.' It is a legacy of poverty. Even the house interiors, though cosy in their way, are simple. The traditional peasant home has just one living-room with a huge chimney piece, and no real bedrooms, merely bed-alcoves or press-beds in cupboards. Today, however, this is changing, and farm-ers are building modern multi-roomed houses. Often a farmer will use his old home as a barn and build a new villa beside it.

There is little industry, except in the urbanized Cler-mont-Ferrand area and around Limousin's capital, Limoges. Agriculture is still the Massif's main activity. In the lowlands on its periphery, notably the Limagne plain near Vichy, the fertile soil yields crops of wheat, maize, sugar-beet and tobacco, and there are orchards of pears, apples and cherries. The uplands are for livestock – some sheep, but mainly cattle which go for slaughter and for dairy-farming, producing Auvergne's famous cheeses. In the old days the cowherd would live out close to his animals in an isolated stone hut, a *buron*: today, he usu-

Conques, with its fine Romanesque church, is in an impressive situation, clinging to steep slopes above a gorge.

Massif Central

ally prefers more modern comforts. But one tradition still going strong is the big cattle-market, held in spring and autumn, when farmers flock in to a nearby town to bargain and drink. On these occasions many of them still wear the classic local costume of blue cotton blouse and broad black felt hat.

As might be expected, the cuisine of these country folk is not refined or sophisticated, but is based on cheap, simple ingredients, prepared with a peasant ingenuity that brings out their tastiness. The homely cabbage is served stuffed with mincemeat, or is mixed with pieces of pork and chicken to form a thick, succulent soup. Somewhat similar is *potée auvergnate*, an appetising stew. Black puddings and tripe are popular, while *coq au vin* is cooked in a very dark-red local wine, Chanturgue. Over in Limousin, a rather more sophisticated cuisine includes hare stuffed with veal, carp stuffed with *foie gras*, goose served with local chestnuts, and broiled larks.

Auvergne is noted for its cheeses, all made from local cow's milk. The four best known are: Fourme d'Ambert and Saint-Nectaire, both pungent-tasting; the blue-veined Bleu d'Auvergne; and the full-cream Cantal, a big round fairly hard cheese that can weigh up to 40 kilos. It bears some relation to Cheddar – indeed, the Cantal *département* does also produce a cheese called 'French Cheddar', of which thousands of tons are exported under that name to Britain every year. But the Auvergnats prefer to keep for their own use their tasty patisseries and desserts, such as cream tarts and *clafouti* (cherries baked in batter). This upland region has few wines of any note, save Saint-Pourçain from the Allier: but the peasants do

make a curious aperitif from gentian – possibly an acquired taste.

Folk traditions have survived more robustly in Auvergne than in most parts of France, above all the *bourrée*, an ancient folk-dance that is probably Celtic in origin. It is a lively jig in three-time, a little like a waltz, and is danced by groups of men and girls who continually change partners in elaborate patterns of movement. There are scores of different versions of *bourrée*, varying from village to village: but nearly all have the basic theme of courtship and love. The man chases the coquettish girl who first rejects, then accepts him, amid much grimacing, flirtation, bowing low, and doffing of hats.

Until recently the *bourrée* was dying out, even in country areas, in favour of modern dances. But the past 20 or so years have seen a conscious revival, led very often by students and other young people. Today in the Massif Central there are over 50 regular amateur folk-groups who at fêtes will dance the *bourrée* in traditional local costumes – the men in flowery waistcoats or long blouses, bright scarves and wide-brimmed hats, the women in bodices, with flowing, coloured skirts. But the *bourrée* is not merely an animated museum-piece for the folk clubs. Most ordinary country people, young as well as old, know more or less how to dance it, and often at weddings or other parties they will start to jig away in their modern clothes. Often today the *bourrée* is accompanied by an accordeon, to the indignation of purists: but there are still special occasions when the true original local instruments are used – the *vielle*, a kind of viol, and the *cabrette*, similar to bagpipes. 'Our instruments, and our dances', said one Auvergnat, 'are remarkably similar to those you find in Brittany and other Celtic lands. It proves how deep and real are our own Celtic roots.'

In Limousin, a live tradition of a very different kind is the series of religious festivals known as *Ostensions*, which are held in a number of villages every seven years, just after Easter (the next time will be 1988). They date from the tenth century, and take the form of exhibiting the holy relics of certain local saints. The streets are decked out with banners and flowers, and the villagers parade through them in quaint and colourful costumes for festivals.

Like folk-dances and festivals, rural handicrafts too have long been a strong feature of life in the Massif Central. Many of these – for instance, lace-making and copperwork – have been tending to die out under modern conditions. But recently, as with the *bourrée*, there have been some attempts at revival – in this case officially sponsored, in a bid to create new jobs. Thus a lace-making centre has been set up at Le Puy. In the Cantal, a cooperative has begun to produce bellows. Most curiously, at Ambert a little firm is making thick brown medieval-style paper out of rags, and is doing a roaring trade selling it for fancy restaurant menus, invitation cards and handbound books. And at Mende, in Lozère, a new cooperative is encouraging farm families to practise home handicrafts in the winter as a means of adding to their incomes. Local crafts that were in danger of dying out – the making of baskets, lampshades, rugs, pottery and so on – are now being revived under the guidance of trained artisans.

(Opposite above) Milk being cooled at La Fageole. The region is famed for its cheeses, made from local cow's milk.

(Opposite below) Although cattle are the main form of livestock, sheep are also grazed on the upland pastures.

(Right) A village near Les Vans in Ardèche. The buildings are typically simple in style, made of granite with steep roofs.

Massif Central

(Right) The cabrette, a traditional musical instrument, is the Auvergnard version of the Breton biniou, not unlike the Scottish bagpipes.

(Far right) A dry-stone house at Le Tournel in the Lozère.

Unemployment is a serious problem in the remoter parts of the Massif, for there are few jobs available to replace those inevitably lost through farm modernization. Local and state bodies have been trying to find remedies, both by promoting artisan work and by coaxing small-scale modern industries into the area – with some success. Thus a small printing works has started up in one Aveyron townlet; nearby is a new firm making beauty cream; and a young engineer has hopefully opened an electronics workshop with a staff of twelve in a Lozère village. But such ventures do not work easily. Few firms will dare to settle in these isolated regions, fearing *inter alia* that they will not find adequate skilled labour. It is indeed a vicious circle.

Much of the southern part of the Massif suffers severely today from depopulation. Lozère, emptiest of any French *département*, has only 14 people per square kilometre: its number of inhabitants, 140,000 in 1900, fell to 72,000 by 1980 and is still slowly falling. In some such areas, the population has dropped below the minimum

needed for making a social life possible and for keeping up basic services. If the farms depopulate, then the village shops and schools close, and the post offices and churches too. It is especially hard on poorer elderly people without cars. Most younger people today would like to stay in the region, but cannot find the jobs: some 80 per cent of school leavers seek work elsewhere.

Since 1975 the Government has been trying to take matters in hand with a new long-term development programme for the Massif. Besides promoting small industries and handicrafts, its main aims are to encourage tourism and forestry. The Massif contains 15 per cent of the Common Market's forest area, mainly pine, oak, beech and chestnut. So there is a huge potential, but it is still very under-used and ill-organized. Some forest land belongs to the state or big private estates; but most of it is parcelled out between small owners, over 30,000 of them. What is more, the land is hilly, not flat as in the Landes, and this does not make tree-felling any easier. Yet there is much that could be done. The Government

Massif Central

In recent years there has been a
revival of traditional handicrafts
such as lace-making.

has been trying to persuade the small owners to regroup rationally, with a little success. But although there are plenty of sawmills in the Massif, there is not one wood-pulp factory or paper-mill. All the wood for pulping has to be sent to factories elsewhere that dictate their price. It is an absurd under-use of local resources.

Probably the area's future lies more with tourism than with forestry. Rural tourism has made great strides in recent years. For winter, there are several modern ski resorts on the volcanic heights, used especially for the popular sport of cross-country skiing (*ski de fond*). In summer, the season is fairly short but busy, and the moors and forests are specked with the blue-and-orange tents of *les campings*. A tourist can go on any one of a series of long-distance hiking tours over the plateau, either in a group with a guide, or on his own following signposted tracks, maybe spending the night in simple upland hostels. Or he can hire a horse and carriage and

Oradour-sur-Glane

No name evokes the horrors of the German occupation of France more than that of Oradour-sur-Glane. The modern rebuilt village of Oradour, 14 miles northwest of Limoges, is an ordinary kind of place. But, just beside it, the charred ruins of the old village have been preserved as a memorial to the most terrible of the Nazi massacres in France. A notice reads, 'This village was burned down by the SS "Das Reich" Division, June 10, 1944, and 642 inhabitants, men, women and children, were savagely murdered.'

Just after D-Day, the infamous Das Reich Division was facing constant harrassment from resistance guerilla units as it struggled northwards across central France to join the Normandy front. So its senior officers decided that mass reprisals against the innocent might be the neatest form of defence. First on 9 June they hanged 99 hostages in public in Tulle. Then they decided to make a special example of Oradour. Why this particular village was selected has never become clear, for it was not a resistance centre. Nonetheless, in the early afternoon of 10 June an SS major arrived there with 120 men, plus incendiary weapons and high explosives. The entire population was rounded up. The men were divided into groups, herded into various buildings and there machine-gunned. All died save five, badly wounded, who at first lay still, pretending to be dead, and later managed to escape.

More frightful still, the 241 women and 202 children were shut up in the church, where the SS placed a crateful of lethal smoke-bombs on the altar-piece and exploded it. The terrible scene lasted a few minutes as the victims struggled to escape from the foul smoke which was burning their eyes and lungs. All died, save one woman who climbed out of a window despite having five bullets in her body. She hid, and survived. At sunset the SS set the whole village on fire.

There is some evidence that the SS major had exceeded his brief. At all events, many non-SS Germans were genuinely distressed when the news of the massacre leaked out. The chief German military attaché at Vichy even told the Swiss Minister there that he was ashamed to be wearing German uniform. And yet, when the Oradour war crimes trial was held in 1953, of the 43 SS men, many of them officers, who were condemned to death *in absentia* by the court, not one could be found and executed. All had disappeared.

A visit to the village today is a macabre experience. All has been left just as it was. In and around the ruins are mementoes of daily life in 1944 – a few rusty old cars, a charred sewing-machine, advertisements for chocolate and motor oil, a faded shop-front sign, 'boulangerie'. The church still stands, roofless, with wreaths and flowers inside. In a memorial crypt beside the cemetery, a small museum contains such relics as old banknotes, coins, penknives, and toys including a small girl's bicycle.

'Nicht vergessen', says a notice. In summer, tourists come here in thousands, French, British, American . . . even quite a few Germans.

---

jog for days down forest paths like a gipsy.

It is also possible for the holidaymaker to mix on close terms with farming life. There are some places where he can take courses in local handicrafts – iron-forging, basket-making, or distaff wool-spinning – and there are even one or two farms where the tourist can spend a few days learning how to milk cows, make hay and practise local recipes. Ideal for the weary tycoon. And the farmers are getting extra labour for free!

As elsewhere in France, there are also plenty of *gîtes ruraux*, which are old farm cottages or stables converted by farmers for summer rentals or paying-guests. It adds usefully to their incomes. City dwellers come gladly to these country lodgings, and lasting friendships are often formed with the farmers: there have even been one or two marriages. It is one more aspect of the new yearning of the urban French for country life, and of the narrowing of the old gulf between *paysan* and *citadin*.

Another and surprising new aspect of the narrowing of this gulf can be found today in the Cévennes uplands of southern Lozère, an area where the peasantry is still strongly Protestant. Centuries ago the Protestants fled into these lonely hills, and were repeatedly persecuted by armies sent from Paris. Today those wars of religion are long past, but not forgotten: the Cévenol Protestants still retain a mistrust of Paris and all its works. But into their midst in the late 1960s there came a strange new assortment of peaceful invaders – hippy middle-class drop-outs from Paris and other cities, disillusioned by the failure of the May '68 revolt, seeking a new 'pure' way of life in the country.

These newcomers set about trying to scratch a living from hillside farming on a few stony acres, or from handicrafts, or both. It was all rather romantic. But they soon found that such a life was not the idyll they had supposed, especially in the long, icy winters. Many grew fed up and drifted back home. Moreover, frictions tended to develop with the devout local Protestant peasants who were often shocked by their free-living, free-loving ways. However, a fair number of these dropouts have stayed on, and gradually they have adapted to local ways and been accepted by local society. One girl who arrived in 1972 as a hippy rebel has now become a municipal councillor. She, and others like her, just about manage to make a modest living, breeding goats, selling cheese or honey, making rugs or pottery. And they are happy, probably happier than they would be back in Paris. There are only some 3,000 of them in the Cévennes, and their arrival can help only marginally to solve the basic problems of Lozère and the rest of the Massif Central. But they provide a fascinating footnote to the study of changing French rural society.

Massif Central/Roquefort Cheese

The village of Roquefort-sur-Soulzon straggles along the foot of a great limestone cliff in the *causses* region of southern Aveyron. And it is in caves deep in this cliff that every cheese bearing the genuine Roquefort label is matured. Roquefort, blue-veined, slightly oily in texture, with a uniquely heady, tangy taste, is to other cheeses what champagne is to other wines. It is arguably the king of Europe's cheeses. Its very special quality derives from a unique combination of factors found only in these caves. First, the ancient fissures in the rock which permit a cool, even temperature all the year and a high degree of humidity. Second, and most mysterious, a penicillin fungus which grows naturally in the caves and is added to the young cheese to produce its special aroma.

According to an old legend much cherished locally, Roquefort was invented by chance, many centuries ago, when a young shepherd deposited his frugal lunch – a chunk of ordinary cheese on a slice of bread – in a cleft in the rock, while he went off to court some damsel. This urgent task made him forget about his lunch, which he

The village of Roquefort-sur-Soulzon at the foot of the limestone 'mountain' of Combalou seen from within one of the caves.

(Opposite above) Sheep at a rainwater drinking trough on the plateau near Roquefort.

(Opposite below) Roquefort is one of the greatest French cheeses. Casanova enjoyed it with iced ham.

(Opposite far right) Cheeses at the second maturing phase in the limestone caves at Roquefort.

chanced on months later and was startled to find that it had grown blue veins and a fungus and tasted delicious and unusual. Maybe this tale should be taken with a pinch of salt (if not of penicillin). What is certainly true is that cheese was matured here in Roman days, and its qualities were known later to Charlemagne who had shipments of it sent to his court at Aix-la-Chapelle.

Roquefort is made only from the milk of ewes, more pungent than the milk of cows or goats that is used for 'lesser' cheeses. These ewes belong to private farmers, and mostly they roam the chalky uplands of the Aveyron and the adjacent Tarn and Lozère; just a few are farther afield, in the Pyrenees and Corsica. Some 8,000 farmers own a total of 800,000 ewes milked for Roquefort; four litres of milk is needed to produce a kilo of cheese, and each ewe's output is enough for some 30 kilos a year.

The milking season is December to July, with a high point in February to May when the lambs are born. The fresh milk is taken each morning to a cheese-making dairy near the farm, where morsels of the *penicillium roqueforti* are added to it, and then it is churned and curdled. After a few days, the young cheeses are then moved to the huge caves at Roquefort where they are stacked in rows and left to mature for three months. During this time the fungus grows and spreads inside the cheese, creating the veins and the fermentation. The process is helped by the moist climate in the caves which stays at a steady 8°C all year, without human help, and whatever the weather outside. This is due to the deep natural fissures in the caves, created by subsidence in prehistoric days. Here in these damp clefts the fungus grows, today specially cultivated on rye bread.

Once matured, the cheese is wrapped in tin foil to keep it fresh, and is kept in cold storage so that it can be sent for sale at any time of the year. Each of these great round cheeses, some three inches high by ten across, weighs about 3 kilos. And some six million a year are made by the major Roquefort firms, of which the biggest bears the somewhat odd name of Société ('company') – as if were the only company in the world! They are a proud and vulnerable breed, these Roquefort cheese-makers, as proud as the haughty barons of Champagne and Cognac.

Production has been rising steadily, reaching an annual 16,000 tons in 1981. Ninety per cent of this total is sold inside France; the rest goes for export, to Europe, and above all to the United States. But this trade to the United States poses problems of hygiene control, for Roquefort is not pasteurised – indeed, it could not be so, without losing its taste. For some years, then, the American authorities banned its entry. Then they agreed to let it be a special case, and today Roquefort is one of the very few non-pasteurised dairy products which is allowed into the United States.

Even today, some American visitors to Roquefort are horrified at the way the cheese is made – all that live fungus! One local cheese-maker enjoys telling the true story of a tourist who was shown round the caves and then, perplexed, asked why that special aroma couldn't be produced by more 'hygienic' means. 'Well', said the guide, somewhat piqued, 'we have another secret ingredient besides the fungus. Before the milk is churned, the ewe pees into it. *That* is what gives the special flavour you have just tasted. If we pasteurised the pee, there'd be no taste left.'

Massif Central/Spas

The volcanic soil of Auvergne is exceptionally rich in minerals and underground springs. Hence, this is the main region of France for thermal cure centres and mineral waters: in the valleys of north-east Auvergne, around Clermont-Ferrand, are no less than 20 spa towns. They receive many thousands of *curistes* a year who come to take the waters in the hope of easing their ailments, and each spa has its speciality depending on its minerals – Vichy for liver complaints, Royat for the heart and arteries, Saint-Nectaire for kidney troubles, Le Mont-Dore and La Bourboule for asthma, and so on.

Underground streams, fed by rainwater, flow through clefts and channels deep in the soil, mingling with the volcanic gases and absorbing the chemicals in the rocks. The deeper the stream, the stronger the pressures on it which cause the water to rise in temperature: so, at the surface, the hottest springs are those that have come from deepest underground. At the aptly-named spa of Chaudes-Aigues the water reaches 82°C, while at La Bourboule it is only 40°C.

With rising prosperity, the French since the war have become much more concerned with personal health and keeping fit. And despite the growth of modern forms of medicine, a good deal of this new health vogue is directed towards the old-established spas, which used to be the smart resorts of a rich few, but are now popular centres. Most cures are paid for by the national health service. Today some 500,000 French *curistes* per year attend spas, though this is small compared with Germany's two million. Auvergne has shared fully in the boom: La Bourboule, for instance, had 13,000 *curistes* in 1950 and 24,000 in 1982.

Oddly enough it is Vichy, best-known spa not only in Auvergne but in all France, that alone has failed to benefit. Its clientèle has been falling sharply, and today it ranks a mere fourth in Auvergne in terms of numbers of *curistes*, behind Royat, La Bourboule and Château-Guyon. Is this because of Vichy's wartime political stigma? Hardly. Or because the French, far more diet-conscious than they used to be, today have less need for their swollen livers to be treated at Vichy? Maybe, a bit. But, above all, it seems that Vichy is victim of its own success in selling across France and the world, in huge quantities, its famous bottled mineral water with its subtle, refreshing taste of sodium bicarbonate. Said one thermal expert: 'If people can drink the water from a spa in their own homes, they feel less need to go and visit it.'

Two thriving and typical spas are Le Mont-Dore and La Bourboule, sedate little Victorian towns that nestle in the verdant valleys of the Mont-Dore foothills, amid a backdrop of wooded uplands. Both lie on the banks of the upper Dordogne. Both specialize in asthma cures: the main difference is that Le Mont-Dore caters mainly for adults, and its rival mainly for children (due to its milder climate, and because it also treats skin diseases).

La Bourboule used to be very fashionable, notably with the British upper classes: Queen Victoria would stay here at the vast Hotel Metropole, now a block of flats. Today the only relics of that golden era are the names of some surviving hotels – Les Iles Britanniques, des Anglais. The white cupolas of the imposing Grand Baths still gleam proudly in the sun, but La Bourboule is hardly chic. In summer it is crowded with school children who come to be treated for asthma or eczema by waters that have the highest arsenic content in Europe (this is not poisonous: it is the basis of the cure). After hours in the warm baths, the children must then wrap their heads warmly to avoid sudden exposure to the cooler outside air, even in summer – and it is a bizarre sight, on an August day, to see crocodiles of them trooping back to their hotels, their faces masked in thick scarves like Arctic explorers.

Le Mont-Dore, nearby, was first used as a spa by Gauls and then Romans: in the main baths are remains of a huge Roman column, with friezes. The town calls itself 'the world capital of asthma'. Its main baths look ugly outside – 'like a provincial railway station', someone said – but inside they are palaces of marble. Here *curistes* generally come for a three-week course of steam baths, gargling, nasal sprays and inhalation, under the guidance of a doctor. The local waters are used also for treating rheumatism, and for improving the vocal chords. There are steam showers that allegedly can cure certain neuroses. And it is even claimed that Le Mont-Dore can alleviate hypochondria – although Dr Coué was never on the staff.

The hot-water springs at Vichy, the most famous of all French spas, are renowned for their beneficial effects in the treatment of liver and stomach disorders.

Massif Central

A Village in Cantal: A Personal View

With its church, two cafés-restaurants, grocery, town hall, sub-post-office, telephone box and two small primary schools (one state, the other Roman Catholic), the village is fairly typical of present-day south-west Auvergne. Before the last war, when cars were relatively rare, there were four groceries, two smithies and a bakery. Today, bread is delivered twice a week from a neighbouring village. And, curiously perhaps in such a small community with no great sea-food tradition, a weekly fish van does a thriving trade in ultra-fresh tunny, turbot, shrimps and squid as well as the more familiar trout and salt cod.

The village is located in the southern Cantal, an area that never suffered a massive rural exodus like the Lozère. True, the population has halved in the last century. But there is little visible sign of this: the modern peasant requires far more spacious living conditions than his forbears, so the number of derelict houses are very few.

The village has been dragged unwillingly but ineluctably into the twentieth century. The number of households with a telephone has tripled since 1975. All the farms now have milking machines. The local *patois*, the natural language of anyone over 35, is now hardly ever spoken by the young, though they understand it. This is the result not so much of schooling in French, which the older generation also received, as of the exclusively French television programmes now received in almost every village home.

Yet stubbornly, affectionately, the villagers cling to their traditional values wherever possible. Although farmers are forced by the extremely steep terrain to rely mainly on their dairy herds for income, many of them have recently installed modern pig-rearing batteries. Any suggestion, however, that they might themselves eat the battery-reared animals is met with scorn (*'Ça, c'est pour les Parisiens!'*). Every farmyard houses two or three privileged pigs, which are pampered with Jerusalem artichokes, beets, windfalls and so on, and often allowed to roam in the woods and grub for acorns and chestnuts. When a pig is slaughtered – still an important event – it is turned, as it always has been, into succulent raw ham and dry sausages (though the pattern has changed slightly with the advent of the deep-freeze, now as common a piece of equipment as the television set in the village home).

Similarly, the villagers prefer their farmyard chickens, turkeys and rabbits to the bought product, not so much out of Auvergnat thriftiness (they realize that when time and the cost of feed are calculated the price

(Left) A buron, *a stone hut in which shepherds used to take shelter. They are particular to the Auvergne.*

(Right) The small village of Orcival set in a wooded valley at the foot of the Mont–Dore contains a fine Romanesque church.

A Village in Cantal: A Personal View

difference is minimal) as out of wariness: they like to know exactly what they are eating. Thrift there is, and this shows in their eagerness not to squander the bounty of nature – chestnuts, wild mushrooms, game.

Several other traditional aspects of village life are unlikely to die a sudden death. Traditional French male chauvinism continues to flourish. There is still at least one farmer's wife who follows the old custom of eating standing up, while ministering to her seated husband's every culinary whim. And women of the older generation are never totally at ease when at table.

There are three or four masses a week at the village church, including a 'farmers' mass' on Saturday evening. After the service on Sunday morning, the menfolk repair to the café, leaving their wives and children to wait in their cars for anything up to half an hour.

On the rare occasions when 'Monsieur le Ministre' – a local man made good, who was fleetingly housing minister under De Gaulle – is in residence in his 'château', a massive eighteenth-century pile that dwarfs all else on the tiny village square, he and his wife naturally attend mass. As they descend the steps from their gate and distribute stiff handshakes to those villagers in their path, there trots behind them the middle-aged unmarried farmer's daughter who acts as their servant, for a pittance, whenever they stay in the village.

Weddings tend to be rather low-key, often because it is common knowledge that the bride is already pregnant. Things do loosen up a little, though, after the wedding feast is over and the swirling Auvergnat dances get under way. Sometimes the ice gets broken at an earlier stage, such as when the hard-working *curé*, who conducts mass in this and several neighbouring villages and is famed for the celerity with which he can down several rounds of Ricard, muddles up the order of service and apologises with an awkward joke.

Another traditional aspect of village life that has survived unscathed is its sense of community. Good turns are invariably repaid in one way or another, and ritualistic exchanges of gifts are common. Talk of money causes immediate embarrassment.

The villagers are observant, in a protective rather than an inquisitive way. If anyone returns after an absence of a few days and opens his windows to air the house, someone is bound to drop in to make sure that a burglar is not at work. However secretive one is, it is almost impossible to do anything unobserved.

Lurking almost inevitably behind all the protectiveness and solidarity there are, as in any self-respecting rural community, long-standing and often bitter feuds between families. Sometimes no one really knows how they started, though property of some kind is usually involved and politics often dragged in.

From time to time, such feuds erupt into the open, as happened recently with the affair of the sawmill. The owner of the sawmill, which was very small when he

took over from his father, is a man of great ambition and little sensitivity to local feeling. He recently expanded his business considerably. When he had used up all the space on his own land, he began to pile wood on the communal car park and took to loading juggernauts on the road in front of the mill, often blocking it completely and coating it with a dangerously slimy layer of sawdust (the local gendarmes became inexplicably lax in enforcing the rule that it should be hosed down daily). He illegally stored a dangerous wood preservative in an open tank next to the garden wall of the school next door. He installed powerful bark-stripping machinery so noisy it virtually prevented classes from being held in the school and greatly irritated holidaymakers staying at the café-restaurant opposite the mill.

The schoolteachers and the hotelier, exasperated at the way their complaints fell on consistently deaf ears, organized a petition calling for the sawmill to move. It was signed by the great majority of people living in the village itself. The sawmill owner (a municipal councillor and Gaullist militant) immediately claimed it was all a leftwing plot hatched by a former Socialist mayor of the commune and implemented through that traditional hotbed of leftwing sedition, the state school. Experts came from the prefecture, measured the decibels and decreed that the sawmill move elsewhere – which it did, eventually, to its proper place amid fields in a remote part of the commune.

The affair even caused rifts within families. One village girl (a recent university graduate and now a senior bank clerk), who had helped organize the petition, was

fiercely scolded by her first cousin, a woman who left school at 15, had a shotgun wedding at 18, and has since borne five children (one of whom herself married in similar circumstances at 17): 'A fat lot of use your education has been to you!' The bank clerk has a modern attitude to sex now shared by a gradually increasing number of young people in the village, though it has to be said that for most unmarried girls pregnancy still automatically means the altar.

Thirty years ago attitudes were even more deeply rooted in the past. One village girl was so terrified of telling her father she was pregnant that she camou-flaged her swelling belly and, on giving birth to the child, left it in a field to die. After serving a year or two in prison for manslaughter, she returned to the village but, out of shame, cut herself off entirely from the community. She now scrapes a very modest living running her late parents' small farm single-handed. Any offer by friendly souls of a lift to market at the nearest town is firmly turned down. Instead, she makes that daunting trek of 15 miles on foot, sometimes pushing a wheelbarrow. Solitary, bow-legged, striding along at an astonishing pace, she cuts a tragic figure – one last straggling victim of French rural life in the past.

PROVENCE

Provence and its famous coastline, the Côte d'Azur, are so popular with visitors of all kinds that in some people's eyes they have been irretrievably ruined. But this is not really so. Much of this lovely coast today may be crowded and over-built; but just inland there begins a vast and hilly hinterland, rolling for miles, much of it still remarkably unspoilt. This is the true rural Provence, a land intensely meridional, bathed all year in that special clear light which has so fascinated painters. It is a land of great scenic diversity, from the snowy Alps in the east to the marshes of the Camargue in the west. A land, too, of bright colours and strong scents – above all, the scent of pine that lingers in the air. Some hills are covered in deep forests of pine or oak; others are bare limestone massifs. Many hillsides are terraced with olive groves and vineyards; and many valleys are luxuriant with flowers. Nature in Provence is as prolific and varied as anywhere in Europe.

The people of rural Provence, as meridional as the land they live in, are usually dark and stockily built, and talk with the harsh accent of the Midi. Since pre-Roman times their land has been a crossroads, the scene of repeated invasions, and maybe this is why they are often wary at first with strangers. But their true temperament is passionate and volatile. Tempers flare up quickly, but arguments are as quickly forgotten, and end over a friendly drink of *pastis*. Gossipy but seldom malicious, the Provençaux are as individualistic as any Frenchmen, earthy and humorous, and strongly traditional. In country areas, some of the older ones still speak their ancient language, Provençal, which is a version of Occitan, the main tongue of all southern France in the Middle Ages. Provençal is a gentle, melodious language – the troubadours sang in it – and so it is sad today to see it dying out, despite efforts by some local intellectual patriots to revive it. The younger generation today find French a more useful daily tool, and few bother to learn Provençal.

Many of the villages of Provence stand on hilltops, and despite the influx of modernism they preserve their medieval aspect. They are built of pale local stone, and the roofs are made of curved red brick tiles. Usually there is a small main square shaded with plane trees, where old men sit at outdoor café tables drinking *pastis* and eating black olives. Somewhere, a game of *boules* may be going on too. The siesta hour is long, the pace of life is slow, and only the local teenagers' revving of their motor-bikes disturbs the silence. Dogs laze in front of shop doorways where bead curtains hang as a protection against the heat. The village church is usually very old, a handsome Romanesque or Early Gothic building; and in some places the churches were cathedrals in the Middle Ages but have long been demoted. Senez, near Digne, boasts a tiny thirteenth-century former cathedral with fine Flemish tapestries; today there is not even a resident *curé* and the village has only 126 inhabitants.

Outside the villages, the countryside is dotted with farmsteads and villas. They have stone walls and gently sloping roofs of terra-cotta tiles. Their north walls are often blind, as a defence against the *mistral*, the icy wind that periodically sweeps through Provence in winter; the front door and windows are on the south side, and even these are usually small, as protection against the summer heat. Outside, there may be a line of slender cypresses, one of the most graceful and distinctive of the region's trees. A larger farmhouse is known as a *mas* (from the same Latin root as 'mansion' or '*maison*'); a smaller one, often square-shaped, is a *bastide*.

The post-war tourist and residential boom has thrown

Provence

up a mass of new building, as well as the restoration of old buildings, both in villages and in the open country. Happily, this trend – with some sorry exceptions – has disfigured the landscape much less than one might have feared. This is partly because in many areas there are strict regulations whereby all new building or alterations must conform to traditional styles. Indeed, several of the big new holiday developments – notably Castellaras, near Cannes – are a pleasing pastiche of traditional architecture, harmonizing with the landscape. However, in other cases eyesores have been permitted, and not only on the coast: a rash of ugly modern villas now surrounds some villages. This is because some local mayors are lax in their interpretation of building regulations, and permit this new building for the money it brings into their communes. But other mayors do try to protect their environment. 'Here', said one of them, 'I forbid farmers to sell off part of their land for holiday villas, as they'd often like to do.'

Agriculture in Provence is diverse. The lower Rhône valley, thanks to its sunshine and fertile soil, is France's leading market garden, and exports mainly peaches, melons, strawberries and asparagus. This brings prosperity, except that no one has yet solved the problem of the surpluses in a good season, notably of peaches, which send market prices tumbling. Provence, with its chalky soil, is also France's main region for growing olives and almonds; wine too is produced in abundance. But few of these are fine wines that command high prices, and rising costs of harvesting have been causing worry to the farmers; some have recently moved over to mechanical grape-picking which is cheaper than hiring labour. Fewer problems beset sheep-grazing, which remains one of Provence's most prosperous activities. The sheep spend the summer on upland pastures (where their diet of wild herbs gives its special succulent flavour to the *agneau de Sisteron* found on many menus), and then in autumn their herdsmen lead them down through the villages to their winter pastures near the plains. This twice-yearly transhumance is a picturesque sight.

The agriculture of Provence is rich and diverse; the old methods of cultivation still persist on some upland farms.

The cuisine of Provence is as varied as its agriculture, thanks to an exceptionally varied local produce. Much use is made of garlic, as well as of the many wild herbs of the region such as basil, thyme and fennel. Olive oil is usually used for cooking rather than butter. In rural areas, stews are common, especially in winter – *civet de lièvre*, for instance, or *boeuf en daube*. Rabbit, chicken, some fish, and even frogs' legs are often prepared *à la provençale*, that is, in a tomato and garlic sauce. Rabbit is also cooked in a mustard sauce, while the *agneau de Sisteron* mentioned above is frequently grilled with herbs on a wood fire.

Villagers will often begin a meal with a hearty soup such as *soupe au pistou* (vegetables with basil and garlic), or with the ubiquitous *salade niçoise* (green peppers, eggs, black olives, tomatoes, tunny, anchovies and much else, all mixed together) or maybe with a basket of raw vegetables (*crudités*) with a vinaigrette and mustard sauce. Local fresh vegetables are plentiful, including artichokes and aubergines. And Provence is above all famous for its fish. The greatest fish dishes, notably *bouillabaisse*, also *bourride* and *loup au fenouil*, are found mainly on the coast; but in inland villages *soupe de poissons* (a rich stock of various fish, served with garlic sauce) is not uncommon, as well as local river fish such as trout and crayfish. One very special Provençal dish, indeed one of the region's symbols, is *aioli*, a garlic mayonnaise usually offered as a sauce with boiled cod.

As elsewhere in France, the post-war decades have brought huge changes to rural Provence. The farms are now far more modern and comfortable, but far fewer people work there. The villages have grown more prosperous and far less isolated, but have lost some of their old warm community spirit. The young people leave for the towns to find work. Many small local industries have died, but others survive if they can specialize, using local resources – for example, ochre quarrying near Apt, and the making of corks and *marrons glacés* amid the cork-oak and chestnut forests of the Maures hills.

Inevitably, many of the old folk traditions have been disappearing under the impact of modern life. No longer, except for special fêtes, are women seen wearing the lovely old Provençal costumes and head-dresses. At one smart hotel in Arles, the waitresses until recently were expected to dress up in them daily, to please the tourists; but now the girls refuse to do so, saying that the elaborate dressing process takes far too long.

Yet some traditions do survive. One is the making of *santons* ('little saints'), costumed clay figurines some 18 inches high. Some represent the figures of the Nativity story, others a range of Provençal stock comic characters. Today *santons* are still used in private homes as ornaments, or at Christmas for cribs. They are made locally by village craftsmen, and sold to local people as well as to tourists. Many churches still have elaborate and charming cribs full of *santons* at Christmas. And a few villages preserve the tradition of a 'live crib' – a Nativity pageant on Christmas Eve, with villagers in the roles of the Holy Family, the Shepherds and the Wise Men. The best known is at Les Baux.

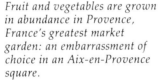

Fruit and vegetables are grown in abundance in Provence, France's greatest market garden: an embarrassment of choice in an Aix-en-Provence square.

Provence

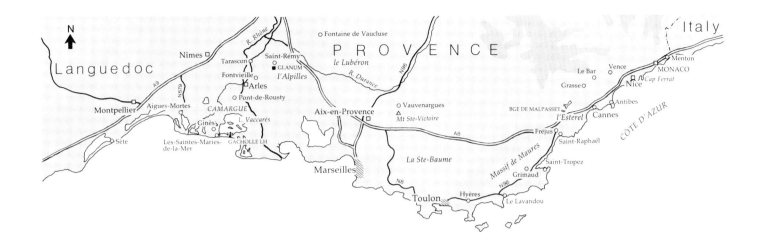

The gipsies at Les Saintes-Maries-de-la-Mer for their annual procession.

Among traditional sports, there are real bullfights at Arles, Nîmes and some smaller towns of that area. The bulls (which get killed) come from Spain, as do the matadors, but the toreadors are often Provençal. A more harmless local sport in the Arles area is the *course à la cocarde*, where the bull has a rosette stuck to its horns and agile young men compete to snatch it off. And throughout Provence, as in most of southern France, *boules* (and its variant, *pétanque*) is still an immensely popular local game. Every village has its *boules* pitch, a stretch of earth where men young and old can be seen earnestly playing this version of bowls, using metal balls. As in bowls, the two rival teams compete to see who can roll its balls closest to the jack. But they must not hit it.

Every village has its annual fête, usually a three or four day affair, prepared weeks in advance. Some of these fêtes are elaborate pieces of pageantry, dating back centuries, religious or secular in origin. Among the best known of these: the two *bravades* at Saint-Tropez, where the bust of a local saint is carried round the town in procession, escorted by a large troupe of locals in eighteenth-century uniform, and accompanied by much merriment and noisy music and the firing of blank shots; the religious pageants at Roquebrune, dating from the fifteenth century, where costumed villagers enact scenes from the Passion in alleys lit with luminous emblems; the fête of the Tarasque at Tarascon, also fifteenth-century in origin, where a bizarre green papier-maché monster is paraded round the town; and, most important, the gipsy pilgrimage in May at Les Saintes-Maries-de-la-Mer in the Camargue. Their caravans today may be almost all motorized, but the gipsies themselves with their gay clothes and dark exotic looks are still a fine sight, as in procession they converge on the church to honour their patroness, Saint Sara.

An ordinary village fête, held often to mark some saint's day, will still sometimes include Provençal folk-dancing (the *farandole*) to the sound of local instruments, the *tambourin* (a narrow drum) and *galoubet* (a three-holed flute). There will be competitions and games of various kinds, and a big open-air communal feast known as an *aioli* after its main dish. The fête is still the high point of the village year, but it no longer excites the inhabitants as it used to in the days when they had few other forms of entertainment. A middle-aged woman in the Var said, 'The young now have cars and go to discos every Saturday, they've grown blasé about the fête. We still dutifully prepare an *aioli*, but few of us take it seriously the way we used to in my childhood.' And the

mayor of a village in the Vaucluse said, 'The folk-orchestra of drums and flutes has been replaced by a noisy modern pop band, and the folk-dancing by American style majorettes brought up from Avignon. It's sad.'

It is the same story all over Provence. The old folk traditions are dying away in the villages – killed partly by television – despite the sporadic efforts of a few students and intellectuals to revive them.

The revival of handicrafts has possibly been more successful. Provence has many traditional crafts, notably ceramics, weaving and olive-wood sculpture. Thirty years ago these were mostly in decline. But now in many places they have been given a new lease of life by the arrival of artists and artisans from Paris and other points north, eager to make a living if they can in the warm southern climate. Today they are probably as numerous as the indigenous craftsmen. And so, in many of the fashionable hill villages (Tourette-sur-Loup, Saint-Paul-de-Vence, Roussillon, and others) today you will find chic boutiques and adjacent studios run by these immigrant artists. You can find sundials being made at Coaraze, silk-painting at Tourette, stained glass at Gordes, olive-wood sculpture at Sospel and Cabris, glassware at Biot, and much besides. It is a major aspect of the recent renaissance of rural Provence due to the influx of new blood from those who have come from the north to settle in the hill villages.

A face from an era rapidly passing in Provence; the older inhabitants have many misgivings about the new prosperity of the villages.

Many Provençal traditions still flourish, however: a game of boules in Saint-Paul-de-Vence.

135

Provence/Hill Villages

(Left) The ruined eleventh-century church at Oppède-le-Vieux in the Lubéron hills.

(Right) One of the many old hill villages which are characteristic of Provence.

Terraced along mountain-sides or perched on hilltops, many hundreds of old fortified villages dot the Provençal landscape, forming one of its most distinctive features. Often they are girt by the remains of ancient ramparts and nestle beneath some half-ruined château. And in some cases their alleys are so narrow and steep that cars cannot enter. Inside is a labyrinth of vaulted archways and winding stone stairways, of shady arcades and little squares where fountains splash. All very charming. Yet today only some of these places are lively communities of real local villagers. Many others are derelict, silent, falling into ruin. Others again are overlaid with a new chic, their alleys lined with smart boutiques and restaurants, their stone façades expensively restored – and the strollers in their alleys look less like local peasants than denizens of Paris, London or New York, which is probably just what they are. For a revolution has recently hit the Provençal hill village, causing a kind of death, and a kind of rebirth.

These villages were built on high ground for security, first against Saracen pirates, then against the invaders and marauders of the Middle Ages. The peasants would sleep within the ramparts, moving out by day to till their fields. Some villages are spectacularly sited, such as Èze, perched above the Côte d'Azur, and Saorge which clings to a cliff near the Italian frontier, its houses standing one on top of the other. Most villages are made of local stone, so that some of them, such as Gordes and Les Baux, seem to merge into the rocks on which they are built.

With the coming of settled conditions in the nineteenth century, the villagers began moving down into the valleys. More recently, the exodus from the farms has greatly reduced the population of rural Provence, as in the rest of France. As a result, many of the remote villages have become entirely or partly abandoned. And yet, at the same time, very different trends have been giving some villages a new lease of life. A few, such as Les Baux and Èze, have become major tourist centres, filled with souvenir shops and cafés. Hundreds of others – and this is the major trend – have been affected by the post-war vogue for buying up country homesteads and converting them into summer or weekend residences. Middle-class Parisians and other French city-dwellers, as well as Britons, Germans, Dutch and others, all eager for a place in the sun, have acquired literally hundreds of thousands of these secondary homes in Provence, so that land and house prices have rocketed, far outstripping inflation. Some of these restored villages are now very chic, haunts of the rich and famous, especially those near the coast such as Mougins, Grimaud and Bormes-les-Mimosa. Their alleys, formerly rough cobbles, are now smartly paved; their stone façades are embellished with fancy ironwork and neat flower-pots. It is an artificial renaissance, yes, though better than letting the villages die. But it can lead to tensions.

Bargemon is a sizeable village on a wooded hillside in the Var, thirty miles from the coast. Two elegant church steeples, a sea of red tiled roofs, a main square shaded by venerable plane trees, with a mossy fountain in the middle. Before 1914 Bargemon was a busy centre, with 3,000 people and some little factories making boots and pasta. Then the factories closed, killed by modern competition; the branch railway line closed, too, in the 1950s, the farm workers drifted away, and by 1970 the population was down to 850. Since then it has risen again to 1,140, due to an influx of retired well-to-do people from Paris and elsewhere; and in summer it is much higher still. One alleyway is nicknamed the 'promenade des Anglais', because of the number of houses which are now owned by English families.

Provence/Hill Villages

The influx has revived local commerce. Some food shops which had closed have re-opened; there are now estate agents, too, and even a branch of Lloyd's insurance. A former peasant/artisan economy is moving towards the suburban or the tourist-resort model, full of service industries. But the boom is a fragile one, for though some of the newcomers live at Bargemon all the year, the majority are there only in the brief summer months; and in winter the shops can do little trade. The mayor, an elderly Socialist schoolmaster, officially encourages the *résidence secondaire* invasion, for he knows how much his village now depends on it, and he claims that the newcomers are easily accepted locally. This is true, to a degree: but integration is far from total. Of the two cafés in the main square, one remains the preserve of the village locals, mostly old men playing cards, while the other is used by tourists and the neo-residents.

The Provençaux are wary of those they call in their *patois 'les estrangers'* (and that term includes French from other parts, notably Parisians), and there are some Bargemonnais who feel that the new influx has spoilt the true character of village life. 'In my youth,' said one woman, 'all the villagers took part eagerly in the village fête, but now we can't be bothered. Nowadays nine in ten of those who attend the fête are tourists and summer visitors, or from nearby towns.'

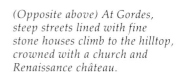

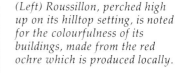

(Left) Roussillon, perched high up on its hilltop setting, is noted for the colourfulness of its buildings, made from the red ochre which is produced locally.

(Opposite above) At Gordes, steep streets lined with fine stone houses climb to the hilltop, crowned with a church and Renaissance château.

(Opposite below) Medieval alleys link shady squares in the old town of Bargemon in the Var.

Some of the same reactions can be found at Gordes, over in the Vaucluse, east of Avignon, a famous village on a rocky outcrop with a fine Renaissance château dominating the broad valley. It still has many elegant stone buildings of the sixteenth and seventeenth centuries, evidence of its patrician past. But later it fell into decline and many of its houses into neglect. Then in the 1930s a number of artists, intellectuals and others, mostly from Paris, began to buy up cheaply the ruined houses below the castle, as well as outlying farmsteads abandoned by the peasantry. Today, Gordes is *à la mode*. Many artists, writers and musicians have summer houses there, including the painter Victor Vasarely who has turned part of the château into a museum to house his idiosyncratic art. Héliard, the smart Paris delicatessen, has even opened a branch in Gordes. All this has brought the village a new prosperity, but not all the locals are completely happy about it. Some are annoyed at the *nouveau riche* invasion by the wealthy middle-class of other European nations whose new swimming-pools use up the water which is so badly needed by the farms in summer.

'The character of this place is changing fundamentally,' said one villager, 'it used to be truly Provençal – and so it still is, visually. But socially it's becoming a commuter suburb of rich northern Europe. The new population is gradually overwhelming the old.' This same point was put more precisely by the elderly Socialist mayor of the nearby village of Saint-Saturnin: 'Over half of the electors here are newcomers, but they're not all full-time residents. Many Parisians who come just for the summer succeed in registering this as their main domicile, not Paris, for it saves them money on car insurance and some taxes. This is quite legal, alas: but it's a scandalous dodge which the Government ought to forbid.' He did not hide his anxiety that these middle-class interlopers, few of them left-wing voters, were imperilling his majority. The old 'rotten borough' in a new guise. It is a complaint heard in many parts of Provence today.

Yet there are other cases where the new immigrants have come as saviours. Across the valley from Gordes, the ancient village of Oppède-le-Vieux clings to the side of a rocky cliff in the Lubéron hills, crowned by a ruined eleventh-century church and château. By the 1940s it was almost totally deserted; but then a few artists and architects began to take over some of the semi-ruined stone houses and restore them for their own use. And today the village presents an odd aspect: in its rough, cobbled alleys, tastefully renovated homes alternate with dilapidated ruins, for some of the old houses were too far gone to be recuperable. Unlike Bargemon or Gordes, there is no indigenous village life left in Oppède at all: yet, unlike Èze or Les Baux, the place is not touristy either – no souvenir shops or charabancs. Oppède is a ghost village now lovingly brought back to a kind of life by the efforts of a few fastidious lovers of *les vieilles pierres*. By contrast, there are scores of villages like Evenos on the limestone crags behind Toulon: it is now totally ruined and empty, and rather creepy. No one has yet dared try to resuscitate it.

Provence/Writers and Artists

A province with so potent a personality has not surprisingly produced a number of fine poets and novelists whose roots were in the soil of Provence and whose genius was nurtured on their love for its people and traditions. The greatest of these was Frédéric Mistral, who in 1854 was the leader of a group of young poets active in the Arles/Avignon area who founded the movement called the Félibrige. This was the major cultural event in modern Provençal history. Though not political nationalists, these poets hated the way that Napoleonic centralism had been stifling Provence's own ancient culture, and so – with some success – they waged a campaign for its revival.

Mistral was a poet of genius and has been compared to Homer and Dante. Detesting French, he wrote only in Provençal – epic poems of local rural life, notably *Miréio* (*Mireille* in French), the tragic love-story of a girl in the Camargue. This passionate, warm-hearted man became a cult figure in Provence in his life time, and indeed still is today (the fact that he bears the same name as the region's unpleasant wind is no more than coincidence). In 1904, aged 74, he was awarded the Nobel Prize for literature. He was born and spent his whole life at Maillane, a village near Saint-Rémy; the house where he lived for 38 years is now a Mistral museum. His spirit also infuses the wonderful Arlaten folk museum at Arles, which he created himself.

Mistral's contemporary, Alphonse Daudet, preferred to write in French, and in prose. But he too had a vivid pen for chronicling Provençal rural life, in a slighter and more humorous vein than Mistral. He is remembered for the *Tartarin de Tarascon* burlesques, for the play *L'Arlésienne* with music by Bizet, and for the sentimental sketches of *Letters from my Windmill*. This famous mill still exists, on a rocky hill outside Fontvieille, east of Arles. Daudet never owned it: but when staying with friends in the village he would often go to spend long hours there, wrapped in thought, or listening to the miller's tales. The mill is now a Daudet museum.

The revival of good indigenous regional writing that began with the Félibrige has continued into our own day – even though Mistral may be turning in his grave to note how little of it is written in the Provençal tongue he sought to sponsor. Marcel Pagnol, playwright and film

Frédéric Mistral.

Mistral (left) and his wife Marie Rivière outside their house at Maillane in 1906.

director, wrote earthy comedies of rural life (such as *La Fille du Puisatier*) as well as his famous plays of Marseilles low-life (the *Marius* trilogy). René Char, of the Avignon area, is one of France's best modern poets. And Jean Giono wrote serious pastoral novels about man in communion with Nature, set in his homeland around Manosque. Gide called him 'the Virgil of Provence': but his philosophical studies of human endurance in face of cruel fate, amid a brooding landscape, surely give him more in common with Hardy.

The earliest of a line of non-Provençal writers seduced by Provence was the Italian poet Petrarch, who grew up at the Papal court in Avignon in the early fourteenth century. He spent 16 years at the famous Fontaine de Vaucluse, where a torrent of water gushes out of a cavern in the rock; and the majesty and solitude of this setting was an inspiration to his poetry. In the eighteenth century, Tobias Smollett and Arthur Young were two travellers who wrote memorably about Provence. More recently, fleets of English and American writers have come to live or stay in the region, mostly on the Riviera. They have written mainly about its sophisticated urban life; and yet, the pages of Maugham, Mansfield and Fitzgerald contain eloquent descriptions of local landscape and rural ways. Today, Lawrence Durrell is spending his old age in a village west of Nîmes.

(Above) Alphonse Daudet.

(Left) The famous windmill near Fontvieille, where Daudet spent much time pondering and preparing his stories.

(Below) Petrarch.

Provence/Writers and Artists

La Baigneuse, *one of Renoir's best-known paintings.*

The landscape of Provence, with its dazzling clear light and bright colours, has understandably long been a source of inspiration to great artists, both those who were natives of the region, such as Cézanne, and those who came as immigrants, such as Van Gogh and Picasso. In some cases, painters' former homes and studios can be visited today; and in the region's many modern art museums the sensuous canvasses bear witness to the magnetic appeal of Provence to artists.

Auguste Renoir's old home at Cagnes-sur-Mer, just west of Nice, is today a small museum devoted lovingly to his memory, and has been carefully preserved just as it was when he spent the final years of his long life there, between 1907 and 1919. It still breathes the spirit and the gentle charm of this wonderful life-loving genius, and a visit is a moving experience. Renoir was in extremely severe pain from rheumatoid arthritis during his time in this quiet villa, Les Collettes, and in fact could paint only by moving his arm, with the brush strapped to his paralysed fingers.

This handicap did not prevent him from reacting passionately to the vivid Provençal world around him, and the result was a profusion of paintings of fruit, flowers, girls in gardens, olive groves, hillsides shimmering in the heat. These works are today in museums around the world, and at Les Collettes there is only one of Renoir's own paintings, plus a few drawings and sculptures. But there are some fascinating souvenirs (including his coat, easel and wheelchair) and photos of those close to him such as his son Jean, the film director, and the voluptuous Gabrielle who was his maid and favourite model. Out in the garden are the great olive trees that he adored.

Aix, Rocky Landscape *by Cézanne. The landscape of this part of Provence formed the subject of many of his paintings.*

But the view down to the sea, that he also loved dearly, is today unfortunately marred by numerous high-rise blocks of flats.

Picasso too was inspired by Provence. Born in Malaga, he returned to his beloved Mediterranean in 1945, aged 64, and for some months he worked in a studio in the château/museum at Antibes. It was an especially fertile period for him, as joyously he painted fish and fishermen, fauns and centaurs, and other subjects evoking the sea and Greek mythology. These works today hang in the museum at Antibes. Between 1947 and 1953 he lived at nearby Vallauris, a village that for centuries had been a centre of pottery. Picasso became fascinated by this local traditional craft, and for the next years spent much of his time making ceramics. His creations which resulted from this fertile creative period are today exhibited at Antibes and Vallauris.

Matisse and Dufy both lived at Nice, and both now lie buried at Cimiez in its suburbs. Both in their different ways were influenced by the Riviera. Matisse's feeling for colour matured under the Provençal sun, while Dufy wittily depicted local life in his light-hearted paintings. Another modern master, the Russian-born Marc Chagall, did not move to the Riviera till his later years, when he settled at Vence; he too reacted intensely to Provence's bright colours, as can be seen from his *Biblical Message* in his museum at Nice. Jean Cocteau had a summer home at Cap Ferrat, which he loved: his frescoes in the sailors' chapel at Villefranche and in the town hall at Menton bear witness to his feeling for the local fisherfolk and their lives.

The Côte d'Azur had first begun to be popular with artists in the 1890s, when Paul Signac, the Neo-Impressionist, came to live in Saint-Tropez, then almost unknown. He set a fashion: soon Matisse, Bonnard and others of the Ecole de Paris were spending the summer there. Picturesque Saint-Tropez and the lovely coast around it made a strong impact on their work and that of many other artists, as can be seen today by a visit to L'Annonciade museum in the town: it has vivid Provençal landscapes by Braque and Vlaminck, and charming scenes of Saint-Tropez by Manguin, Camoin and Dunoyer de Segonzac.

Western Provence, around Aix and Arles, is associated with two slightly earlier artists, Cézanne and Van Gogh. Cézanne was born at Aix, and though he spent many years in Paris, it was in and around his native town that he lived much of his later life. Here the landscape he cherished was the subject of much of his best work – red-roofed farmhouses, limestone hills, solitary cypresses, and above all the lofty pyramid of Mont Sainte-Victoire which he painted so often in ever-changing light. His studio outside Aix can today be visited. Vincent Van Gogh was another Post-Impressionist fascinated by the light and colours of Provence's sky and scenery. He spent only two years there, at Arles and Saint-Rémy, but it inspired some of his finest work, such as *Sunflowers* and *The Bridge at Arles*.

Provence/Wild Massifs

Provence's landscape is marked by a low mountain range of limestone or schistous rock, all running from east to west parallel to the coast – the Alpilles, the Lubéron, the Mont Sainte-Victoire, and the massifs of La Sainte-Baume, the Maures and the Esterel. Their white or red jagged crests, their lonely heights or deep forests, help to give this province its epic quality, and each of them holds some special place in its history, whether as a centre of early Christian legend or as a refuge for invaders, bandits or heretics. These are massifs redolent of mystery and magic.

The Alpilles run for 20 miles between the Rhône near Arles and the Durance valley. They never rise above 1,200 feet, yet their barren white crags give them the aspect of real mountains in miniature – the name means 'little Alps'. They have long been popular with rock climbers: indeed, here Alphonse Daudet's comic 'hero' Tartarin de Tarascon did his training as a mountaineer. Above all, the Alpilles have long exerted a fascination on writers and artists alike. Daudet would gaze at them philosophically from his mill in the valley below, and Van Gogh when he lived at Arles painted them often, intrigued by their beautiful changing hues in the varying Provençal light.

Other visitors have fallen under the spell of the Alpilles' ruined monuments of past ages. On their northern slopes are the remains of the Gallo-Roman settlement of Glanum, with its vestiges of baths, temples and villas and its imposing Roman cenotaph and triumphal arch. High on a spur on the southern side stands the famous ruined castle of Les Baux, where in the fourteenth century the cruel Viscount Raymond de Turenne would force his victims to leap to their deaths in the chasm below and laugh at their agony. With these and other memories, at night the Alpilles seem a ghostly, haunted place. By day, sheep graze placidly on their upper pastures, above the groves of olive, almond and cypress that stretch down to the valleys.

To the east, beyond the ugly Durance river, there stands another limestone range, the Lubéron, less wild and craggy than the Alpilles but just as mysterious. In the Middle Ages it was the stronghold of an early Protestant sect of 'heretics', the Vaudois, who translated the Bible into Provençal. Though truly religious, they would also defend themselves by pillaging and burning abbeys and churches in the valleys below. Finally in 1545 François I sent a crusade against them, and nearly 2,000 were hanged, beheaded or stoned to death.

The eastern part of the Lubéron is wild and forested, with some palaeolithic cave-dwellings and ruined Ligurian forts on the heights. The western part is a lush and gentle plateau, with vineyards, beehives for honey, lavender fields and a superb forest of tall cedars. Scattered across this plateau, as well as on the slopes around Gordes to the north, are scores of very curious igloo-shaped stone huts called *bories*, unique to this part of France. Their history is somewhat obscure. Some of them probably date back to pre-Roman times, but some were inhabited as late as the 1820s, and it is thought they were sometimes used by townsfolk escaping the plague, or at

(Left) The fantastic craggy slopes of the Dentelles de Montmirail are an outcrop of Mont-Ventoux, the highest peak of north-west Provence.

(Below left) The limestone ridge of the mountain of Sainte-Victoire from the Route Cézanne.

other times by shepherds. They are made of dry stones without mortar, and look like a cross between a large beehive and an Apulian *trullo*.

Some way to the south of the Lubéron, just east of Aix-en-Provence, there rises up the great white hulk of the Mont Sainte-Victoire. Viewed from Aix it looks pyramid-shaped, but in fact it is a limestone range ten miles long, and for lovers of art it is one of the world's best-known mountains, for Cézanne was mesmerized by it, and when he lived in Aix he painted it scores of times, in different hues. Picasso too lived in this area for a while, though the mountain never inspired *his* brush; he lies buried in the park of the château of Vauvenargues, where he spent some of his final years. In 102 B.C. the Sainte-Victoire was the scene of a mighty victory by the Roman general Marius over invading Teuton hordes (hence its name).

Further to the south-east, a score of miles inland from Marseilles and Toulon, the landscape is dominated by La Sainte-Baume, longest and loftiest of Provence's limestone massifs and in many ways the most striking. The world *baume* comes from the Provençal *baoumo* (cave), for ancient legend has it that Mary Magdalene, after landing at Les Saintes-Maries-de-la-Mer, took refuge in a lonely cave near the summit and here spent her final years entirely alone.

Today the visitor can walk up through the woods to this cave, which has been looked after by Dominicans since 1295. Midnight mass is celebrated in a chapel here every 22 July, for this is still a place of pilgrimage just as it was in the Middle Ages when popes and kings would make the ascent to the blessed spot. For Provençal Christians today, it is still a place of awesome sanctity. Near the cave, on the crest of the mountain, stands the

Provence/Wild Massifs

A borie, *an igloo-shaped stone hut, at Gordes.*

(Opposite) The harbour and sea-front at Saint-Tropez.

lofty stone monument of Saint-Pilon (3,800 ft), visible for many miles around. Northwards down the slope there stretch glorious woodlands of beech, lime and maple, trees rarely found in the south of France.

The ancient Gauls worshipped these trees as sacred. Here on this smiling plateau just below the summit there are tidy farms and well-tilled fields. Yet a mere three miles to the west the massif changes dramatically to a lunar landscape of towering white crags, with sweeping views towards the coast. Few corners of Provence are so rich in contrasts as the Massif de la Sainte-Baume, or so haunting in their appeal.

Beside the coast from Hyères to Fréjus there sprawls the mighty Massif des Maures, which is not limestone but schistous rock and one of the most ancient chunks of Europe. In the Dark Ages it was invaded and long occupied by Saracen marauders whose ruined strongholds are still visible, notably at La Garde-Freinet. The massif's name is often said to come from these Saracens or Moors (*Maures* in French): but in fact probably derives from the Provençal *maouro* meaning dark wood, for the range is covered with deep forests of Aleppo pine, cork oak and chestnut. These supply two of the main local industries: the making of corks for bottles, and of *marrons glacés*.

146

The coast here, though now heavily built-up, is still beautiful. There are famous resorts, including Le Lavandou, Port-Grimaud and of course Saint-Tropez. The interior of the massif contains some surprises, such as a ruined eighteenth-century monastery and a Club Méditerranée holiday 'village'.

Just as ancient as the Maures massif, and also made of schistous rock, the Massif de l'Esterel lies along the coast between Saint-Raphaël and La Napoule. Its miles of jagged red crags are one of the most curious and unforgettable sights in Provence. It is composed of a single block of volcanic rock, mainly porphyry, which across millions of years has been eroded into bizarre shapes. These can be seen either from the coastal road or by going inland along the modern A8 autoroute or the older N7 main road. Smaller roads wind up into the wild heart of the massif, from where a bold walker can clamber to the summit of the russet crags and find glorious views.

The old Roman highway from Rome to Arles, the Aurelian Way, was built along the northern fringe of the massif and until modern times this was the only throughway here near the coast. The N7 today follows much the same track, and to this day some local peasants still call it 'lou camin aurélian'. In the old days the Pax Romana protected the area; but in more recent times the history of the Esterel has often been one of violence and disaster. For many centuries, escaped convicts would hide out in the wooded ravines and attack travellers. Highwaymen also infested the area, such as the notorious Gaspard de Besse who used the Auberge des Adrets on the N7 as his base; he was finally captured and broken on the wheel at Toulon in 1781. His head was then nailed to a tree by the road.

The twentieth century brought security, but added a new hazard: forest fires, started either by careless tourists or even by saboteurs. Sometimes motorists were trapped in these raging fires and burned to death. And today the fires have left large parts of the massif a scarred wilderness, where the replanting of trees is a slow process. As if all these calamities were not enough, in 1959 a huge dam burst after heavy rain at Malpasset, on the western edge of the massif: the waters surged down to the coast at Fréjus, killing over 400 people, and an enquiry found some engineers guilty of negligence. So the blood-red rocks of the Esterel stand as a cenotaph to man's imprudence and savagery across the ages.

Provence/The Camargue

The Camargue, in the Rhône delta, a wide expanse of lagoons and marshy plains, is a strange region like none other in France. Birds and animals in marvellous variety here lead their own special life, and so do humans. Here orange-purple sunsets glow and linger on the far flat horizons; herds of black bulls and half-wild white horses roam across the salty marshes, where few buildings are visible save the lonely cottages of the local herdsmen, the *gardians*; and at dusk a flock of pink flamingoes may suddenly fly up from the reeds of a lagoon.

The plain of the Camargue comprises some 300 square miles between the Grand Rhône to the east and the ancient walled town of Aigues-Mortes to the west, on the borders of Languedoc. The northern sector towards Arles was desalinated after the war and is now France's main rice-growing region. To the west, vines too grow in the sandy soil, yielding a *rosé* with a greyish tint and a mildly gritty flavour, known appropriately as *'gris de gris'* or *'vin des sables'*.

At the heart of the Camargue is the great lake of Vaccarès, separated from the sea by a maze of little islands. This whole area is now a National Reserve of Zoology and Botany, and is open to visits only by naturalists and students who must seek special permission in advance. If you can produce a good reason, it is well worth applying, for the reserve contains many wild plants and flowers which are found in few other parts of Europe, as well as a fascinating variety of birds living freely in the open – among them, storks and cormorants, martens and purple herons, and above all the flamingoes for which the Camargue is famous.

Even without entering the reserve, some of the flowers and birds can be seen by driving along the east side of the lake to the Gacholle lighthouse, from where in dry weather it is possible to walk along the dunes to Les Saintes-Maries, the Camargue's only town. The best time to see the birds is very early in the morning, or just before dusk, and you need patience, for they do not always show themselves readily.

The main part of the Camargue is divided into some thirty privately owned ranches, each with its own *manade* (herd) of black bulls and white horses, peacefully cohabiting. Though these agile bulls are really fighting animals, they are not bred to be killed in the *corridas* of Arles, Nîmes and other nearby towns, but are used simply for the harmless sport of *courses à la cocarde* where man and beast alike are rarely hurt. The bull is far more likely to meet violent death in the *abattoir*, to be sliced up for a spicy local stew of *boeuf gardian*.

Everywhere on these plains you see groups of the renowned white horses of the Camargue – hardy, stocky animals with broad flanks and short legs, yet nimble of foot and very manageable. Some are still wild and ownerless; but even those belonging to *manades* are left free to roam about in the open at night, not put in stables. They are hired out to tourists: there are several good ranch-hotels in the area, notably just north of Les Saintes-Maries, where one can enjoy an equestrian holiday, going out in groups for long horseback excursions across the marshes, led by a *gardian*.

The *manades* are supervised by these *gardians*, who have been called 'the aristocrats of the Camargue'. They are lithe, tough men and women with weather-beaten faces and a somewhat gipsy-like appearance. They spend much of their time in the saddle, rounding up their herds with their long staves, and most of them live out on the marshes in remote *cabanes*, which are whitewashed thatch-roofed cottages, each topped with a cross. One key activity of the *gardian* is the *ferade*, or branding, when the yearlings are detached from the rest of the herd and brought to an enclosure to be laid on their side and branded with their owner's mark. In summer this is a popular tourist spectacle, usually accompanied by a great deal of drinking and merriment.

There are also still some true gipsies in the Camargue, though they are less picturesque than of old and their caravans now are all motorized. But every May they still gather at Les Saintes-Maries-de-la-Mer for the great gipsy festival. This little windswept town beside the sand-dunes and the beaches is a curious place, part popular bathing-resort, part mysterious centre of legend and folk-tradition. It is dominated by its high fortified church, a curious edifice built in the eleventh century as a defence against the Saracens. Close beside it, the Baroncelli museum contains much of interest on the customs and wildlife of the Camargue, as do two other museums, northwards along the road to Arles, at Ginès and Pont-de-Rousty.

(Above) The famous white horses of the Camargue are left free to roam in the open.

(Left) A bull being baited in the arena at Les Saintes-Maries-de-la-Mer.

(Right) The herds of black bulls are in the charge of mounted gardians *who live in remote huts on the marshes.*

Provence/The Perfume Industry

The elegant city of Grasse lies terraced on a hillside, facing south towards Cannes and the sea. Perfume-making was established here in 1595, and today Grasse is still the world capital of this industry. Why? Above all, because its balmy, sheltered climate gives a special fragrance to the flowers cultivated here in such profusion – jasmin and roses, mimosa and others. Grasse's 30 scent factories treat almost 90 per cent of the world's flower essences for perfumes, and most of these flowers are grown locally, in the lush valleys between Grasse and the sea.

The figures are amazing. Some 500 tons of roses, 250 of violet, 250 of jasmin, 200 each of mimosa and orange-blossom, plus 130,000 tons of lavender from the plateaux, go each year to feed the Grasse distilleries. And there are 120,000 rosebuds to a ton. Yet this ton of roses makes just one kilo of pure perfume essence. No wonder good perfumes are expensive.

Each flower has its season, and its area. In January and February the Tanneron hills, due south of Grasse, are ablaze with golden mimosa, mostly wild but some of it cultivated. The latter goes to the florists, largely for export: but the perfume trade prefers the wild mimosa, whose scent is stronger. April is the month for violet and orange. The orange groves are mostly around Le Bar and Vence to the north-east of Grasse: these oranges are the bitter Bigarade variety, not for eating, and their trees are grown solely for blossom for essence, which is a basis of eau-de-cologne.

Roses are cultivated on the slopes near Grasse, and usually are picked in May and June. Then July to October is the high season of jasmin, a white, not very pretty flower, but highly prized by Grasse perfumers for the subtlety of its scent. August/September is the time for tuberoses, which grow mostly between Grasse and Cannes. Finally, high summer is also the season for lavender, but this is grown not around Grasse but on the plateaux to the north and north-west as far as the Durance valley, and in huge quantities. It is cut by machines, whereas most other flowers are culled by hand.

In the Grasse area you will not see wide plantations of flowers as in Holland. The terrain is hilly, the fields small, and the produce comes from some 600 different local farmers who rarely have more than three or four acres each. Many families have owned and tilled the

same plot for centuries. The flowers, especially roses and jasmin, have to be picked very early in the morning, or else their scent fades in this hot climate. Farmers and their workers – some of them Italian seasonal migrants – develop a skill for picking the flowers at tremendous speed, maybe 100 jasmin blooms a minute which yields a kilo in 90 minutes. It is back-breaking work.

Flowers for perfume are grown in the open air. This is an entirely different world from the cut-flower industry down along the coast, just a few miles away, where roses and carnations in vast numbers are nurtured in greenhouses for sale in Paris and abroad. Very few growers work for both markets – and those who supply Grasse with its essences tend to look down their finely tuned nostrils at the 'mere' cut-flower producers. As one of them said with cheerful arrogance, 'Cut roses last just a few days, while perfume is eternal. And those people who love perfumes will seldom stoop to the bad taste of putting cut flowers in their homes. In fact, the two trades are as different as wood for log-fires is from wood for high-quality furniture!'

And yet, this proud industry is today menaced, and for

50 years has been in decline. The local production of jasmin has dropped since 1935 from 1,000 to 300 tons a year, while roses and orange blossom have registered similar falls. There are several reasons. One: the growing competition, even in Grasse, from synthetic essences, which are much cheaper to produce. Two: competition from flowers imported from countries such as Egypt and Morocco where labour costs are far lower. Three, and most important: the post-war boom in holiday housing in the Grasse/Cannes area has pushed up land prices so high that many farmers have fallen to the temptation of selling or renting their fields for new building – and so, in this now overcrowded and over-exploited area, there is simply far less space for flower-growing. Sad, in a way.

And now on top of this has come economic crisis, along with new taxes on luxury goods, both severely hitting the market for quality perfumes. In 1979-82 sales of Grasse's flower-based essences fell by 50 per cent and gloom deepened. If all these trends continue, in a few decades these gorgeous valleys will have lost the redolence of their famous scents, and the local cabaret singers will be left to lament, 'Where have all the flowers gone?'

LANGUEDOC-ROUSSILLON

The ancient province of Languedoc used to cover a wide swathe of southern France between the Rhône and the Garonne: its historical capital, Toulouse, lay on its western fringe. Today, rather confusingly, the modern French *région* of Languedoc-Roussillon comprises only the eastern or 'lower' Languedoc along the coast around Montpellier, plus bits of the Massif Central and Provence to the north, and Roussillon (French Catalonia) to the south. We are here concerned mainly with Lower Languedoc, a sun-parched land that lies astride one of Europe's oldest through-routes, for commerce, invasion and, today, tourism.

The coastal plain is filled with mile upon mile of vineyards. Behind, lies the country of the *garrigues*, dry stony hills, covered with scrub and wild flowers, that form the lower slopes of the Cévennes. Save that its coast is flat and dull, Languedoc in many ways resembles Provence – the same bold sun and clear light, the same scent of thyme and whirr of the cicada, the same kind of rural dwellings with stone walls and red-tiled roofs, the same sleepy villages where old men play *boules* in the shade, the same intensely meridional people, volatile yet easy-going.

To understand these people, one must know their history. Languedoc in the Middle Ages was not part of the French kingdom but an independent principality with a brilliant civilization, exemplified by the troubadours and their 'courts of love'. It was also the centre of the Cathar heresy. And tribal memories today still run so deep that local people have not forgotten nor forgiven the bloody suppression of the Cathars by Paris in the thirteenth century and the brutal annexation of Languedoc to the Crown. Today this remains the most anti-Paris of any French mainland region: many people still feel 'colo-nized', as they put it. Yet, though proud, they are also a slow, wayward, not very enterprising breed, who in modern times have done less than they might to develop their own economy themselves and thus escape the dread 'tyranny' of the technocrats sent from Paris. This applies especially to the vinegrowers, as we shall see.

Languedoc is so called because its ancient tongue, Occitan, was known as 'the language of *oc*' ('yes' was *oc*, as opposed to *oui* in northern French). It was also the heartland of the vast and vague region known as Occita-nia. And since the war, with the growth of regional feeling in France, there has been quite an Occitan revival, both political and cultural. A lunatic fringe of extremists are separatist, seeking to create an Occitan nation; 'OC' slogans can be seen daubed on walls. However, most local people know this is a senseless daydream: they want to remain part of France. But they do also demand a better deal from Paris. Some of them have been taking part in the Occitan cultural revival, which has thrown up new Occitan theatre and folklore groups, writers in Occi-tan, even Occitan pop singers. But attempts to revive the Occitan language seem unlikely to get very far. It is true that in the towns more young people are now studying Occitan, which has even become an option in secondary school examinations: but meanwhile in country areas it is fast dying out as a vehicle of daily speech. The net total of Occitan speakers is thus still in decline.

Lower Languedoc produces 40 per cent of all France's wine, including most of its cheaper non-imported table wine. The vine has been described as the area's 'sole wealth, and its tragedy', for the grape grows here so pro-lifically, needing so little care, that the many thousands of small farmers have been used to a leisurely life and are ill-disposed to seeking other sources of revenue. Their

Languedoc-Roussillon

The wine harvest at Saint-Guiraud in the Hérault département.

chronic problem is over-production and unsaleable surpluses, for output has been rising faster than demand.

Since the creation of the Common Market, they have grown alarmed at the flooding into France of imports of cheaper but stronger Italian wines; in 1976, a farmer and a policeman were killed in severe riots near Narbonne, in protest against these imports, and the Government was forced to yield to local demands by placing for a while a partial ban on Italian wines, in defiance of Common Market rules. Since the late 1970s, the farmers have become even more panicky at the prospect of being undercut by even cheaper and more robust Spanish wines, within a free European market: 'Without special rules to protect us', said one local grower, 'Spain's entry into the Common Market will wipe out a large part of the Midi vineyards. And the unrest here then would be more than all the police in France could control.'

For some years, official policy has been to encourage the uprooting of the poorest vines, good for thin *ordinaires*, and their replacement with 'nobler' vines capable of producing the rather better *vin de pays* and VDQS grades. This is to meet the demands of a French public that has been turning from basic plonk towards more palatable wines. And the policy has met with some response: 30 per cent of vineyards have been thus upgraded since 1962. But the bizarre economics are such, that this does not necessarily bring the grower more money, since outputs per hectare are severely limited by law for the classified grades, but not for *vins courants*. The farmer thus retains some incentive for still producing a mass of poor, unsaleable plonk. The Common Market today pays for the surpluses to be bought up for distillation, so the grower has some protection. But it is a wasteful solution and costly for the taxpayer.

The hillsides can produce goodish wines: but there are wide areas of plain that should not be under vine at all, for the terrain is just not suitable. Official policy, today backed by Common Market grants, is to persuade farmers to replace their vines with more useful crops such as fruit and cereals. This is going ahead, slowly: some 5,000 acres per year are uprooted. But too often the process falls foul of the conservative farmer's emotional attachment to his ancestral vines. It is true that two brothers on the coast at Cap d'Agde changed their vineyards not into orchards, but into a tourist site which then became part of Europe's largest nudist city. But this was an exceptional case of local enterprise.

In the 1950s the Government created the biggest irrigation network in Europe, based on a new canal from the Rhône delta to Montpellier, and dams in the hills behind Béziers. The aim was to help diversify the monoculture of the vine by encouraging fruit-growing. But this led to other problems, owing to Common Market fruit surpluses, notably of peaches and apples. Today the emphasis is on more marketable crops such as rice, soya, asparagus, tomatoes and other vegetables – and output has been rising. But few of the indigenous farmers are responsive. In fact, most of the farming dynamism in the region in the past 25 years has come not from locals but from repatriated *pieds noirs* from Algeria who have bought up declining farms and have made them buzz with a new enterprise.

Vinegrowers may resist 'progress'; yet the rural life of Languedoc has changed hugely in the past decades. The extensive modern tourist resorts along the coast, the new factories and motorways, the urban spread of Montpellier and other cities have all brought new activity to which the villages have not remained immune.

Languedoc-Roussillon

A professor at Montpellier University, who for the past 20 years has lived in a tiny village 12 miles north of the city, says: 'The mutation here has been total. This place used to be a world apart, in the middle of nowhere: now, on the edge of the Montpellier commuter belt, it's been dragged into the modern world. It used to be a small enclosed society, gossipy yet protective, a true caring community: now ''les estrangers'' (city commuters and weekenders) have moved in, the fields have filled up with estates of modern villas, and the farm population has dropped by two-thirds. Local people used to spend the warm evenings sitting outside their houses in the narrow streets, and chatting: but TV has killed that kind of social life. Farmers used to get up at 5 a.m. to look after the horses: now they have just cars and tractors. And they are buying machines for the grape-harvesting, as it's cheaper than hiring pickers. So the old social ritual of the grape-harvest, which used to be a two-week fête, is now more like an impersonal factory operation.'

Yet the old traditional village carnivals of Languedoc are managing to survive. A few years ago, they had seemed in danger of dying out: but now conscious efforts have been made to revive them, pioneered often by local teachers, students or others. Each village has its own special fête usually dating back centuries – and very odd some of them are.

(Right) The cuisine of Languedoc is highly spiced, with much use of garlic and olive oil. Sunday lunch is still a family ritual.

(Far right) Bread being made in a traditional bakery in the Languedoc.

At Cournonterral, west of Montpellier, men wearing special clothes are rolled in a pool of lees of wine at harvest-time. In some villages, people are thrown into heaps of mud, or pelted with flour and eggs; or, as in the Basque country, wild bulls are let loose in the streets and people run for their lives. In contrast to these pranks, sometimes a costumed folk society (probably city students) will perform the graceful old folk-dances of Languedoc that today, alas, are seldom danced spontaneously by villagers. At the carnival's *bal*, the music nowadays is more likely to be provided by a modern pop group than by a local orchestra with traditional instruments.

However, traditional gastronomy is very much alive –

with garlic and olive oil supreme, as in Provence. In the west, around Toulouse and Carcassonne, the supreme country dish is *cassoulet*, a white bean stew with *confit d'oie* (preserved goose), pork and mutton, spicy sausages and pork rind. The delectable *saucisses à la languedocienne* are skewered, sautéd in goose fat, and served with spicy tomato purée. In the hinterland, the country people have a range of unusual soups, such as *ouillade* (cabbage, potato, mushrooms and salt pork) and *mourtaîrol* (chicken bouillon with saffron). On the coast, you find much the same fish and shellfish dishes as are common in Provence, though the port of Sète has its own specialities, notably cuttlefish in garlic sauce.

Rural tourism is being developed to help the visitor gain insights into country life. In the Aude, you can go on a 'cheese weekend', where you stay in a farm cottage and are taught cheese-making by the farmer. Or you can take a wine-tasting tour of the Corbières, guided by an expert. Or – if you are brave – explore deep caves with fellow-speleologists. As in other upland regions of France, in the Cévennes there are guided excursions either on foot or horseback: bed and board, for humans and horses alike, is provided in fairly basic hostels.

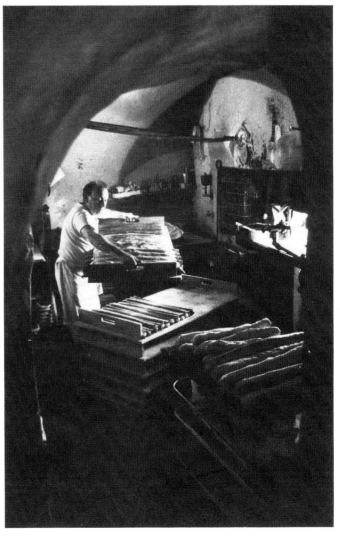

Languedoc-Roussillon

There is plenty for the tourist too in southerly Roussillon, which lies along the Spanish border. Culturally and historically it is quite separate from Languedoc, being part of Catalonia, and its people are close cousins to the Spanish Catalans across the frontier. They are more serious, dour and hard-working than the Languedocians. The Spanish flavour is strong, both in the architecture (cool, elegant arcades) and in the folk traditions. Country people still often dance the *sardaña*, Catalonia's national dance: they join hands in a circle, and the tempo alternates between joyous jig and stately ritual. You can see spontaneous *sardañas* in almost any village square in summer, as well as at the big festivals such as that at Arles-sur-Tech.

Coastal Roussillon around Perpignan, a very fertile area with a mild climate, is one of France's leading market gardens for fruit and early vegetables. There are good wines, too. Farming is far better organized than in sleepy Languedoc. Inland is the gorgeous mountain scenery of the Pyrenean foothills, where amid the spas and ski resorts are several surprising man-made marvels, ancient and modern. Odeillo, on the Cerdagne pastoral plateau, is the site of Europe's leading solar furnace where 62 swivelling mirrors reflect the sun. Near Prades, the isolated eleventh-century abbey of Saint-Martin-de-Canigou stands high in the folds of the Pyrenees, lost to view, accessible only by jeep or a steep walk. It is a place of austere beauty, breathing spiritual grace, today much used for retreats by both priests and laity.

Another religious centre, much larger than Saint-Martin, and more ambitious and unusual, is to be found up in the lonely hills of the *causses* region of Languedoc, 40 miles north-west of Montpellier. This is the famous Community of L'Arche, founded by the late Lanzo del Vasco, a leading disciple of Mahatma Gandhi. Here a multi-national group of some 150 people practise the shared, simple life in an atmosphere of joyous serenity.

Del Vasco was a Sicilian nobleman who met Gandhi in India in 1936 and was converted to his philosophy of non-violence. After the war, he founded the L'Arche movement in Europe where it now has eight centres. The largest, and its headquarters, is in an isolated red-and-ochre converted farmhouse. Since del Vasco's death aged 80 in 1981, the leader of L'Arche – 'the Pilgrim', as he is called – is a Corsican doctor, Pierre Parodi, who explains the movement thus: 'We are religious, but totally oecumenical: we have Muslims, Hindus, Buddhists, as well as Christians of all kinds. We try to live non-violence. Not only are we against nuclear arms and war of every kind, obviously; but we also oppose a modern society where profit, competition, class conflict and mechanization seem to us forms of hidden violence. Gandhi believed in decentralization into small self-sufficient rural communities as a way of avoiding violence – and this we try to practise.'

L'Arche aims for the maximum autarchy. Members pool all their money, have no private possessions, and live very simply. There is no electricity, just candles; no motor transport save an old Renault 4, used very rarely. The community weaves its own clothes, makes its own bread and cheese, grows its own vegetables, and buys the minimum from outside. Everyone is vegetarian. Meals are taken communally – but this is no kibbutz, for members live in their own families, many are married and have children. Even non-married couples are accepted if their relationship is serious. The community runs its own school. It practises homeopathy, and will only call on a doctor from outside in case of serious illness. Young Americans, French, Germans, with joyful smiling faces, singing as they wash clothes in the open air, tend the cows, work the printing press – the mood of happiness is patent.

(Opposite) The abbey of Saint-Martin-de-Canigou in its spectacular setting high in the Pyrenees.

A traditional farming scene in Roussillon.

Languedoc-Roussillon/Catharism

The Cathar heresy was suppressed by fire and sword in the thirteenth century, and it would not be unreasonable to expect it to have been virtually forgotten today. Yet 'Catharism' is today *à la mode*, not its religious practice, but the cult of what it represents in this strange Languedoc: the spirit of dissent. The tourist will be invited to drink *'le vin des Cathares'*, or be taken on a guided tour of the ruined Cathar fortresses such as Montségur; or he can read the many recent books on the subject, notably Le Roy Ladurie's bestseller *Montaillou*.

The Cathar heresy (known also as the Albigensian heresy, for one of its main centres was Albi, near Toulouse) spread into southern France from the Balkans in the twelfth century. It took root mainly in independent Languedoc, land of the troubadours. Oddly in this elegant setting, the Cathars themselves preached a doctrine of purity and asceticism in reaction and revulsion against the Church of Rome, which at the time was undeniably corrupt, licentious and widely despised. The Cathars were Manicheans: that is, they held that the universe was made up of two contending forces of good and evil, each equally strong. All that was spiritual was good; but the world and the human race were in the hands of the powers of evil. This led the more extreme Cathars to assert that procreation itself was evil and the human species had better die out.

Catharism was not a formal church but a loose network of sects. It did, however, have its élite, the *parfaits* (perfect ones), ascetic celibates. Around them were the mass of ordinary lay believers who in practice were permitted to lead normal, earthy lives, so long as they turned to asceticism on their deathbeds (which, after all, was not too hard). So Catharism was an odd mixture of rigour and tolerance. This helps to explain the apparent paradox of its flourishing side-by-side with the romantic culture of the troubadours. The two were not really opposite extremes. After all, the courts of love were not erotic harems, but places where the troubadours would sing of their pure and chaste love for some virtuous – and probably unattainable – lady.

An infuriated Rome saw Catharism as a dangerous threat to its hegemony and a challenge to its own doctrines. In 1208 Pope Innocent III ordered a crusade against the Cathars; and he found willing allies in the Capetian rulers of France who gladly seized this chance to extend their own domains. Under the command of Simon de Montfort (whose homonymous son was later to play a key role in English history), an army of 30,000 knights and infantry descended on the south, and the entire Languedoc rallied against them in the Cathars' defence. What had begun as a war of religion soon became a mainly colonial war. The Languedoc ruling nobility had long been sympathetic to the Cathars: indeed, the Count of Toulouse's sister was herself a *parfaite*.

The crusade was ferocious and merciless, as town after town fell to the invaders. At Béziers, over 15,000 men, women and children were butchered. When one officer enquired of his superior how he could tell the heretics from true Catholics, he was told, 'Kill them all: God will then recognize his own'. Finally in 1229 Languedoc sur-

The ruined castle of Montségur, the scene of one of the final episodes in the Albigensian crusade.

rendered and was formally annexed to France; thus ended a glorious civilization, which was now drawn back into the barbarism of most of the rest of Europe at that time. Little pockets of Cathars continued to hold out in the high fortresses to the south, towards the Pyrenees. It was not until 1244 that the mountain citadel of Montségur finally yielded, and 200 *parfaits* were burned alive. The fortress of Quéribus held on till 1255. After this, outward Cathar resistance seemed to have been wiped out completely, but its spirit and practice still went on underground, rather like dissent in modern-day Poland or Russia.

Years later, in the early fourteenth century, Catharism was still so much alive in some upland villages around Montségur that one local bishop staged an Inquisition to try to wipe it out. The verbatim transcripts of his detailed enquiries in one village, Montaillou, have survived to this day; and the famous French historian Emmanuel Le Roy Ladurie has recently edited and reworked them into a fascinating account of medieval rural life.

The bishop's Inquisition was successful: after the trials and purges at Montaillou, nothing more was heard of Catharism for centuries. Yet in a sense it has refused to die, and the many mysteries surrounding its tragedy haunt the modern imagination. The relics of its martyrdom can still be seen, mainly in the Aude around Carcassonne and in the eastern Ariège. Here the gaunt ruins of Montségur castle still stand in lonely splendour on their hilltop; at the foot is a stele inscribed in Occitan, 'Als Catars, als Martirs del Pur Amor Chrestian'. Further east, in the austere mountains of the Aude, are other ruins of the fortress eyries used by the Cathars as their final hideouts, notably Quéribus and Peyrepertuse.

According to one legend, a mysterious Cathar treasure was smuggled out of Montségur before it fell, and was buried in the area. Some have connected this with the true story of the nineteenth-century priest in the nearby village of Rennes-le-Château who seemingly found the key to some hidden treasure in his church. And some have gone on to link this enigma of the Cathar treasure with the mystery of the Holy Grail.

Germans in particular have always been fascinated by possible connections between Catharism and the Grail. Wagner visited Montségur when he was preparing his opera *Parsifal*, which is precisely about these legends and is set in a castle called Montsalvat, probably based on Montségur. More recently, the Nazis tried to appropriate Catharism as an element in their Aryan creed; one Nazi philosopher and SS officer spent some time at Montségur during the war and wrote a book on this theme. In the past few years young neo-Nazis have taken to coming to Montségur and trying to steal stones from its ruins as souvenirs, and the French police have been obliged to restrict access to the castle.

Happily, all this has little to do with the upsurge of real interest in Catharism, in France itself and notably in the Languedoc, in the past 20 years or so. This is much more closely linked with the post-war regionalist revival in the area. Many Occitan leaders have been exploiting the Cathar heritage to promote and justify their own cause: sometimes they hold Occitan 'nationalist' rallies and ceremonies at Montségur. They have even stirred up the militant vinegrowers to regard themselves as the true inheritors of the Cathar dissidents – *'les cathares de la vigne'* – but such phrases really mean little.

Some people who know the region well, however, do claim that traces of the Cathar philosophy have survived in the popular psyche, across all the centuries. 'The feeling of good versus evil, of *le mal* as an active force, is still embedded in the local temperament', claims one local intellectual, 'and this is subtly different from Catholicism. Catharism still has deep popular roots, even among ignorant peasants who are not aware of it rationally.' This may be far-fetched – local people today are far from ascetic – yet it is true that the flame of Catharism has been kept alive by a few small groups of dedicated people. The revival dates from the 1890s when Jules Doinel, an intellectual, created a 'neo-Cathar church' at Carcassonne. In the 1890s a Centre for Cathar studies was set up in the village of Arques, near Limoux, and this has remained to this day a meeting-place for intellectuals, some of them scholars with a purely objective interest in Catharism, others true believers seeking to propagate its creed. One of these was the Occitan writer René Nelli, who described himself half-humorously as 'the new Cathar pope'.

There are persistent rumours today, hard to confirm, that an active Cathar freemasonry, with its own clergy and bishops, still secretly exists today in the Aude, around Carcassonne and in the Corbières hills. The Aude has long been a land of magic and witchcraft. And today at Carcassonne there is said to be a neo-Cathar group that holds strange midnight ceremonies, dabbling in the occult. Of course, Catharism is perfectly legal in France today, where all religions are tolerated and no one is burnt at the stake for his beliefs. None the less certain of the old Cathar rituals are *not* legal (such as the practice of burying the dead wrapped only in a shroud in ordinary ground) and therefore these have to be practised in the darkest secrecy.

AQUITAINE

When the Romans came they called it Aquitania, 'land of waters', because of its many rivers and its Atlantic coastline. Historically this vast province used to stretch far to the north, beyond Poitiers: but the modern region runs just from Périgord to the Pyrenees, with Bordeaux as its capital. It is a gentle, sunny, southerly land, fanned by Atlantic breezes, less dry and hot than Provence, but greener, a varied land of forest and meadow, vine and mountain. In the north-east is Périgord, where the Dordogne river flows; in the north-west, the vineyards of the Bordeaux district. South from here lies the forest of the Landes, France's largest, created out of marshland in the last century. Even further south are the lands that border the high Pyrenees – the Basque country, and the districts of Béarn and Bigorre where spas lie in the narrow mountain valleys.

Aquitaine's modern history has been fairly calm and peaceful, unlike that of north-eastern France. In the Middle Ages, however, it was a turbulent area. Béarn then was a powerful semi-independent state. And so was the neighbouring duchy of Gascony, which really belongs to Aquitaine, though by a French administrative quirk much of it today lies across the border in the Midi-Pyrénées region; its heartland is the Gers *département*. The English controlled much of Aquitaine for 300 years, on and off, until finally defeated and driven out in 1453, at the end of the Hundred Years' War. They have left many memorials: for example, a village called Hastingues in Béarn, where in the thirteenth century John of Hastings built a fortified gateway that still stands.

The saga of the Landes is an extraordinary one. Until the nineteenth century this vast flat area south-west of Bordeaux was an insalubrious marshy plain. Atlantic rollers had piled up high dunes along the coast, and the westerly gales were whipping these inland at the rate of some 50 feet a year. The sand blown across the plain was creating a desert and even menacing the Bordeaux vineyards. Then the French authorities took action. First in the early nineteenth century they managed to fix the dunes by setting up palisades of stakes and planting gorse, broom and shrubs. Later they settled the plain with vast plantations of pines, plus a few oaks, and steadily the marshes disappeared.

Today this great forest stretches for 150 miles along the coast and up to 60 miles inland. It has brought prosperity to a hitherto poor area, for the trees are used for timber and paper-making, while their resin is tapped for glue and synthetic products. Forest fires have sometimes caused damage; but techniques have now been evolved for preventing these from spreading, and the last severe one was in 1950. The forest is monotonous, a little gloomy for some tastes, and very thinly populated except on the touristy coastal strip. Here and there in a clearing one comes across a traditional farmer's cottage, a simple low building of wood and plaster, surrounded by a vegetable patch and a cornfield. At Marquèze an 'ecological museum' has now been set up, giving details of the life of the Landes both before and after the coming of the pines. It tells how, in the days before the marshes were drained, the shepherds used to walk on stilts to keep their feet dry.

The dunes along the coast are impressive: at Pyla, south of Arcachon, are the highest in Europe (375 feet). This 'Silver Coast', as it is called, running all the way from the mouth of the Gironde to that of the Adour, has superb sandy beaches lined with little bathing resorts. Just inland are a string of shallow freshwater lakes, popular for boating: they were formed by the blocking of the

163

Aquitaine

streams draining the forest. Here the Government today is embarked on a new ecological scheme, master-minding the creation of a series of new resorts, carefully sited so as to blend with the landscape: no building can be more than three storeys high. The aim is to avoid the high-rise *gigantisme* that arguably has spoilt the holiday coasts of Languedoc and the Vendée.

South-east of the Landes is the Armagnac district, at the heart of old Gascony. It is attractive undulating country, with villages built of golden-brown local stone. Many still have fortifications dating from the Hundred Years' War when they frequently changed hands between French and English. The local brandy, armagnac, is rated by connoisseurs as equal to all but the greatest cognacs. In this area, to ask for a cognac and not an armagnac can be taken as an insult.

South again and we are in Béarn, around Pau, a lushly pastoral area where the hills are gentle and salmon leap in the fast-flowing rivers that gush down from the Pyrenees. Béarn breathes *douceur de vivre*. The mildness of its winters was what above all drew thousands of Britons to settle here after Wellington's officers returning from Spain had discovered Béarn around 1815. By the 1860s a third of Pau's population of 9,000 was British; it was in fact the largest British colony outside the Empire, with its own tea-parties, balls and fox-hunts. Today the British are gone, but the French have kept alive the fox-hunt, which meets on Saturdays in winter.

Béarn and its neighbour, Bigorre, are today tourist areas, especially where the Pyrenees rise to the south. Visitors come to ski, or to gaze at scenic wonders such as Gavarnie's towering circle of rocks. Others come to Lourdes to be cured by a miracle, or to one of the many local spas for a possibly more scientific cure. In country areas, some people still practise traditional nature cures. Henry Myhill in *North of the Pyrenees* (Faber & Faber, 1973) tells how an English lady living in Béarn was cured of shingles by being placed at night at a north-south, east-west cross-roads. This the healer traversed seven times, throwing down his cummerbund and repeating the words, 'Je porte', to which the lady replied with the strange formula, 'Le zona'. She was completely cured, to the amazement of her doctor.

Agriculture in Aquitaine takes less bizarre forms. The farms are mostly small, but the land is fertile and the produce abundant: in the wide valley of the Garonne they grow peaches, plums, tomatoes and melons. Béarn too is rich, a land of orchards and vineyards as well as livestock. Here transhumance is still practised: the herds of sheep and cattle spend the winter in the valleys, then are taken up to the higher pastures for the summer. Above all, Aquitaine is noted for its poultry and notably for the geese which are assiduously stuffed to make *confit d'oie* and *foie gras*. Today the unpleasant process of stuffing the poor geese, to make their livers swell, is done mostly on an industrial scale by big farms. But there are still plenty of small-holdings where the wife or daughter will turn her hand daily to this traditional local chore.

It follows that *foie gras* features prominently in the *cuisine* of Aquitaine, though it is so costly that country folk will not eat it often. Served hot in a sweet wine sauce, with small grapes, it is especially delicious. In the Bordelais, many dishes are cooked in red wine, such as *entrecôte bordelaise* (with marrowbone fat and a sauce of wine and shallots) and *lamproies* (lampreys) *au vin rouge*. The cuisine of Béarn is quite different, often spicy, due to the Spanish influences. One country favourite here is *garbure*, a thick soup of beans and salt pork. The Basques have their own dishes, as they have so much that is special, among them, *civet de palombe* (jugged wood pigeon), *pipérade* (a spicy omelette with pimentoes and tomatoes) and *ttoro*, a thick fish stew.

Outside the Basque country, Aquitaine folk traditions and festivals are not especially lively. But on 15 August it is worth visiting the Ossau valley in Béarn, for the festival at Laruns where the old costumes are taken out of mothballs and the old dances performed. To the south of the Landes they hold *courses landaises*, where frisky heifers held on ropes are baited by mock-toreadors; it is all very friendly. A more violent sport is *le rugby*, introduced by the English a hundred years ago and today highly popular all over south-west France.

(Left) The spectacular sand-dunes of the 'Silver Coast' stretch from the mouth of the Gironde to the mouth of the Adour.

(Opposite) An attractive farmhouse in Armagnac built of the local golden-brown stone.

Aquitaine/Basque Life

Politically the Basques belong to Spain and to France. But ethnically they are a race apart, with their own strange language, thought to be the oldest in Europe and linguistically unrelated to any other. No one quite knows where the Basques come from. They are not Latin. Since the Dark Ages, or earlier, they have been living in the mountain valleys on either side of the Pyrenees. They have kept their individuality and their sense of nationhood, which today they express not only in their language (still widely spoken) but in their customs: the game of *pelota*; the Basque beret and sandals; the red, white and green folk costumes; the high-leaping folk-dances.

Of the million or so Basques, nearly 90 per cent live in the Spanish provinces which are relatively industrialized, with big towns such as Bilbao and San Sebastian, whereas the strip of Basque territory in France is more rural. Here the coast around Biarritz and Saint-Jean-de-Luz is touristy and sophisticated, overcrowded in summer, and not typical. The true *pays basque* lies inland, where charming villages nestle in the Pyrenean foothills: Ascain, Aïnhoa, Sare, Saint-Jean-Pied-de-Port. This is a remarkably unspoilt country of meadows and knobbly hills, as brilliantly green as Ireland and with far prettier houses, all clean white walls and red roofs. The Pyrenean

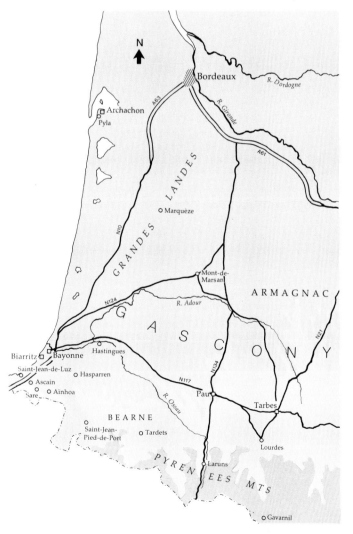

The village of Sare lies in the foothills of the Pyrenees, in the true pays basque.

Aquitaine/Basque Life

(Right) Saint-Jean-Pied-de-Port on the river Nive. The town used to be a central place of pilgrimage on the way to Compostella.

(Far right) In the western part of the region, as here in the village of Espelette, the houses are built in a style reminiscent of Switzerland, with red-tiled roofs and white-washed walls criss-crossed with beams.

peaks attract the wet Atlantic weather, so the climate though mild is damp, often misty, sometimes stormy. But it is rain followed by sun that gives the fields and villages their washed, fresh, sparkling quality.

The houses are in chalet style, sturdily built and spacious, with gently sloping roofs of bright red tiles, and red or brown beams criss-crossing the white-washed walls. It is all very spruce, with more than a hint of the Swiss Alps. The houses face east, for protection against the westerly gales; and each bears its owner's name on the lintel, as well as its date of building. The villages are pleasingly harmonious, for all new housing must by law conform to the local style. In the eastern part of the Basque country, known as Soule, the houses are of local stone, with steep roofs of grey slate – very different, but almost as picturesque.

Basques are a tough and hard-working people. The coastal dwellers used to be deep-sea whale-hunters. Today they still catch tunny, but devote themselves mainly to tourism. Inland, the principal activity is farming: corn, apples, and the keeping of sheep and light-brown dairy cows. Some cottage industries and crafts still flourish, too, such as the tanneries of Hasparren, and the making of *espadrilles*, the Basques' traditional springy rope-soled shoes. Smuggling is another time-honoured activity, at least in the villages near the frontier where numerous remote forest paths lead over the mountains into Spain, and dodging the customs officers is not very difficult. Until not long ago, many people earned a living from contraband in sheep and cattle, brandy and other drinks. Today, the traffic tends in the main to be in electronic and mechanical goods and parts. But smuggling on any large scale has ceased.

Basques were one of the last peoples in Europe to be christianized. Their conversion did not happen until

Aquitaine/Basque Life

sometime in the twelfth century and to this day the word in their language for 'nothing at all' is 'deus', the Latin for God! This used to be a land of witchcraft, where witches would gather on the misty Rune mountain to hold their orgies and sabbaths: this went on even until the seventeenth century, when finally the French authorities launched a crusade against the wild ladies, executing over 600, so it is said. Today there are no more witches. But even Christianity in the Basque country still bears traces of an earlier paganism. The curious disk-shaped tombs (fifteenth to nineteenth centuries) in many churchyards are believed to date in inspiration from some pre-Christian past: some are decorated with the Basque cross, in the form of an inverted swastika, its origins as mysterious as those of the Basques themselves. However, today this race is more devoutly Catholic than the low French average, and the *curé* often keeps more influence than elsewhere. In church, women and men are separate: the women and children in the nave, the men up in wooden galleries around the sides.

Basques are generally tall, slim and dark. Many still wear the traditional beret, red or black; and some country people still carry the *makhila*, a strong leather-handled stave used for herding cattle or – in the past, at least – as a weapon. Perhaps because of their unknown history, or their misty climate, Basques are sometimes regarded as a mystical people. But in fact they are rather down-to-earth, even taciturn much of the time, though given to expressing their emotions through singing and dancing. They are much attached to their language, known as Euskara, which has been retained as a vehicle of daily speech more successfully than any other regional tongue in France. In the villages, notices of sporting or social events are frequently posted up only in Euskara.

The richness of Basque traditions can be studied by a visit to the folk museum at Bayonne, which has rooms devoted to *pelota*, to dance-costumes, and to local farming and farm dwellings. Like other French minorities, Basques have recently been turning back with a new eagerness to their old customs, notably to the national game of *pelota* which is played passionately all the year, and not just put on for tourists. Somewhat resembling squash or fives, *pelota* is a fast game played on an open-air court against a high white wall, the *fronton* – and every village has its *fronton*. The players, usually three-a-side, are dressed in white; and apart from their red or green berets they look remarkably like an English cricket team. They use a small hard ball made of wool and rubber, bound with dog's hide, and this they strike (the game has many variants) either with a gloved hand, or with a thin wicker basket (the *chistera*) strapped to the wrist, or even, despite the blisters, with the bare hand. *Pelota* has become very popular with Basque emigrants to the Americas who have introduced an even faster version, *cesta punta*.

Basques also enjoy bull-fights, like their Spanish brothers, as well as mock bull-fights similar to the *courses landaises*. In autumn they have their own special hunting sport, the *chasse à la palombe*, at the time when these wood-pigeons are migrating down from the north in thousands. Some of them are shot with guns in the usual French fashion. Mostly, however, they are trapped with nets that are spread between the trees in the mountain defiles. The birds then go to make that local delicacy, wood-pigeon stew. The sport may seem cruel, but Basques argue that the birds do damage to the crops and so their numbers must be contained.

Above all, young Basques have been reviving their famous folk-dances. Several new folk-groups have been created: these perform for the summer tourists, yes, but also for the Basques' own enjoyment at local festivals. Here the visitor may well be struck by the strange similarities between these ancient Basque dances and those of many other parts of Europe, including Britain. Young men with jingling bells on their ankles do handkerchief-waving and stick-beating dances, not unlike Morrismen. Girls in yellow skirts do a kind of Sir Roger de Coverley, or what seems to be a Highland jig, accompanied by flutes, drums and whistles. Then a comic character will prance on, wearing the kind of wicker-framed horse round his middle that one finds in some English dances. This is not imitation; it is a shared European folk-culture dating back into the mists of time.

Other dances, however, are more exclusively Basque. There is a comic dance with a stuffed pig, and a mournful fishermen's dance with a coffin. There is the curious dance where everyone must pirouette round a full glass of wine on the ground, without knocking it over. And there are the joyous high-leaping dances, a Basque trademark, to the sound of strange whooping cries which are how Basque peasants signal to each other in their lonely mountain valleys. The dancers' costumes are always colourful and varied: the men in white, maybe with red berets and green cummerbunds, the girls in red or green skirts, black bodices and white caps.

The Soule area in the east, around Tardets, has preserved an even more complex tradition: a series of medieval charades called *pastorales* and *mascarades*, with an array of richly costumed characters divided into 'reds' and 'blacks'. These Gallet-plays go on for hours, and are so complicated that today they are performed only once every few years. To watch one of these performances is a rare and impressive experience.

However, more everyday expressions of Basqueness can be seen on almost any occasion. After a *pelota* match or a bull-fight, young Basques will spontaneously burst into their national songs, or parade around waving their red-white-and-green national flag, or do their leaping dances. At Bayonne's midnight carnival in August, the whole city centre is a sea of heads bobbing rhythmically up and down in the bouncy Basque dance-ritual.

Young French Basques today are glad to give vent so exuberantly to their Basqueness, but very few of them are politically separatist. They feel a close kinship with the Basques in Spain, while deploring the terrorism which has marred that region and happily has never spread into France. Though they might want more devolution, the vast majority of French Basques are happy to remain within France, a France that freely allows them to express their national culture.

A craftsman making a chistera, the thin wicker basket which is used in the game of pelota.

Aquitaine/A Wine Town

Saint-Emilion is renowned both as a wine centre and as a historic and ancient town.

(Opposite) Steep cobbled streets lined with well-preserved and interesting buildings add to the charm and atmosphere of the town.

Saint-Emilion is both a town and an appellation. As a town, it is probably the most ancient wine centre in France; as a wine, it is one of the best known and most respected of the French appellations. The history of the wine and the city were as interwoven in the past as they are to this day, as is evident from even a first visit to the town.

Situated 35 km from Bordeaux and 7 km south-east of Libourne, the Saint-Emilion region covers a surface of about 5000 hectares. Vines were first planted in Gallo-Roman times, making Saint-Emilion one of the oldest vineyards in France. Although often outclassed in the public's mind by the grander image of the Médoc, the region produces almost one-sixth of all red Bordeaux from nearly 1000 different châteaux. This concentration of small *propriétaires* (while many of the well-known châteaux cover more than 50 hectares, the average hold-ing is less than 10 hectares) is very characteristic of the region, where vine-growing (apart from a little macaroon-making) is the only activity.

It would be misleading, however, to think that with only one appellation all the wine is the same. The different châteaux have been classified into a hierarchy of Premiers Grands Crus Classés, Grands Crus Classés, Grands Crus and generic Saint-Emilion. Each year the wines are 'blind' tasted by a panel of experts to make sure that they justify inclusion as a Cru Classé, and are disqualified if they do not come up to the required standard. Such concern for quality has always been at the heart of the wine-making tradition in Saint-Emilion.

Over the centuries these controls were the duty of the 800-year-old Jurade de Saint-Emilion. Founded in 1199 by a charter from the English King John, the Jurade had almost total administrative power over the nine parishes of the region. The 'Jurats', as the members of the Jurade were called, were rigorously active in the propagation of fine wine: deciding when the vintage should commence, regularly visiting cellars, checking barrels, punishing abuses and generally controlling production. In 1948 the Jurade was reconstituted by the growers of Saint-Emilion with the aim of maintaining the quality of their wines, by eliminating anything that could harm their reputation. Every such brotherhood holds a series of fêtes throughout the year, the two principal ones for the Jurade being the 'Jugement de Vin Nouveau' in mid-June and the 'Ban des Vendanges' in mid-September. At both of these, lengthy enthroning ceremonies are held in the Monolithic Church, followed by a procession through the streets of the city.

The city is a historical monument in itself. Already famous in Gallo-Roman times, there are traces of a prehistoric civilization, Saracen and Normand invasions, not to speak of the centuries of occupation by the English. The streets are cobbled and winding and at every corner there are buildings of great interest. Perhaps the most extraordinary is the Monolithic Church, a place of worship built during the ninth to eleventh centuries, hewn out of the rock beneath the town. This is the centre of what is known as the 'lower town', which was dedicated to Saint Ermite by the Benedictines. Nearby is the Ermitage de Saint-Emilion, the Catacombs and the Chapelle de la Trinité, this last built in the thirteenth century. In the upper town one finds the Eglise Collégiale with its famous portal and beautiful cloisters (twelfth- to sixteenth-century), the Maison de l'Abbé, the Chapelle de Châpitre and the Maison du Doyenné, off the Place des Creneaux, which is now used for the banquets of the Jurade. The outskirts of the town are dominated by the powerful twelfth-century fortified Château du Roy, of which only two towers still exist, and the ruins of the Couvent des Jacobins. A little further from the centre are the romantic cloisters of the Couvent des Cordeliers. Much has been lost, but much more remains of this historical ensemble to bear witness to a unique and lasting cooperation of Church and State, both of whom saw their best interests in the continuing propagation of the vine.

CORSICA

Corsica, which has been called 'a mountain in the sea', is an island of contrasts: high peaks, dramatic gorges, secret valleys and secluded villages, vast forests cut by rushing torrents, expanses of marshland. Above all, and perhaps most memorably for the tourist, Corsica has a thousand kilometres of coastline, hidden coves enclosed by steep cliffs, beaches of soft, golden sand. It is the visitor who arrives by ship, either on one of the car ferries which ply to and from the mainland, or by yacht, who enjoys the most spectacular visual introduction to this Mediterranean isle.

The island is divided into two main geographical areas: high mountains in the north-west, rising to their highest point of 2710 metres on Mount Cinto, with further mountainous country in the south-east which declines to the lower plains in the east. The mountains play a dominant part in the landscape and life of Corsica, bringing rain to temper the dry Mediterranean climate and dividing the island into self-contained, autocratic regions. It is a climate of scorching-hot, dry summers and clement winters, with regional variations: more humid and brisk on the western coast, warmer and drier in the north-east, with a typical alpine climate at altitudes above 1500 metres. The island is watered by numerous rivers and streams, fast-flowing in spate after the rains, reduced to a trickle in the dry season. The vegetation varies according to region and altitude; exotic species such as the prickly pear, aloe and eucalyptus on the warmer slopes, the *maquis* which covers vast areas of the coast and interior with a riot of wild flowers and herbs, extensive forests in the centre of the island. Of the tree population, the holm oak is the most widespread on the lower slopes, with chestnut and *laricio* pine predominant at the higher altitudes. The *maquis*, tinder-dry in sum-

mer, represents a constant fire hazard, and thousands of acres of undergrowth and forest are destroyed each year. On the upland pastures sheep, cattle, goats and pigs roam freely; transhumance is practised, and herds are driven up on to the higher ground to pass the summer, returning to the plains in October. The beauty and variety of the island's flora and fauna are here shown off

Corsica

A typical village surrounded by terraced vineyards in the region of La Balagne, north-western Corsica.

(Below left) Traditional rural life still continues in many parts of the island.

(Opposite below) The lovely bay of Girolata with its small fishing village on the western coast.

to best advantage, with berries, mushrooms and wild flowers in season.

The Corsicans are a fiery yet friendly race, partisan with a highly developed sense of family and clan loyalty, fiercely jealous of personal territory. They are, perhaps inevitably, inward-looking, religious yet superstitious, aware and proud of their island separateness. Personal vendettas and family feuds can persist over generations: honour is a real concept to the Corsican. Physically, the typical Corsican is short and stocky, with dark hair and eyes, though by contrast most of the shepherds in the northern Niolo region are taller and slimmer with fair hair and blue eyes. The most famous Corsican is undoubtedly Napoleon Bonaparte, born at Ajaccio on 15 August 1769. It was during his education at the *école militaire* at Brienne on the mainland, and later at Paris, that Napoleon become imbued with patriotic longing and decided on a political and military career on his native isle. The Revolution of 1789 gave fresh impetus to his ambitions, but partisan hostility forced the whole Bonaparte family, including Napoleon, to leave Corsica in 1793. The history of his subsequent meteoric career is well known.

Corsica is the least populated of the larger Mediterranean islands. More than a third of the total population of 220,000 is concentrated in Bastia and Ajaccio, the capital and main port. Emigration from the island has increased since the middle of the last century, as a result of agricultural disasters and the effects of World War I, and

The Regional Park

A vast Regional Park, covering about a quarter of the island's surface and including the main mountain belt and forestland of the interior, was created in 1970. Its specific aims were nature conservation, particularly of the many rare species of flora and fauna which flourish on the island, revival of the rural economy and the creation of fire zones to help combat the annual forest fires which regularly ravage the countryside. Tourism has played a major part in the organization of the park's facilities with the creation of skiing and climbing centres and walking and horse-riding itineraries. A long-distance path (*grande randonnée*) runs for some 170 kilometres through the park from Calenza, south of Calvi, to Conca near Porto-Vecchio, providing walkers with an exhilarating means of exploring the most spectacular scenery of the island. Huts offering accommodation have been established at various points along the signposted route. The itinerary is a demanding one, at an altitude of over 2000 metres for much of its length, and the full traverse takes two weeks. It is an expedition which should only be undertaken by experienced walkers, and only in the summer months.

The needle crags of Bavella are one of the many outstanding features in the Regional Park.

large colonies of Corsican ex-patriots have grown up in the southern part of France – in particular Marseilles, Toulon and Nice – and around Paris. On the other side, there has been a regular influx of Italian immigrants since the nineteenth century.

Agriculture has declined as a profitable economic activity and the two main crops are now wine and citrus fruits, both of which have seen major expansion in recent years. The new vineyards, planted in the 1960s, are concentrated in the east and south, while the older vines grow on the terraced hillsides. From the area around Ajaccio come mainly red and rosé wines made from the Sciacarello grape, while Patrimonio produces a range of wines including a full-bodied red. Some excellent and celebrated dessert wines – among others – with the appellation Coteaux du Cap Corse come from the slopes of the north-eastern promontory. These local wines go well with the traditional cuisine using local produce and olive oil which still flourishes all over the island. The emphasis is on plain, substantial food such as soups of vegetables or fish (notably *aziminu*, the Corsican *bouilla-baisse*), shellfish, goat's-milk cheese (such as Broccio and Niolo) and *pâtes* (reflecting the Italian influence). Pork is used in various forms, from *lonzu*, made from fillet, to *prisuttu*, raw ham similar to the Italian *prosciutto*, usually eaten with fresh figs. Game is another speciality: for example, roast lamb with herbs, kid meat, roast boar with chestnut purée. Chestnuts add a distinctive note to the Corsican cuisine and are used in a variety of dishes, including pastries (*frittelle* and *torta castagnina*).

Outside the few large towns, in the villages and country districts, the rural architecture shows the face of Corsica as it has been for centuries. The traditional house is tall and solid, built of local granite or schist. The style is typically austere, with little ornamentation, the windows narrow to keep out both summer sun and winter wind. Most houses have an external staircase leading to the first floor. Traditionally, houses are grouped together in villages or hamlets around the church. Another typical feature of the Corsican landscape is the sheepfolds with their dry-stone walls which are scattered through the mountains. They are still used by the shepherds from May to October when the herds are driven to the upland pastures.

Les Petits Vins

Whenever the average Frenchman takes a liking to something, he gives it the endearing epithet *'petit'*. Thus the phrases *'une petite amie'* (girlfriend), *'la petite maison à la compagne'* (weekend house), *'le petit chien'* (dog of any size), and, of course, *'un bot p'tit vin'*, are in everyday use. The last phrase has none of the condescension of the literal translation into English, 'a nice little wine'; the French are proud of their *'petits vins'*, and have every reason to be so.

Petits vins should not be confused with *vins ordinaires*. The wine served from litre bottles in city cafés is anything but endearing. Sold on the basis of its alcohol content rather than any specific quality, it has certainly earned the name *'gros rouge'*. It is viewed more as a necessary, as opposed to enjoyable, part of French life, seeming to get nastier, but perhaps more necessary, the further one travels from the vineyards. It is not surprising that the largest producers of this stuff, the vine-growers in the Midi, tend to avoid it in favour of Pastis.

Petits vins are better described as the 'local' or 'country' wines of France. They have a definition of origin based on where they are grown and what they are grown from. They have a style, a feel about them that is local, specific to their region, a recognisable *'terroir'*. Another definition could be that these wines are essentially drunk *'sur place'*, that they fit in with the local way of life as much as the cuisine, the architecture and the people. Good, bad or indifferent, they have an individuality about them that is typically French.

This individualism is the key to the renaissance of *'petits vins'* that is one of the most encouraging elements in the wine industry in France today. And a renaissance it really is. The tendency is to think, with regret, that things were always better in the past, but for French wines, especially the everyday sort, this was not the case. Following the economic crash, a series of poor but often prolific vintages in the early 1930s caused chaos in the wine industry, leaving many wine producers faced with ruin. The system of *appellation contrôlée* was proposed in order to protect the finer French wines from extinction and to bring order to a collapsed market. Strict rules were imposed on the growers as to which grapes could be planted where, maximum yields, minimum degrees of alcohol, and methods of planting and pruning, so that the classic wines of France lived up to their reputation.

Very little interest was shown in the lesser wines, for which there was a healthy (in the economic sense) market in an era before bottled water and soft drinks, when wine was the principal family thirst-quencher. Yet, however romantically one looks at the past, everyday

Wine is an essential, and integral, part of the French way of life. The petits vins, *local wines, are today enjoying an increase in popularity.*

The major areas producing vins de pays.

The wine harvest near Limoux, in the Aude département.

179

Les Petits Vins

wines in the 1930s were anything but good. Questionable grape varieties, many of them now restricted or banned, ignorance of wine-making techniques, poor storage conditions and general lack of enthusiasm all led to low quality. Even the cooperative system (still the largest producers of *petits vins*), with large wineries built with Government finance, led more often than not to a loss of individuality in a *passe-partout* blend. Finally, most of the producers were losing money, and had no reason to feel that they might lose less if their wines improved.

The change began in the late 1960s. France was prosperous and, while wine consumption had fallen considerably, the French were becoming more informed about and more interested in the better *appellations*. The classic wines were already well known and 'new' wines were being discovered in the Loire, the south-west and Provence. At the same time, there was growing interest mainly among young vine-growers in experimenting with different grape varieties. The basis of quality in French wine lies in the soil, and the more noble the vine you plant in it, the finer will be the wine. Certain soils suit certain varieties of grape, yet within legal and climatic limits, most noble grape varieties can be planted all over France. The exciting development in the late 1960s was the possibility of making different, better wines from the vineyards in the Midi, the classic producer of *gros rouge*. In less than twenty years Provence has been transformed from an area which was known principally for its 'pink plonk' to what has been described as 'the California of France'.

Yet while the Midi can claim to have seen the most marked progress in producing better wine, the heartland of *petits vins* still remains the Loire valley. From its source in the Massif Central, to its mouth on the Atlantic coast, come an unparalleled range of wines: red, white, rosé and sparkling; from very dry to fully sweet. They are the perfect *petits vins*, refreshing, charming, with a certain elegance to balance a touch of rusticity. Their character is as different from the robust, masculine wines from the south, as the soft luminous light along the Loire river contrasts to the glaring sun of Provence. This is a country made up of smallholdings and mixed farming, where a few acres of vines supplement the family's income from *élevage* or *primeurs*.

Historically, the Loire valley wines shared the important Paris market with Burgundy and Champagne, and its wines were being served in Paris bistros while Provence was still a part of Italy. The general style makes them attractive to drink at any time, for the most part within a year or two after the vintage, and the local market for these wines has always been strong, so that the vine-growers in this region never knew the problems which were suffered by the producers of bulk wine in the Languedoc. But many of these local wines are ignored outside their own appellation. For every Sancerre, Vouvray and Muscadet, there is a Châteaumeillant, a Coteaux-de-Giennois and a Jasnières that in a few years may be just a memory. Yet these wines that have been part of the way of life of their region of origin for centuries are in fact the quintessential *petits vins*. This is perhaps summed up in the newly created *appellation 'Les Vins du Pays du Jardin de la France'*. How can one resist a wine with a name like that?

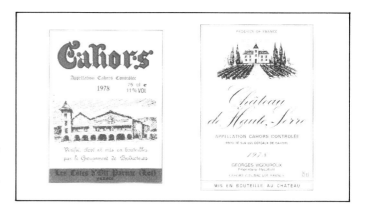

The reputation of the famous wine regions in France (Bordeaux, Burgundy, Champagne and the Rhône valley) often makes one forget the lesser wines that are produced alongside the grand *appellations*. The minor wines which come from around Bordeaux perhaps lack the charm of the whites from the Loire valley and the sunniness of the reds from Provence, but they go wonderfully well with the local oysters from Arcachon and the lamb from Pauillac. The vast Entre-deux-Mers vineyards produce the kind of Bordeaux that the French drink everyday, the *'p'tit Bordeaux'* which their doctors recommend is good for them.

From other vineyards in the south-west come some well-known wines, like Cahors and Bergerac, and many others that are beginning to be seen outside France: Madiran, Côtes-de-Buzet and Gaillac. As in the Midi, this is an area which is dominated by large cooperatives of a generally high standard, with a few small properties making hand-made wines of fine quality. These are bottled at the château or domaine of origin, with the label proudly showing the name, address (and sometimes telephone number!) of the producer, or they are sold in bulk, to appear under the label of the *négociant*. Such wines obviously have to be well made, as they have no established reputation to fall back on. The more they are faithful to their *terroir*, the more reason there is to drink them.

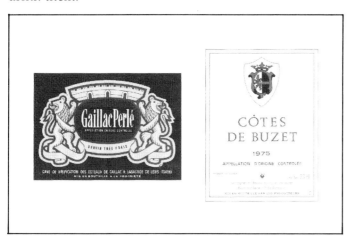

The Burgundy region is not known for its *petits vins*, but there is some clean, crisp Sauvignon from Saint-Bris and some rather sinewy red from Irancy, both in the north around Chablis, while several of the important estates in the Côtes-de-Nuits and Côtes-de-Beaune have an acre or two of Aligoté for their everyday white wine, and Gamay (to be blended with Pinot Noir to produce Bourgogne Passetoutgrains) for their red. Up in the hills, the Hautes-Côtes-de-Nuits and Hautes-Côtes-de-Beaune make genuinely attractive wine, and consequently keep a good meal in Burgundy an affordable pleasure. In southern Burgundy, Mâcon Blanc and Beaujolais are *vins de comptoir* par excellence, but they have achieved such an international reputation that one seldom thinks of them as *petits vins*.

On either side of the Rhône valley, there are wines of all styles that show off the local cuisine to great advantage. Many of these have improved substantially over the years, and have been upgraded from the *Vins Délimités de Qualité Supérieure* (VDQS) category to that of *Appellation d'Origine Contrôlée* (AOC). They include the Beaujolais-like *vins du Lyonnais*, the light, white *vins du Bugey*, the slightly smokey *vins de Savoie*, the rough, fruity reds from the Ardèche, Coteaux de Tricastin and Côtes-du-Vivarais and the sparkling, muscatty Clairette de Die. And, of course, the best-known wine of all, Côtes-du-Rhône, from around Orange and Avignon, where every different village produces a wine of a different character. The quality and popularity of these wines has led to much replanting, and often the *cuvées* of young vines are declassified from their *appellation* Côtes-du-Rhône to *vins du pays*.

A little further west, an alternative to the rather sturdy wines of the Rhône can be found in the soft, scented Côtes-de-Ventoux or the spicy Côtes-de-Luberon from Haute-Provence. As the Rhône river flows south, the vineyards of Coteaux-des-Baux and Coteaux d'Aix give way to the Costières-du-Gard and the vast expanse of wines from the Midi.

With the huge, almost unlimited range of *petits vins* which exists throughout France, the traveller could spend a lifetime visiting the country, and could be sure that he would never taste the same wine twice. And they will seldom, if ever, taste better than they do in the area of their production. For, although these little wines, with much the same level of alcohol as the grander *appellations*, should travel equally as well, sometimes part of the essential charm is missing.

Rural Cuisine

The French still have a deep respect for food. Though hamburger bars and 'le hot-dog' have gained a foothold in the cities, and supermarkets stacked with processed products have their place in every town, the French tradition for eating well lives on. Witness any market-place on Sunday morning: the colourful display of vegetables and fruit, the vast array of cheeses, meat, charcuterie in slabs and pots, fresh fish and piles of shell-fish strewn with ice. The modern world has robbed us of the authenticity of so much and in some western countries traditional food has all but disappeared. Not so in France, however.

On Sundays, many French families still gather to dine in the conservative style: an *hors d'oeuvre* of local pâté or a dish of boiled sliced potatoes doused with an oil and vinegar dressing (*vinaigrette*); this may be followed by *blanquette de veau*, roast chicken or a casserole; a dish of slender green beans served simply with a knob of butter; and to end the meal, a little cheese or fruit, or both. This is not *haute cuisine*, nor *la cuisine nouvelle*, the more recent simpler, lighter innovation; it is the normal *cuisine bourgeoise*, the age-old food of the French, with its roots in the rural traditions of each region. For the authentic cookery of France is still its country cooking.

Vegetables play an important part in French cooking and are used to create many imaginative and tasty dishes.

(Far right) Sea-food in all its varieties dominates the cuisine in coastal areas.

The true country cooking is simple, honest and nourishing. The ingredients are seasonal and fresh. Indeed, the entire tradition of regional cuisine is based on what is locally available. What could be more natural than for the farmer's wife to make good use of every scrap of meat at slaughter time, or serve young spinach leaves or artichokes straight from the garden, or bake the fallen apples into an autumn *tarte*? Nor is it any different for those who buy their produce in the market place, except perhaps that at many a supermarket you can now find apples twelve months of the year, flown in from South Africa and elsewhere, Israeli strawberries in win-

ter, and Bulgarian *pâté de foie*. Those who live off the beaten track, however, and the many more who prefer to buy local produce anyway, take little advantage of these privileges and stick to their standard traditional fare.

Let us look at a simple dish from the Auvergne, an *omelette compagnarde*, eggs beaten lightly, a sprinkling of herbs and a bowlful of *boudin* (black pudding), chopped into pieces, all briefly cooked and served hot. But pause to consider for a moment the powerful tradition that lies behind just one of the ingredients, the blood sausage, *boudin*. The Auvergne is a craggy, wind-swept, rather infertile place, where the farms are small and the pig thrives. So important is the pig to the economy that he has earned the title of Monsieur, and the day of his slaughter – just before Christmas – is a day of celebration and hard work for the whole neighbourhood. The farmer's wife knows how not to waste a thing: the pig's meat yields not only bacons, pork and ham but also brains and tripe for special dishes, backfat for pâté, trotters to boil into gelatine and the lifeblood of the precious beast, the blood for sausage.

Within days of the slaughter there will be a pig's head soup, which is the local version of *potée* – a meat and vegetable soup which is eaten with a chunk of home-made bread or a crisp, fresh baguette from the village bakery – a dish that appears in a dozen different guises throughout rural France.

In the Auvergne, it also contains the heart of white cabbage, carrots, turnips, leeks, potatoes, even a handful of lentils to add substance.

North in the Morvan, which borders on the lowland pastures, there is rib of beef and neck of mutton, long stalked kale instead of cabbage, and the local *cervelas*, a lightly cured pork sausage; and in the Landes, towards the Atlantic coast, where *potée* goes by the name of *garbure*, the tail of the pig and butter beans are also added.

On the coast it is the *fruits de mer* which dominate the local cuisine, fish and shellfish in all their variety. At their humblest (and often most interesting), they appear

Rural Cuisine

among the cheapest item on the harbour menu – *friture du port* or *fruits du golfe* – a ragbag of tiny fish dipped in batter (made of flour and beer in the north) and deep-fried, tails and all, until crisply golden-brown.

The Frenchman may take his fish as an *hors d'oeuvre* with a glass of white wine, an appetizer at the start of the meal, or as a main course. Elaborate preparations abound in recipe books, such as *sole Dieppoise*, poached in sea-soned butter and wine then served with prawns and mussels in a sauce of all the juices, but most of the tradi-tional fish dishes are simple. Like the famous grilled red mullet of Corsica (*rougets grillés aux olives*) or a pink sal-mon trout of the Jura, baked in its own juices and served with a simple green sauce, perhaps made with chervil and tarragon or sorrel, or with a spicy walnut and horse-radish sauce (*raifort aux noix*) in the Pyrenees. If you are lucky, your fish will be fresh from the river – wild fish that put their tank-bred cousins in the shade. Fish-pond trout are especially bland, consequently needing to be fried in butter or studded with almonds before they taste of anything. Not so the real thing, however, that only need to be simmered in a vinegar *court-bouillon* with thyme and onions (*truite au bleu*).

And then there is game, the real countryman's delight, pungent and if not always tender, at least never dull. Aquitaine offers a broad range, the commonest being hare, browned in goosefat or porkfat, or further south in olive oil, and casseroled slowly in the good company of shallots, bacon, garlic and wine for 2-3 hours (*civet de lièvre*). Long cooking, yes, for the meat of all but the youngest game is fibrous and rather dry. Young pheasants you can simply *sautée* in butter, season with salt and pepper, herbs and lemon peel, before baking them for a brief ten minutes in individual pots or greaseproof paper bags (*perdreau en papillotes*), but the older bird, on the other hand, needs something more to soften and moisten the meat, such as wrapping it in cab-bage leaves and bacon for a long, slow simmer in good beef stock (*perdrix aux choux*).

Game is not an everyday affair of course, no more than are the famous traditional dishes of beef and veal and poultry. Nor is the farmer's kitchen any longer poetically dark and smoke-stained as the travel writers might sug-gest, with a pot of *daube* – that wonderful stew of meat laced with lard and cooked with herbs, onions and car-rots all through the night – simmering endlessly on the black kitchen range. Electricity and Common Market subsidies have changed all that. At Christmas, the far-mers of Gascony may still sit down to their annual *daube* of beef and pork – the meat marinated in red wine and local Armagnac before cooking – but for the rest of the year an occasional frozen *daube* will do. Indeed, where the factory chef is given leave to use the best ingredients, the latter is often as good as anything which can be pro-duced in the kitchen.

Vegetables are accorded minor roles in the drama of the *daube*, but elsewhere they enter into more equal part-nership with meat. In the *caillettes* of the Ardèche, for example, little cakes of finely chopped spinach and pork are baked in the pig's caul, its stomach lining. But vege-

tables are often given a major role in France, either as an *hors d'oeuvre* to relax and refresh and entice the diner on to more serious things, or after the main course on their own. In summer, try a platter of *crudités*, a colourful, care-fully selected array of raw vegetables: thinly sliced cucumber with dill, artichoke hearts and finely grated carrot, beetroot sticks and endive, all lightly dressed at the table with a *vinaigrette*, served in the north with her-ring fillets and pickled gherkins, or in the south with anchovies and glistening black olives. And after the meat or fish, how sensible that plate of tender carrots *sautéed* in butter and glazed with caramelized sugar, or the ten-der young leeks stewed in oil with tomatoes; onions stewed in wine or beetroots baked in their jackets; courgettes fried with garlic, endives sizzled in olive oil or – as a lesson to the world of what may be done with the humblest of ingredients – cabbage in any one of a thousand forms. Red cabbage is sliced fine in Limousine, where they cook it in lard and wine with chestnuts and a

pinch of nutmeg; or it may be braised in the style of Alsace with apples, sugar, cloves and redcurrant jelly; winter cabbage fermented in brine to produce the many varieties of sauerkraut (*choucroute*), to be served in the Jura with a beer and pheasant, or fried in Roussillon with Toulouse sausages and juniper berries; cabbage fried in lard and spiced with *piment rouge* in the Pyrenees, or stewed with ham in beef stock and vinegar in the Péri-gord. These hardy dishes may lack the grace of young artichokes *à la Barigoule* – boiled in spluttering olive oil until they emerge bronzed with crisp leaves – but the cabbages are still barons of the country vegetables: ubiquitous, reliable, versatile – and cheap!

Each French region has its style which has evolved from the soil, the climate, the spirit of the people, and in no other food is this more evident than in France's great traditions of cheese. From the high, lush pastures of Savoie and Franche-Comté with their subtly flavoured Gruyères (*Comté, Beaufort* and *Emmenthal*) to the salty

(Above left) Old-fashioned styles of grocery and bakery still survive in some villages.

(Above) The making of gateaux and confectionery has been elevated to a national art.

France has a great tradition of cheese. Here the curd is being moulded in the production of Roquefort.

Rural Cuisine

Open-air markets selling
everything from live game to
flowers are a common feature in
French towns.

(Far right) There are many
varieties of charcuterie and
pâtés, often special to the
region of origin.

goats' milk Venaco from the sun-baked scrubland of Corsica, the variety is legion. From Normandy come a hundred breeds of Camembert; from the limestone caves of the southern Massif Central, Roquefort and the personable blue cheese of Aveyron, Thiezac and Laqueuille; and then Boursin, Brie and Bosson, the Picardon and Pont l'Evêque, Saint-Nectaire and Saint-Paulin.

Bread also has its regional variety but here the differences are not so much of flavour or texture but rather of form. The *épi* of Charente is shaped like a stalk of wheat, the Saint-Ouen is short and fat, while the *tourte d'Auvergne* is like a crown. While you may find whole-wheat bread (*pain complet*) served with your mussels at the port, and rye bread (*pain de sègle*) in the larger towns, the basic ingredient is white wheat flour. For the French are the world's most conservative bread eaters, placing far higher value on the proper baking than on the flour. The crust must be crisp and firm, the interior light and soft, and above all the loaf must be fresh. Is there another nation in the world where the baker is expected to bake twice a day – every day of the week?

Of course, there are variations around the theme of bread: *croissants, brioches,* soft Provençal rolls. And at the butcher's a feast of pastry-case charcuterie: goose pie, pâté (which properly speaking is always in a crust) and little quiches, egg tarts with ham in the style of Lorraine.

Pastry-making is a national art. It also forms the basis of the French dessert, providing a crusty container for the fruit, with which the meal is usually ended. In season, you will always find tarts of strawberries, cherries, plums, apricots and peaches, and often enough throughout the year the *tarte aux pommes*, for France is Europe's foremost apple-producing nation. Apples cooked in Normandy cider or baked with brandy in the Berry speciality *gouères*; or thinly sliced into an apple pancake – the *crêpe* of Normandy and the *jacque* of Gascony. Once in a while, to please a guest or celebrate the passing of another year, there may be *mousse au chocolat, crème caramel* or *baba rhum*, or even a Corsican chestnut pastry called *fritelli*, but simple fruit is often enough.

Waterways

To those who have previously only travelled through France by road, a journey by canal or river will prove a revelation. Boating is a blessedly slow affair, giving the traveller time to take in something more than just the general scene, the panoramic view. Many waterways may boast grand and spectacular features, but the memories that live on are built up of the steady accumulation of small details collected at leisure. And the waterways world is a private, self-contained world, having its own life which is obviously set apart from that of the rest of the country.

All this is true of waterways everywhere, but the French canals and rivers differ from, for example, their counterparts in Britain, in that they still play an important role in the commercial life of the nation. It is often said of British canals that they lost their trading life simply because being built so long ago, they became out of date. How could one expect a system devised in the eighteenth century to answer the needs of the twentieth? What then should one think of the French system which was begun in the seventeenth century? Indeed, the plans for the first French waterway to be built since Roman times were made by François I in the sixteenth century, when a route was surveyed to join the river Garonne near Toulouse to the Mediterranean. There were technical problems which prevented its building until Paul Riquet, Baron de Bonrepos, came along a century later. In 1666, he applied to Louis XIV for permission to build the canal: permission was given and the Canal du Midi duly built. For over two hundred years, it has continued in use as a trading route, but increasingly the trading vessels have been joined by the motor cruisers of those who come to the canal for pleasure, and a different way of penetrating to the heart of France.

The Canal du Midi is by far the most popular of the holiday routes, and it is easy enough to see why. It offers Mediterranean sun without Mediterranean crowds, yet it takes the traveller to such splendid places as the ancient walled city of Carcassonne. Those are the obvious pleasures, but they could be obtained by anyone prepared to desert the main road for the side roads or, better still, leave the roads altogether and travel on foot. But the canal does have something more to offer: it has itself. This venerable undertaking has its own quite distinctive personality. The way is lined with pine and poplar, for Riquet himself insisted on the trees being planted to shade the boatmen and their horses. Then there are the bridges of a rich, pinkish stone and the locks, quite unlike those of any other canal, built on an oval plan. Most important of all, perhaps, is the sense the pleasure boater has of joining in the working life of France, for it is primarily for the working boat that the system is not just preserved but regularly improved as well. It is all too easy to get lost in a somewhat sentimental daydream while chugging quietly along, the alternation of light and shade as the sun shines through the trees stripes the water, setting up a soothing rhythm. But nothing brings back a sense of reality faster than the sight of a *péniche*, one of the big French barges, often with a little Citroën 2CV on deck, storming towards you round a bend.

The different canals and rivers all have their own special characteristics. Some, such as the canals of Brittany, are very little known; others such as the Loire, with its famous procession of châteaux, have long provided popular tourist routes. It is not possible to give even the briefest description of all the navigable waterways, which cover literally thousands of miles. This, however, is a book about rural France, so that if one could assume

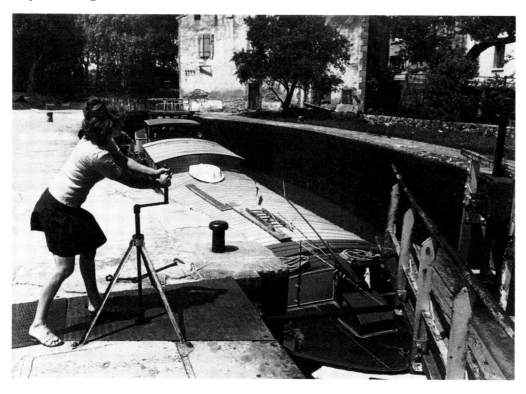

A barge leaving a lock on the Canal du Midi.

(Opposite) A lock at Montargis in the Loiret département.

Waterways

N

Gravelines

Arras

Saint-Valery

C. DE LA SOMME

R. Meuse

Le Havre   Tancarville
Rouen

C. DES ARDENNES

R. Aisne

Reims

C. DE L'EST   R. Moselle

Caen

R. Oise

R. Seine

R. Marne

C. DE LA MARNE
AU RHIN

Nancy

PARIS

C. DE
LA MARNE

Troussey

Strasbourg

Brest

Saint-Malo

Rennes

C. DE NANTES
A BREST

R. Mayenne

Orléans

C. DE LA MARNE
A LA SAONE

C. DE L'EST

R. Rhin

Mulhouse

R. Sarthe

R. Loir

C. DE
NIVERNAIS

C. DE
BOURGOGNE

C. DU RHONE
AU RHIN

Angers

Tours   R. Loire

C. LATERAL
A LA LOIRE

Saint-Nazaire   Nantes

Chalon

C. DU CENTRE

R. Saône

Marans   Niort

R. Ain

R. Charente

R. Rhône

Lyon

Angoulême

Bordeaux   Castets
R. Garonne

R. Rhône

Mont de
Marsan

C. LAT. A LA GARONNE

Bayonne   R. Adour   Saint-Sever

Toulouse

C. DU RHONE
A SETE

Arles

Sète

C. DU MIDI

that the reader was searching for peace and quiet, together with that elusive 'Frenchness' which can so easily be lost or at best swamped in the popular resorts, where should one start? Some would claim that popularity has already begun to erode the special character of routes such as the Canal du Midi though, if so, the forces of destruction have still a long way to go before they can claim success. There is, of course, no single canal that could epitomize all that is best, but among them all, there are a few which, sitting in the centre of France, might be felt to show the best of the rural heartland. And as good a starting place as any would be the Canal du Nivernais.

The Nivernais forms a link between two rivers, the Yonne, which is followed closely and even, on occasions, joined, and the Loire. There are towns at either end, Auxerre in the north and Decize in the south, and a great variety of scenery in between. In the northern Yonne valley, steep limestone cliffs border the river and the land, with its fortified farms and manors, can have a stern appearance. But as the canal continues south, the land softens until by the time the old town of Clamecy is reached, it has become gently undulating and the waterway slides through a remote and private world.

The most southerly section sees the canal take on a more dramatic visage, with some astonishing, narrow, deep cuttings, tunnels and long flights of locks. The Nivernais, it seems, has everything except crowds. For commercial traffic has all but ended on the canal, and those who travel in spring or early autumn will be lucky if they see more than half a dozen other boats on the move. Yet every lock has a lock-keeper to work it, and this provides one of the special pleasures of the canal. Several things are expected of the boater by the lock-keeper: he, or more likely she, will expect a hand with the work, which is a fascinating experience, since there is a bewildering variety of mechanisms in use at different locks. A tip will be expected at the end of the exercise, but most importantly of all, the lock-keeper will expect conversation. And there is no shortage of topics, for most locks provide the topics themselves, whether it be a herd of goats or the flower garden. The chances are that you will leave the lock with a sample of goat's milk cheese or a bunch of flowers to brighten the boat. One soon starts to look foward to the locks as highlights of the day and if by chance one arrives during the sacred lunch hour, then there is little hardship in sitting out on deck with a bottle of wine and the *chèvre* from the last lock.

On the canal, one seldom feels that awful urgency, that need to get somewhere in a rush that is the bane of civilized travel. A canal such as the Nivernais demands that you take your time: time to meander up to the nearest village for the morning *croissants*, time to stop and look around. It is a way of life that ensures that you become involved in the everyday life of the regions, for with few towns along the way you have no Michelin starred restaurants for luxury living. Here it is local produce from the farm or a good, plain, honest meal at the local café. There can be few better ways to make the acquaintance of the true rural France than to travel through it by one of its waterways.

Pleasure cruising on canals and rivers has become a popular form of holiday in recent years.

Forests and Wildlife

Almost one-half of the forestland of the ten member countries of the European Economic Community is in France. Forest covers some 14 million hectares, about a quarter of the country's area. They are forests of extraordinary beauty and diversity: the magnificent stands of beech around Compiègne; the oaks of the Bourbonnais, some of which are the fruits of the policy set out by Colbert in his famous edict on water and forests of 1669; the majestic conifers of the Jura; the pines of the Landes, France's most wooded *département*; Fontainebleau, the Ardennes, and many more.

At the beginning of the Christian era, the great Gaulish forest that forms the background of so many myths and legends probably covered over 60 per cent of what is now France. Julius Caesar records the terror which this oppressive and seemingly endless expanse of woods inspired in his legionaries.

In early medieval times this hostile forest began to recede, largely through clearing which was carried out by monastic orders, and gradually gave way to the plough and to livestock. Its composition was affected by human intervention: oak and beech were favoured because their acorns and mast could be used as fodder for the pigs. It became a playground for the nobility, and a refuge for hermits, the pestiferous, the marginals of medieval society.

It was exploited anarchically until Colbert lamented, 'France will perish for want of wood'. His edict, which aimed at the reconstitution of the French forest, was not inspired by the principles dear to today's ecologists but by the need for timber to build ships to keep up with the British navy. The forest, however, continued to shrink, stoking the fires of early industry, until by the eve of the Revolution it covered a mere six million hectares. The tide did not really begin to turn until the promulgation of a strict Forest Code by Charles X in 1827 brought a strong political commitment to forest protection.

Although at a glance they may seem ancient and spontaneous growths, many French forests are actually the result of a sustained reafforestation policy which began about 150 years ago, hardly the age of a good oak. The great pioneer of this movement was an engineer of roads and bridges named Brémontier. In the late eighteenth century long stretches of the coast of Aquitaine consisted of vast dunes of shifting sand which were not only unproductive but threatened the hinterland, burying entire villages. In 1776 Brémontier proposed that the sands be fixed by planting a species of deep-rooting wild grass and a quick-growing variety of pine. Supported by the Government, which took possession of the land until it had recouped its costs through forestry development, Brémontier's plan was carried out, often in the teeth of opposition from land-owners and shepherds who tried to recover their pastureland and sometimes went so far as to set the plantations on fire. The work took fifty years. Then the insalubrious marshes inland were drained and also planted with pines. The result was the greatest continuous forest expanse in western Europe, over a million hectares of productive woodland.

Another spectacular example of reafforestation is the massif of Aigoual in the Cévennes. This apparently spontaneous growth is a forester's mecca, planted on eroded slopes in the nineteenth century by a pioneer named Georges Fabre. In 1977, when the Paris Mint struck a medal to mark the 150th anniversary of the Forest Code, it was to Aigoual that the Minister of Agriculture went on pilgrimage. As a result of such efforts, by 1880 the French forest had expanded to eight million hectares; by 1900 the figure was ten million.

Today the French State owns some 1,700,000 hectares of forest, known as 'Forêt Domaniale', which consists largely of former royal domaine forest originally belonging to the Church but nationalized during the Revo-

lution, and forest bought as the result of an active acquisition policy. These 'showcase forests' are directly administered by the Office National des Forêts (ONF), created by the Government in 1964. The ONF is also responsible for seeing that the State's norms for forestry are applied in some 2,500,000 hectares of forest belonging to local communities.

The rest of the forest, between 65 and 70 per cent of the total, is in private hands. The State tries to influence the exploitation of this land, mostly owned by small proprietors, through a system of incentives, and also tries to buy forestland whenever possible; between 1975 and 1980, 31,450 hectares were acquired.

French foresters aim to husband a multi-purpose forest, and try to reconcile three imperatives: economic, ecological and social. In some forests one function is likely to take pride of place: facilities for walkers in the Paris area, hunting in the Sologne, the protection of the soil in mountainous areas, wood production in the pine forests of the Vosges and the Jura. But in most forests a balance is struck between the three aims.

In 1946 the Fonds Forestier National was created to encourage planting, and today, not counting natural regeneration, over 100 million trees are planted each year. Since 1946 two million hectares have been planted with the aid of the Fund, but in recent years more emphasis

The Trou de Rat, near the Massif des Cèdres, in Vaucluse (Provence).

Forests and Wildlife

has been put on converting existing coppice and scrub into forest than on the conversion of new land.

Reafforestation has been criticized because it has tended to favour resinous trees. Nostalgic landscape-lovers in regions like the Morvan have complained bitterly about the replacement of beloved oaks and beeches by monotonous stands of conifers. However, in recent years the State has been making efforts to introduce a proportion of broadleaved trees into new resinous plantations, not so much for aesthetic reasons as because the mixed forest is more resistant to disease. But planting a broadleaved forest is more expensive; growth and profits are slower. In addition France imports some two million cubic metres of resinous sawn wood annually. (It should be noted that the market in wood, unlike that in farm products, is not protected by the Treaty of Rome.)

Every year, as regularly as Bastille Day, come the great forest fires in the South of France. Of the 60,000 hectares of forest destroyed by fire in 1979, 50,000 were in the Mediterranean area. Why should this be so? Forest fires, after all, affect all forest areas.

In 1949, for example, fire devastated over 300,000 hectares of pine forest in Aquitaine, and 82 fire-fighters were killed. But since then the problem has been mastered by the provision of access roads, fire-breaks and watch-towers, and by the creation of teams of specialized firemen. Furthermore, the forest of the Landes is productive and well tended by its owners.

The Mediterranean zone, on the other hand, contains some of France's most unproductive forests. About 75 per cent of it is privately owned. According to the old forester's maxim, fire is destructive when three conditions are combined: drought, wind and bush. If one of them is absent it can be mastered. Since the first two cannot be controlled, we must act on the third. In other words, the widespread and costly clearance of undergrowth will be the only way to master the Mediterranean fires. (This problem is not confined to France. If 50,000 hectares were ravaged by fire in 1979, the toll in the Mediterranean forests of Italy and Spain was far heavier: 100,000 and 300,000 hectares respectively.)

Wildlife
The last free-ranging wolf to be shot in France met its end in 1934, but from time to time there are rumours that 'the ecologists' have let a wild one loose. Thus between March and December 1977, the mysterious 'beast of the Vosges', thought by some to have been a wolf, massacred livestock worth some 150,000 francs (250 sheep, three cows, two goats, a deer and a foal). Another former forest resident is the brown bear, which once roamed over highland and lowland France, and today survives as a protected species in a few pockets of the French Pyrenees. The lynx is another predatory animal which once inhabited the plain and later sought refuge in the mountains. There is lively debate as to whether it should be reintroduced in France. The last Alpine bear was seen in the Vercors in 1937. The *bouquetin* has disappeared from the Pyrenees but flourishes in the Vanoise Natural Park in Savoy.

The great animals of the forest today are the stag, which can weigh up to 200 kilos and likes the great forest groves where there is space between the trees. His smaller cousin the roebuck is happier among undergrowth. The wild boar, contrary to widespread belief, is only dangerous to man if wounded or if it thinks its young are in danger. Constantly on the move, it ploughs furrows in the earth as it searches for worms, fieldmice and acorns.

La chasse
On a given Sunday each September the fields and woods of France are combed by armed men in combat outfits, and innocent strollers tend to stay at home. This is the opening of the hunting season, a reminder that for over two million Frenchmen, 'forests and wildlife' are one side of an equation, the other side of which is *la chasse*. They are the most tightly packed hunters in Europe: one to 27 hectares, as against one to 380 hectares in the Federal Republic of Germany, one to 330 in Belgium, and one to 70 in the United Kingdom. Their targets may be hare, wild boar, deer, pheasant, partridge, or, inadvertently, each other: in 1980, 29 died and 96 were wounded in hunting accidents.

Hunting, although contested, is deeply entrenched because its adepts are drawn from right across the social spectrum. A television debate on the subject in the autumn of 1982 unleashed terrific passions for and against, with the Minister of the Environment trying to hold the ring. A type of hunting that aroused particular controversy is the snaring of woodpigeons in the Basque country. The birds migrate southwards along traditional and unvarying routes, and the hunters capture them in masses, using complicated apparatus of massive nets and decoy birds. One point that emerged from the debate was the symbolism of the right to hunt as an achievement of democracy, a privilege wrested only yesterday from feudal lords by the heroes of the French Revolution.

Pines near Bonaguil, in the Lot-et-Garonne.

(Opposite) Hunting, la chasse, is a popular pursuit throughout France.

Rural Châteaux

'There is not a single sizeable estate in the realm whose proprietor is not in Paris, consequently neglecting his houses and châteaux,' wrote the Comte de Mirabeau, who was later to become the leading political figure of the early days of the French Revolution. Few, certainly, were better qualified than he to discourse from personal experience on the uses to which French châteaux could be put in the eighteenth century. As a result of youthful misconduct he was first detained in the Château d'If, the French Alcatraz of the period. The ruins of this fort built by François I can still be seen on an island in the bay of Marseilles. Then came a spell of incarceration in the redoubtable Château de Joux near Pontarlier where, released on parole, he became acquainted with the young wife of an elderly marquis. He escaped to Switzerland; she joined him there; and he was sentenced to death *in absentia* by the burghers of Pontarlier for seduction and enticement. And finally, before entering political life, came a term in the Château de Vincennes, a return to Pontarlier and a reprieve.

But the point made by the brilliant scapegrace was valid enough. In the seventeenth and eighteenth centuries the attraction of court life for the nobility was such that many châteaux went to rack and ruin through their owners' absenteeism. Contrariwise, until court life declined during the reign of Louis XVI and great lords again began to live on their estates, many a château was beautified as a result of the monarch's frown. The disreputable Bussy-Rabutin (1618-93) embellished his Burgundy château after being exiled from court following the publication of his scurrilous *Histoire Amoureuse des Gaules*, with its scandalous stories about court ladies. The Duc de Choiseul (1719-85), dismissed from office and despatched to his estates, lived in princely style at the château of Chanteloup near Amboise, supervising the construction of a 120-foot-high Chinese pagoda, and otherwise dividing his time between billiards, music, excursions, chess, conversation, and of course hunting.

Neglect is but one of the threats that have weighed on France's vast heritage of châteaux. Others have included dismantling by the centralizing monarchy of the sixteenth and seventeenth centuries, jealous of the power of feudal lords; pillage during the Revolution and sale as building stone; and today the tax on great fortunes.

How many French châteaux are there? Quoted figures range from 4,000 to 50,000; it seems that not even a taxman intent on codifying *signes extérieurs de richesse* has ever publicly drawn a dividing-line between a *château*, a

manoir and a *gentilhommière*. But whatever the statistical truth may be, there is no doubt that all regions of rural France are rich in châteaux of all kinds: fastnesses of the south-west where the Cathars took refuge from Simon de Montfort; neo-classical wine châteaux in the Bordelais; turretted bastions of Brittany; the gracious châteaux of the Loire; stern châteaux on the *puys* of Auvergne and the *ballons* of the Vosges. It also seems likely that general interest in the more obscure châteaux only began to develop in this century. When Prosper Mérimée toured Burgundy in 1834 as inspector of historic monuments he did not visit a single château; and Stendhal in his *Memoirs of a Tourist*, travelling in the same region, speaks only of *churches*. Today, however, interest in them is growing and more and more are being opened to the public for at least part of the year.

The word *château* englobes both the prototype feudal *château-fort* – the English *castle* – as well as the 'open', unfortified country house or 'stately home' which came in with the Renaissance. The first kind was sited with an eye to strategy and its architecture was defined by a single function, the assertion of military power. It had a keep, towers, possibly a moat, postern and portcullis. The transition to the new form was much slower than is often

realized, and even Chambord, begun by François I in 1519, largely follows the medieval scheme.

Thousands of *châteaux-forts* are today simply hummocks of overgrown rubble, Gothic lettering on a map, or, like the ancient château of Saumur, a beautiful idealized miniature in a medieval manuscript. But some have survived virtually intact, like the most extraordinary mountain castle in France, Peyrepertuse, which stands vertiginously on a 2,400-foot-high crag in the Corbières massif not far from Perpignan. It has survived because it was militarily impregnable – in fact it was never really put to the test. Built between the eleventh and thirteenth centuries, it passed into the hands of Saint Louis from the Regent of Aragon in 1239. From then on it was garrisoned desultorily for centuries as a royal frontier fortress, being abandoned just before the Revolution.

Another intact masterpiece of military architecture, Bonaguil in the Lot valley has counted among its admirers Lawrence of Arabia and the nineteenth-century architect-restorer Viollet-le-Duc. Equally spectacular though less preserved is the mysterious fortress of Largoët-en-Elven near Vannes in Brittany; marooned in flat countryside, its massive ruined keep is only thirty feet lower than the towers of Notre-Dame in Paris.

*(Opposite) The château of
Chambord, which Francois I
started to build in 1519.*

*The fifteenth-century château of
Bonaguil in its hilltop setting*

Rural Châteaux

At the end of the Middle Ages many of the *châteaux-forts* were abandoned and fell into ruin. Others survived as the nucleus or foundations of the new type of country house, often because their owners prospered and found favour as the gendarmes of the Capetian and Bourbon monarchy. The story of Anjony, one of the most remarkable of the Auvergne châteaux, is not untypical. An original fifteenth-century keep flanked by four towers was built by a family of furriers. It escaped destruction during the Wars of Religion, and survived a 200-year vendetta with a rival but declining family with a château only a stone's throw away. In the eighteenth century a new wing was added in the name of luxury and today, still in the hands of a descendant of the family which built it, it is open to the public.

Ruined medieval castles came into fashion in the early nineteenth century with the Romantics. In the hands of zealous restorers, the most famous of whom was Viollet-le-Duc, some of them were transformed into gleaming Hans Anderson edifices. The château of Pierrefonds in the forest of Compiègne is the most spectacular example of this treatment. Built in the fourteenth century, it was burned down in the seventeenth and remained in ruins. In August 1832 King Louis-Philippe held a banquet among its vestiges to celebrate the marriage of his daughter to Leopold I of Belgium. Later, when Napoleon III used the château at Compiègne as a retreat for entertaining artists and intellectuals, he became interested in Pierrefonds and commissioned Viollet-le-Duc to restore it and transform it into an imperial residence. Many of the details had not yet been completed when Napoleon III fell from power in 1870, nor even when Viollet-le-Duc died nine years later. Even today, the inside of Pierrefonds, in contrast with the finish of its exterior, has a decidedly sketchy and unfinished look. Haut Koenigsberg, where Jean Renoir shot his classic film *La Grande Illusion*, is another example of over-restoration. An eyrie above the plain of Alsace, it harboured brigands in the fifteenth century. Less imagination was put into the restoration of the fifteenth-century château of Rochepot in Burgundy. Almost totally demolished during the Revolution, it was reconstituted later from its ruins by architects working from drawings made in 1645.

The new gracious country residences whose advent heralded the end of the feudal world began with François I. Many of them, like his châteaux of Fontainebleau and Chambord, were originally hunting lodges before being transformed by the talented artists and craftsmen the king brought from Italy. They were concentrated first of all in the Loire area and then in the Ile-de-France. They were built not only by kings and the great noble families but by newly enriched bourgeois servants of the crown. Azay-le-Rideau, begun in 1518 by Gilles Berthelot, treasurer of France, was so lavish that its owner, like Fouquet later at Vaux-le-Vicomte, was relieved of his functions by a jealous sovereign. Chenonceau was a water mill and fortified manor when bought by Thomas Bohier, another treasurer who would later come to grief. The great sixteenth-century châteaux were often little lived-in. When Chambord was visited for a few days' hunting by the peripatetic court, the king's arrival was preceded by a great baggage train of tapestries, furnishings and utensils; the king and his suite numbered 2,000; the logistical problems must have been vast. By the mid-sixteenth century innumerable châteaux were being built. The Constable Anne de Montmorency, who built the great Renaissance château of Ecouen near Paris and who was, admittedly, for a time the second most powerful man in the realm after the king, is recorded as possessing '130 castles, land and baronies'.

Some of these country houses may have preserved a military appearance, through a desire to impress,

The fortress of Rambures near Abbeville.

architectural conservatism, or more prosaically because they happened to be built on the foundations of a demolished fortress. But gradually towers were replaced by rectangular pavilions and side wings were lowered so that sun could flow into courtyards. By the seventeenth century the keep has become a central *avant-corps,* a mere discreet reminder of its past function. There is a search for harmony and an interplay of forms.

Today the big state-owned châteaux are tourist magnets. Chambord, which is also a Presidential shoot, attracted over half a million visitors in 1981, Haut Koenigsberg 496,000, and Blois 320,000 (in 1980). But the public is increasingly drawn to the smaller, privately owned châteaux. Between 500 and 600 of the latter are affiliated to *La Demeure Historique,* an association which has launched a campaign to make them better known. It has created twenty-three 'Routes de Beauté', circuits which group together the lesser-known châteaux open to the public in such regions as Touraine, the Auvergne, Picardy, the Périgord and Champagne. In conjunction with the official *Caisse Nationale des Monuments Historiques et des Sites,* it is preparing a comprehensive guide to French châteaux, abbeys and gardens open to the public. The first of its kind, surprisingly, the guide (entitled *Ouvert au Public*) combines historical and architectural backround information with practical details regarding location, amenities and periods when open. Most of these châteaux have been classified by the state as historical monuments, which brings certain tax concessions in return for tight control as far as alterations and restoration are concerned. Quite a number of them seem to be owned by families which built, married into, or inherited them long ago, although there are many exceptions.

As far as diversion is concerned, the modern château addict is spoiled for choice: the associations may be historical (death cell of Haitian leader Toussaint Louverture in the Château de Joux); macabre (the ogre Gilles de Rais's torture chamber at Tiffauges in the Vendée); literary (Chateaubriand at Combourg in Brittany); or architectural (the ruins of Anet in Eure-et-Loir, Serlio's Ancy-le-Franc in Burgundy); even devotees of castles in the air being catered for at Balleroy in Normandy (built by François Mansart, 1626; gardens by Lenôtre), where there is a permanent hot air balloon museum.

The château of Laussel in the Dordogne.

Rural Tourism

As the regional chapters will have indicated, today there are hordes of possibilities for the kind of off-beat holiday that makes for real contact with rural France and its people. Rather than simply staying in hotels and driving around, you can, if you wish, spend a week or two on a farm, or have a meal in a farmhouse, or take a course in local crafts. Rural France can be explored by trekking from hostel to hostel on foot or on horseback; by cruising along rivers and canals; or even by hiring a gypsy caravan. All this is in addition to the usual sports such as fishing, shooting and sailing. *'Le tourisme rural'*, as it is called, is today carefully organized in France and much *à la mode*. Any French tourist office will give details.

Farm holidays

These have developed hugely in recent years, in response to the new back-to-nature vogue of the French, while the farmer finds them a useful way of adding to his income. There are three main varieties of this type of holiday: (a) the *gîte rural* (rural lodging), of which thousands now exist. They are farm buildings or cottages converted into guest-houses, and can be hired by the week. Guests do their own cooking and look after themselves. But as most *gîtes* are attached to a farm, there is usually plenty of scope for contact with local life.

The *chambre d'hôte* or *accueil à la ferme*. This is more like the British bed-and-breakfast system. A number of farms – not very many as yet – will let out a spare bedroom or two, usually by the night; levels of comfort may be modest, but prices are far lower than in hotels. A farm breakfast is provided, and sometimes other meals too. In some cases the farmer may allow his guests to share in the life and work of the farm, but without paying for their labour or being paid for 'training' them. Such holidays often lead to lasting friendships between city and country folk.

The *table d'hôte* or *ferme-auberge*. Some farms today run a small rustic restaurant as a sideline, either in the open air or in a converted living-room or barn. The farmer's wife cooks local country dishes and all the family serve. The innovation is highly popular with tourists in summer, especially as prices are very reasonable.

Craft courses. Weaving, pottery, woodwork, painting on silk, French cookery, and many other arts and crafts are taught in summer at one- or two-week courses in various parts of France. Many are held residentially in small châteaux or converted farmhouses. In some areas (Languedoc, Massif Central, Poitou) it is possible for children or adults to stay on a farm and take a brief course in farming.

Outdoor activities

Cross-country hiking. This is highly organized. France today is criss-crossed by a 20,000-mile network of long-distance footpaths and tracks, clearly signposted. Most are in hilly or scenic areas. You can go in a group with a guide (possibly advisable in the mountains); or on your own, equipped with a special large-scale map of the route. In upland areas, such as the Massif Central, every 10 or 15 miles or so there is likely to be a *gîte d'étape* – a basic hostel, with dormitories. It will have showers, cooking facilities, and sometimes a simple restaurant. In the Massif Central you can also hire a donkey to carry your luggage – and follow Stevenson's route through the Cévennes, if you wish.

Horse-riding. In many areas it is possible to hire a horse and go for the same kind of long-distance excursion on horseback; some of the *gîtes d'étape* will feed and shelter your horse. Again, you can go in a group with a guide, or on your own with a map. Local riding-clubs organize the group outings. Residential courses in riding, with trained instructors, are held in areas such as Brittany and Normandy, and by the Club Méditerranée at Pompadour.

Wagon holidays. The romantically inclined can in many places hire a horse-drawn gypsy-style caravan, or a buggy, or a horse-and-cart, and go lazing down forest paths or country lanes. Cars can be a hazard.

Waterways holidays. Brittany, Maine/Anjou, Burgundy and Aquitaine are the principal regions that offer scope for navigating their many rivers and canals in a hired cabin cruiser or houseboat, sleeping maybe four or six. Negotiating the locks can be tiresome. Burgundy also features cruises on small floating hotels.

Shooting. This is a very popular sport in France – rabbits, pheasant, partridge, deer and other game. A permit is needed, which can be bought on the spot (ask at a tourist office). Each animal has its strictly defined open season and there are fines for breaking the rules.

Fishing. Plenty of trout, carp, pike and other fish (but not much salmon) in France's innumerable rivers. You must buy a permit, either on the spot (ask at a tourist office) or preferably via your own angling club at home. The open season varies not per species but per area: thus all the fish in a given stretch of water will come in or out of season on the same date.

Farm holidays have become increasingly popular. Accommodation is available throughout the country, and the visitor can stay in buildings typical of the particular region, from the Dordogne (opposite) to Normandy (above).

The lake at Ville-d'Avray, near Paris, one of the many stretches of water open to anglers.

Rural Restaurants

The tradition of rural hostelry is very strong in France. Probably no other country in the world has such an array of attractive small country hotels, inns and restaurants. Many are idyllically situated amid farmlands. Many, too, are old buildings of character, elegantly converted. In most cases the *patron* or *patronne* does the cooking, and not only provides local specialities but derives much of the raw materials from local farms or from the hotel's own farm and vegetable garden.

Of the many hundreds of these places, this article selects just fourteen: restaurants with a few bedrooms attached, or, put the other way round, small hotels where the accent is on the food. Most are at the upper end of the market, both for price and quality but a few in the medium range are also included.

Of the score of restaurants to which the red *Guide Michelin*, that arbiter of taste, gives its coveted top rating of three stars, only six are in Paris: fourteen are in the provinces, and half of these are in a rural setting. Today, very many of France's leading *patron-chefs* shun the big cities and prefer to run an attractive little country hotel, where gourmets will often travel hundreds of miles to visit them.

Michelin three-star restaurants

So-called *nouvelle cuisine* is a much-abused term, and no longer very *nouvelle*, either. Basically it is not a revolution, but an attempt by imaginative chefs, using the finest ingredients, to adapt traditional dishes to an age wanting a lighter style of cooking. It is nearly always expensive. One of its best-known practitioners is **Michel Guérard**, who first won fame with his bistro in the drab Paris suburb of Asnières. In 1972 he met and married Christine Barthélémy, whose family owned and ran a hydro in the spa village of Eugénie-les-Bains, in Aquitaine, amid the gentle hills north of Pau. Here the Guérards now have their famous little hotel/restaurant, **Les Prés d'Eugénie**, which caters partly, but not exclusively, for slimmers taking a cure at the spa. It is a handsome Second Empire mansion with a park; and house and garden are lavishly and romantically decorated: chinoiserie bridges, carefully placed haycocks in the meadows, elaborately patterned wallpaper in bedrooms with names like 'Nuages' and 'Iris'. Guérard offers two kinds of menu. First, his *cuisine minceur*, a brilliant bid to make a low-calorie slimming diet gastronomically exciting. However, it is his even more inventive and varied *cuisine gourmande*, much higher in calories, that wins him the top ratings in the food guides. He buys his beef, poultry and *foie gras* from trusted local producers, and many vegetables are from his own garden. Guérard is a small, ebullient man, with a love of childish pranks and buffoonery that he shares with some other great chefs, such as Paul Bocuse. But about food he is deadly serious. One English caller, asking to speak to him, was told in hushed tones, 'Le Maître is holding a seminar'.

Roger Vergé, tall, handsome and silver-haired, is another member of the famous *bande à Bocuse*, the clique of top *nouvelle cuisine* chefs with Bocuse as their leader. Vergé ran an airline catering service in East Africa before

LA CARTE GOURMANDE

La Mitonnée de Lapereau à la Cuillère
et sa Gelée de Légumes au Serpolet 55
Le Foie Gras Frais des Landes Préparé en Terrine 80
ou Cuit au Court-Bouillon au Poivre Mignonnette 85
Les Trois Salades Impromptues 65
(Mesclun, Aile de Caille, Foie gras, Cerfeuil, Poisson Fumé...)
Le Feuilleté Léger aux Langoustines 95
Les Escargots en Pots aux Croûtons 60
Les Ravioles de Truffe à la Crème de Mousserons et de Morilles 85

Le Râble de Petit Colin Rôti au Four sur Fondue de Pommes Boulangère 65
La Fine Rouelle de Bar Sauce Simple 80
Le Saumon Grillé sur sa Peau au Fumet de Graves
et la Fricassée de Jeunes Poireaux aux Morilles 80
Le Homard Rôti et Fumé dans la Cheminée 180

Le Jambon à l'Os au Coulis de Truffes de Caussade 130
Le Petit Pigeon Tendre sur un Lit de Choux Verts Frais 85
Le Carré d'Agneau Rôti au Four Parfumé au Thym (2 pers.) 85 par pers.
Le Filet de Bœuf Cuit à la Braise de la Cheminée ou Poêlé à la Bordelaise 90
Le Suprême de Caneton Rôti Croustillant à la Bécassine 90
Le Ris de Veau Braisé à l'Ancienne
et ses Légumes de Cuisson Sautés Meunière 75
Le Râgout Fin d'Eugénie 95
(Coquillettes, Foie Gras, Jambon, Ris de Veau, Morilles, Truffe...)

Quelques Fromages de Terroir 35
La Feuillantine de Poires Caramélisées 45
La Grande Assiette de Fruits et Sorbets du Temps 45
La Pêche Blanche de Casteljaloux au Granité de Vin de Margaux 40
La Marquise au Chocolat et sa Sauce aux Grains de Café 38
Les Crêpes Fourrées à la Crème Légère aux Zestes de Citron 40
Le Millefeuille à l'Impératrice 45
Les Petits Pots de Crème au Chocolat de Monsieur Casau et Mirlitons 35

Service en sus 15 %

taking over in 1969 the **Moulin de Mougins**, a sixteenth-century olive mill in the valley below the hilltop village of Mougins, near Cannes. He has since made it into the Côte d'Azur's most fashionable restaurant. However, the glamorous decor retains a Provençal rustic touch, while Vergé's inventive cuisine, too, owes much to Provence: fish in subtle sauces, brightly coloured salads. Pretty garden, where you eat under parasols. Just three bedrooms, all exquisite.

The brothers **Haeberlin**, who run the **Auberge de l'Ill** at Illhauersen, in Alsace, are more shy and retiring than most of the other *nouvelle cuisine* chefs. For a hundred years their family had a simple country inn on this spot, by a bridge over the river Ill. Now it is a luxury restaurant, with wide windows looking on to lawns by the water's edge. Most guests are from Germany. The cuisine makes much use of local game, in season, but the fish comes from farther afield, as the local rivers are polluted. Soup of frogs is a speciality. There are no bedrooms.

(Above) The dining-room of the Moulin de Mougins.

(Opposite above) The 'non-diet' carte gourmande at Les Prés d'Eugénie.

(Opposite below) Christine and Michel Guérard, proprietors of Les Prés d'Eugénie.

(Left) The elegant mansion of Les Prés d'Eugénie in its beautiful grounds.

Rural Restaurants

Le Mas de Chastelas.

Saumon cru mariné au citron vert
Soupe aux moules et au safran
Compote de lapereau aux arómates
Salade de lotte et d'avocats
Terrine de légumes sauce gribiche
Salade d'artichauts

Grenadin de veau à l'estragon
Filet d'agneau au basilic
Faux-Filet à l'échalotte et au xérès
Ris et rognons de veau à la farandole de légumes
Pâtes fraîches aux fruits de mer
Poisson du jour

Les desserts de Paulette
Les sorbets

Un plat autour d'un plat   170 francs
130 francs vin et service compris   vin et service compris

(Left) The prix fixe *menu at the Mas de Chastelas.*

(Opposite) At La Bonne Etape many dishes based on Provençal cuisine feature on the menu.

Menu Gibier

Mousseline de grive au genièvre
Sorbet à l'alcool de poire William
Rable de lièvre rôti
Les fromages
Les pâtisseries

Menu Château

Soupe claire d'écrevisses
Mousseline de grive à la cuillère
Gâteau de mostelle au beurre d'orange
Sorbet à l'alcool de poire William
Marcassin poêlé aux pignons de pin
Salade Jarlandine
Les fromages
Les pâtisseries

Menu Provence

Terrine de coquilles Saint-Jacques
à la crème d'oursins
Cassolette de queues d'écrevisses
Sorbet à l'alcool de poire William
Agneau de Sisteron
Gratin du Jabron
Les fromages
Les pâtisseries

Menu Durance

Hure de marcassin
Joues d'agneau à la Provençale
Les fromages
Les pâtisseries

❧ PRIX NETS ❧

*Si par hasard un plat manquait
à cette carte, c'est parce que je ne
disposerais pas d'éléments assez
rigoureusement frais pour le
préparer convenablement.*

La Mère Blanc also stands in a garden beside a small river on the edge of the flowery village of Vonnas, in southern Burgundy. Its *patron-chef*, **Georges Blanc**, has recently moved up into the very top class and in 1981 was chosen as 'chef of the year' by the Gault-Millau guide. He runs a friendly *auberge*, luxurious but unpretentious, with bedrooms overlooking the river. His refined cuisine has local roots. He also owns vineyards and sells the wine he makes from them.

Alain Chapel is regarded by some as the greatest of all the great chefs of modern France. He runs a classically sober, stone-floored restaurant in an ordinary-looking building on the edge of the village of Mionnay, north of Lyon. He is a serious, rather austere man, a perfectionist and a tireless innovator, creating wonderful new tastes from simple products, and buying most of his raw materials from local producers whom he knows and trusts. His thirteen elegant bedrooms are usually booked for a number of weeks ahead.

The last two names in this survey of three-star rural restaurants are of men devoted to traditional rather than so-called *nouvelle* cooking. The **Auberge du Père Bise** has perhaps the loveliest setting of any top French restaurant: it is a spacious chalet-like building by the water's edge at Talloires, on the glorious lake of Annecy in the foothills of the Alps. Against this backdrop, **François Bise** keeps up the solid traditions inherited from his father, in a restaurant that has had its three Michelin stars since the 1930s. The cuisine includes many local specialities, such as *gratin savoyard*. There are twenty-four sumptuous bedrooms.

Raymond Thuilier began life as a businessman, and did not enter the hotel trade until he was 51, when in 1946 he took over an old farmhouse in the valley below Les Baux, the celebrated hilltop village in Provence. He has since made the **Oustau de Baumanière** into one of the world's leading restaurants, and even in his old age he still plays an active role in it. The cuisine, strictly traditional, depends on finest-quality local produce: vegetables come from the hotel garden. The style is grand, even baronial – a large garden with cypress groves, regal bedrooms, silver candlesticks in the vaulted dining-room. Queen Elizabeth and Prince Philip dined here on their state visit to France in 1972.

Other outstanding restaurants (not Michelin three-star)

Between Les Baux and Avignon, the **Auberge de Noves** is a nineteenth-century manor in a large, rambling garden, with orchards and rolling farmland all around. The food, served in a bright, flowery dining-room, fully deserves its two Michelin stars: memorable oysters in white wine and gateau of wild strawberries. The owner, André Lallemand, is charming, the ambiance intimate, and the decor has some unusual touches, including caged singing-birds in the foyer.

Another outstanding Provençal hostelry, also with two Michelin stars, is **La Bonne Etape** at Château-Arnoux, in the Durance valley. It is on the main road in the village, but looks on to hills and open fields at the back. It is a

Rural Restaurants

seventeenth-century coaching inn, luxuriously converted, and is run with style and warmth by the Gleize family, who have worked at such London hotels as the Connaught. Father and son share the cooking: splendid Provence-inspired dishes such as *lapéreau farci* and Sisteron lamb. There is a heated swimming pool.

Also in Provence, the **Mas de Chastelas** is just outside Saint-Tropez, but has none of that resort's garishness. Secluded amid vines and pinewoods, it is a graceful seventeenth-century farmhouse, once used for silkworm breeding, now converted into a luxurious little hotel by its cultured Parisian owners, the Racines. The atmosphere is club-like, and guests include many film-stars and other celebrities. Meals, Provençal in flavour, are served by the idyllic outdoor swimming pool, with a garden around it. There is even a jacuzzi.

(Above) La Pescalerie in the Lot valley.

(Left) The imposing Château de Locguénolé in its wooded park.

(Opposite) The extensive and distinguished menu of the Château de Locguénolé.

206

Soupière de rougets et moules safranées
Soupe de poissons de roche et sa rouille

Vinaigrette de légumes tièdes, au magret de canard fumé
Panaché de tourteau et d'avocat au sabayon de tomates
Fonds d'artichauts frais aux petits lardons
Terrine de foie gras frais, fait maison
Huîtres plates de Riec sur Belon
Bouquet de salades de saison, servies tièdes
Gourmandise de crustacés aux œufs de caille
Aiguillettes de saumon frais à l'aneth et fondue d'aubergines

Poêlée de langoustines rôties aux légumes confits
Petits feuilletés gourmands, au retour du marché
Raviolis de tourteau parfumés au curry et à la courgette
Petits farcis d'escargots de Bretagne aux aromates
Coquilles Saint-Jacques sautées à l'effeuillé d'endives (en saison)

Filet d'agneau en noisettes, à la crème d'estragon
Caneton de Challans aux citrons confits et ses cuisses grillées
Mignons de filet de bœuf à la moelle et vin de Beaujolais
Aiguillettes de lapereau, pâtes fraîches et petits navets confits
Rognons de veau et pieds de veau, poêlés au vinaigre de vin
Foie gras d'oie sauté au naturel et poires en aigre doux
Petit sauté de gigot d'agneau "minute" au thym frais
Pigeonneau "fermier" rôti en cocotte et sa chartreuse de chou nouveau
Mignonnettes de veau braisées au blanc de poireau, beurre cresson

Turbot, lotte et daurade rose, aux échalotes rôties
Saumon frais "gros sel" et ses légumes
Langouste rose de "Bretagne" rôtie, au vert de laitue
Marinière de turbotin aux huitres, et son gâteau mousse de persil
Petite nage de poissons et coquillages au citron vert
Joues de morue en fricassée à l'ail doux
Suprême de bar au poivre, mousse d'artichauts
Sole pochée à la fondue de tomates et concombres

Glace aux gousses de vanille et émincé de pommes à la cannelle
Quatre sorbets aux fruits frais de saison
Sabayon de fraises et d'oranges confites
Crêpes fourrées au praliné et à la mousse d'ananas
Fondant au chocolat et aux petits raisins, crème café
et
Le grand dessert du château
comprenant :
Les entremets au chocolat
Les fruits de saison pochés au naturel
Le gâteau ou la tarte du jour
Les œufs à la neige
Les petits fours

Over in Périgord are more delightful hotels. At Champagnac de Belair, near Brantôme, the **Moulin du Roc** is a seventeenth-century walnut-mill converted into a sleek and cosy little hotel, with flowers everywhere and a stream flowing through the garden. The mill-wheel's machinery still works. The owner's wife, Solange Gardillou, provides subtle variations on Périgourdin dishes, and has won two stars in Michelin. Other delights include canopied four-poster beds, strawberries for breakfast in season, and a convivial atmosphere.

At Cabrerets, in the Lot valley, **La Pescalerie** is a handsome eighteenth-century mansion standing alone in the countryside, with a garden sloping down to a river. The manageress-chef, Hélène Combette, does regional cooking using vegetables from the garden and other local produce; she makes her own *foie gras*. The owner is a local doctor who also spends part of his time helping to run the hotel, even serving at table!

Over in the Aube, near Troyes, south-east of Paris, rural idyllicism is again to be found at the unusual **Auberge de la Scierie**: four farmhouse buildings, one of them a former sawmill, all set in a big garden by a stream. There are lots of animals, including horses for hire, a donkey, ducks, peacocks; and a very 'rustic' bar decked out rather like an English pub, with horse-brasses, sheepskins, farm tools. The restaurant specializes in good local cooking at moderate prices.

Finally, to Brittany, where the **Château de Locguénolé** stands in its 250-acre woodland park above the river Blavet, near Lorient. Rebuilt after the Revolution, the property has belonged to the Comtesse de la Sablière's family since 1200, and today she runs it as an exclusive hotel, with marble fireplaces and Aubusson tapestries. Michel Gaudin's distinguished cuisine (two stars in Michelin) leans heavily on local produce: fish of all sorts, rabbit, lamb, pigeon. Try the hot oysters in leek sauce.

Tourist Information

Walking and Rambling
There are some 20,000 kilometres of marked footpaths in France. Detailed guide-books are available from:
– C.N.S.G.R., 92, rue de Clignancourt–75018 Paris
– I.G.N. (Institut National Géographique National) publishes route maps:
107, rue de la Boétie–75008 Paris

1. Some of the routes suggested by the Comité National des Sentiers de Grande Randonnée (C.N.S.G.R.)
Ile-de-France
– GR 1: Tour de l'Ile-de-France, 650 km around Paris
Normandy
– GR 2: Sentier de la Seine, Les Andelys to Le Havre
–GR 223: Tour du Cotentin
Centre
GR 3: Sentier de la Loire
Auvergne
– GR 30: Tour des Lacs d'Auvergne
Brittany
– GR 34: Sentier du Tour de Bretagne 'Tro Breiz'
Poitou-Charentes
– GR 36: Sentier Manche-Pyrénées
– GR 360: Roman art in Saintonge
Auvergne, Languedoc-Roussillon
– GR 4: Sentier Méditerranée/Océan
– Grasse to Manosque via Gorges du Verdon
– Gard, Ardèche, Lozère, Cantal, from Pont Saint-Esprit to Saint-Flour
– Avergne, Cantal, Puy-de-Dôme, Creuse, from Saint-Flour to Aubusson
– GR 40: Tour de Velay
– GR 441: Tour de la Chaîne des Puys, volcanoes of Auvergne
Rhône-Alpes
– GR 5: Sentier Hollande/Méditerranée
Haute-Savoie
Lac Léman–Col de la Croix du Bonhomme
Savoie
Parc National de la Vanoise
Hautes-Alpes–Alpes de Haute-Provence
Modane–Larche
– GR 54: Parc National des Ecrins, Tour de l'Oisans
– GR 58: Tour du Queyras (Hautes-Alpes)
– GR 559: Lakes and Forests of the Jura
– GR 6: Sentier Alpes/Océan
Midi- Pyrénées, Aquitaine
6-60: Lozère, Aveyron, Lot: Meyrueis – Figeac
6-64: Lot, Dordogne, Quercy, Périgord Noir: from Figeac to Les Eyzies
62-62 A: Sentier Causse Noir, Rouergue, from Conques to Maubert
65: Chemin de Saint-Jacques de Compostella, Le Puy to Eauze
Auvergne – Languedoc-Roussillon
Midi-Pyrénées
– Haute-Loire, Lozère, Aveyron, Lot, Tarn-et-Garonne, Gers (Eauze)
66: Tour de l'Aigoual
67: Tour des Cévennes
68: Tour du Mont Lozère
Vosges
– GR 7: Sentier Vosges–Pyrénées
7: Vosges – Ballon d'Alsace
Burgundy
760: Tour du Beaujolais
– GR 9: Sentier Jura/Coté d'Azur
Corsica

– GR 20: Sentier de la Corse
Mont-Blanc
– T.M.B.: Tour du Mont-Blanc

2. The following organizations will give information on specific routes and walks:
– Club Alpin Français (C.A.F.), rue de la Boétie – 75008 Paris
– Touring Club de France, 65, avenue de la Grande-Armée – 75016 Paris
– U.C.P.A. (Union des Centres de Plein-Air), 62, rue de la Glacière–75013 Paris
– Chalets Internationaux de Haute-Montagne (C.I.H.M.), 15, rue Gay-Lussac–75005 Paris

Alsace-Vosges-Lorraine
– Traversée des Vosges–Office de Tourisme, BP 64–68160 Sainte-Marie-aux-Mines

Aquitaine
– Departmental offices of the C.N.S.G.R.
Dordogne
– 15, avenue de Lattre de Tassigny – 24000 Périgueux
Gironde
– Syndicat d'Initiative – 33115 Le Pyla-sur-Mer
Landes
– Cité Galliane – 4000 Mont-de-Marsan
Lot-et-Garonne
– Association Départementale du Tourisme Pédestre, Centre Culturel Ledru-Rollin, rue Ledru-Rollin – 47000 Agen
Pyrénées-Atlantiques
– 83, avenue des Lauriers – 64000 Pau

Auvergne
– Découverte du Massif-Central, 31, rue Eugène-Gilbert – 63000 Clermont-Ferrand
– Association de Tourisme de Randonnée Pédestre et Equestre de L'Allier, 13, avenue de la République – 03300 Moulins

Burgundy
– Club Alpin Français, 34, rue des Forges – 21000 Dijon

Brittany
– C.N.S.G.R. et A.B.R.I., 14, boulevard Beaumont – 35100 Rennes

Champagne-Ardennes
– Délégation Régionale du C.N.S.G.R., 7, rue Linard-Hubert – 10000 Troyes

Corsica
– Club Montagne-Corse, 1, boulevard Auguste-Gaudin – 20200 Bastia
– Parc Naturel Régional – 20000 Ajaccio

Franche-Comté
– C.A.F., 9, rue d'Alsace – 90000 Belfort

Languedoc-Roussillon
– Office de Tourisme de la Lozère, 16, boulevard du Soubeyran – 48000 Mende
– Association du Tourisme Pédestre, BP 4001 – 30000 Nimes
– Délégation Régionale du C.N.S.G.R., Chambre d'Agriculture, place Chaptal – 34000 Montpellier

Limousin
– Association Touristique de Haute-Marche et Combraille, mairie de Mainsat – 23700 Auzances

Midi-Pyrénées
– Grandes Randonnées Pyrénéennes, 4, rue de Villefranche – 09200 Saint-Girons

Nord-Pas-de-Calais
– Délégation Régionale du C.N.S.G.R., 271, rue Constant-Dutilleux – 59500 Douai

Normandy
– Association Départementale de Tourisme Pédestre du Calvados, Chambre Départementale d'Agriculture, 4, promenade de Madame de Sévigné–14000 Caen
– Délégation Seine-Maritime du C.N.S.G.R., Val Pitan, Amfreville-sous-les-Monts – 27380 Fleury-sur-Andelle

Pays-de-la-Loire
– Association Sarthoise pour les Chemins de Petites Randonnées, 18, rue des Acacias – 72700 Saint-Georges-du-Bois

Picardy
– Délégation Régionale du C.N.S.G.R., 18, avenue Thiers–60200 Compiègne
– Association du Tourisme Pédestre de Compiègne, 7, rue de la Gare, Trosly Breuil – 60350 Cuise-la-Motte

Poitou-Charentes
– Délégation Régionale du C.N.S.G.R. – 79330 Saint-Varent

Provence-Alpes-Côte-d'Azur
– Délégation C.N.S.G.R. des Hautes-Alpes, Pelleautier–05000 Gap
– Parc Naturel Régional du Lubéron, avenue des Druides– 84400 Apt

Riviera-Côte-d'Azur
– C.A.F., 15, avenue Jean-Médecin – 06000 Nice

Rhône-Loire
– Comité Départemental du Tourisme 'Loire-Forez', 12, rue Gérentet–42000 Saint-Etienne
– Parc Naturel Régional du Pilat, Moulin de Virieux, 2, rue Benay – 42410 Pelussin

Alpes-du-Nord
– La Grande Traversée des Alpes, C.I.M.E.S. (Centre Informations Montagnes et Sentiers), Maison de Tourisme, 14, place de la République – 38000 Grenoble

National and Regional Parks
1. National Parks
Languedoc-Roussillon
Parc National des Cévennes
Registered office: BP 4 – 48400 Florac

Midi-Pyrénées
Parc National des Pyrénées Occidentales
Registered office: BP 300 – 65013 Tarbes

Parc National de l'Ariege

Normandy
Parc National des Iles Chausey

Provence-Alpes-Côte-d'Azur
Parc National de Port-Cros
Registered office: 50, avenue Gambetta – 83400 Hyères

Parc National des Ecrins

Registered office: 7, rue du Colonel-Roux –
05000 Gap

Riviera-Côte-d'Azur
Parc National du Mercantour
Registered office: 17, rue Alexandre Mari –
06000 Nice

Alpes-du-Nord
Parc National de la Vanoise
Registered office: BP 105, 135, rue du Dr
Julian – 73003 Chambéry

2. Natural Regional Parks
Alsace-Vosges-Lorraine
Parc de Lorraine
Registered office: Abbaye des Prémontrés,
BP 35 – 54700 Pont-à-Mousson

Parc des Vosges du Nord
Registered office: La Petite Pierre – 67290
Wingen-sur-Moder

Aquitaine
Parc des Landes de Gascogne
Registered office: Préfecture des Landes –
40011 Mont-de-Marsan

Auvergne
Parc des Volcans
Registered office: Château du Montlosier-
Randanne – 63120 Rochefort-Montagne

Burgundy
Parc du Morvan
Registered office: Maison du Parc, Saint-
Brisson – 58230 Montsauche

Brittany
Parc d'Armorique
Registered office: Menez-Meur-Hanvec –
29224 Daoulas

Champagne-Ardennes
Parc de la Forêt d'Orient
Registered office: Maison du Parc – 10220
Piney

Parc de la Montagne de Reims
Registered office: 86, rue Belin – 51000
Reims

Parc des Ardennes
Registered office: Chemin des granges
moulues – 08011 Charleville-Mézières

Corsica
Parc de la Corse
Registered office: Préfecture de la Corse –
20188 Ajaccio

Languedoc-Roussillon
Parc du Haut-Languedoc
Registered office: 13, rue du Cloître, BP 9 –
34220 Saint-Pons

Nord-Pas-de-Calais
Parc de Saint-Amand-Raismes
Registered office: Préfecture du Nord-Pas-
de-Calais, mission régionale–59039 Lille

Normandy
Parc de Brotonne
Registered office: 61320 Château de
Carrouges

Pays-de-la-Loire
Parc de Brière
Registered office: 180, Ile de Fédrun – 44720

Saint-Joachim

Picardy
Parc de Picardie Maritime

Poitou-Charentes
Parc du Marais Poitevin, Val de Sèvre et
Vendée
Registered office: Syndicat Mixte, 4, rue
Pasteur – 79000 Niort

Provence-Alpes-Côte-d'Azur
Parc de la Camargue
Registered office: Le Mas du Pont de
Rousty – 13200 Arles

Parc du Lubéron
Registered office: avenue des Druides –
84400 Apt

Parc du Queyras
Registered office: avenue de la Gare, BP 3 –
05600 Guillestre et Relais Inter, rue Carnot –
05008 Gap

Rhône-Loire
Parc du Pilat
Registered office: Moulin de Virieu, 2, rue
Benay – 42410 Pelussin

Parc du Vercors
Registered office: Maison du Parc, chemin
des fusillés – 38250 Lans-en-Vercors

Alpes-du-Nord
Parc du Vercors (see above)

Zoological Gardens
Alsace-Vosges-Lorraine
– Parc zoologique et botanique de – 68100
Mulhouse

Aquitaine
– Parc du Thot – 24290 Thonac-Montignac
– Parc ornithologique du Teich, mairie du
Teich – 33380 Biganos

Auvergne
– Château et Réserve de Saint-Augustin –
03320 Château-sur-Allier-Saint-Augustin

Burgundy
– Parc naturel du Morvan, Parc de Saint-
Brisson

Brittany
– Jardin botanique de Brest, Vallon du
Spangallach – 29200 Brest
– Parc zoologique du Château de la
Bourbansais – 35720 Saint-Pierre-De-
Plesguen
– Jardin du Thabor, mairie de Rennes –
35000 Rennes

Centre
– Parc des châteaux de Chambord 41 – Diors
36 et Valençay 36

Champagne-Ardennes
– Parc de vision de Bel Val – 08240 Buzancy

Franche-Comté
– Parc zoologique de Besançon – 25000
Besançon

Ile-de-France
– Parc de Thoiry – 78770 Thoiry-en-Yvelines
– Parc de Sauvage, Emance – 78120
Rambouillet

Languedoc-Roussillon
– Parc de Sigean – 11130

Limousin
– Parc de l'Avrenne, mairie – 87000 Limoges

Midi-Pyrénées
– Parc zoologique de Plaisance-du-Touch –
31170

Nord-Pas-de-Calais
– Réserve ornithologique d'Ambouts-
Cappel – 59

Normandy
– Parc animalier de la Forêt de Saint-Sever –
14

Paris
– Parc zoologique de Paris 12e, Bois de
Vincennes
– Jardin des Plantes, 57, rue Cuvier – 75013
Paris

Pays-de-la-Loire
– Parc zoologique du Tertre Rouge – 72200
La Flèche

Picardy
– Parc zoologique de Vendeuil – 0200 La
Fère

Poitou-Charentes
– Zoorama européen de la Forêt de Chizé,
Forêt domaniale de Chizé – 79260
Villiers-en-Bois

Provence-Alpes-Côte-d'Azur
– Zoo et vivaquarium de La Barben – 13
Pelissanne

Rhône-Loire
– Parc zoologique de la Tête d'Or – 69000
Lyon

Riviera-Côte-d'Azur
– Parc zoologique de Saint-Jean-Cap-Ferrat
– 06

Inland Waterways
Information:
– 'Tourisme Fluvial en France', brochure
edited by the Ministère des Transports,
Sous-direction des voies navigables, 244,
boulevard Saint-Germain – 75007 Paris
– Syndicat National des Loueurs de Bateaux
de Plaisance, Yacht-House de la F.I.N., Port
de la Bourdonnais – 75007 Paris

Picardy-Champagne-Paris Region
Services de la Navigation:
Paris Region:
– Service de la Navigation, 2, quai de
Grenelle – 75015 Paris
Champagne: – Service de la Navigation, 28,
boulevard Albert 1er – 54000 Nancy

Brittany-Pays-de-la-Loire
Service de la Navigation:
– 2, place de l'Edit de Nantes – 44000 Nantes
Comité de promotion touristique des
canaux bretons et des voies navigables de
l'Ouest:
– 14, boulevard Beaumont – 35100 Rennes
Information:
– Secrétariat, 12, rue de Jemmapes – 44000
Nantes

Tourist Information

Burgundy-Centre
Service de la Navigation:
– Direction Départementale de l'Equipement, 57, rue de Mulhouse – 21000 Dijon
– Direction Départementale de L'Equipement, 2, rue de la Poissonnerie – 58020 Nevers Cedex

Aquitaine-Languedoc-Midi-Pyrénées
Service de la Navigation Midi-Garonne:
– Cité administrative, boulevard Duportal – 31074 Toulouse

Watersports
1. Sailing
Information:
– Fédération Française de Yachting à Voile (F.F.Y.V.), 55, avenue Kléber – 75116 Paris

Organizations which arrange sailing courses:
– Centre Nautique des Glénans, 15, quai Louis Blériot – 75016 Paris
– Union Nationale des Centres Sportifs de Plein-Air (U.C.P.A.), 62, rue de la Glacière – 75013 Paris
– Touring Club de France, 65, avenue de la Grande-Armée – 75116 Paris

2. Cruising
Organizations which arrange sea cruises (see under Sailing for addresses):
– Centre Nautique des Glénans
– U.C.P.A.
– Touring Club de France

3. Canoeing
Information:
– Fédération Française de Canoë-Kayak, 87, quai de la Marne – 94340 Joinville

4. Snorkelling, deep-sea and skin diving
Information:
– Fédération Française des Sports Sous-Marins, 24, quai de Rive-Neuve – 13007 Marseille

Organizations which arrange underwater courses:
– Union Nationale des Centres Sportifs de Plein-Air (U.C.P.A.), 62, rue de la Glacière – 75013 Paris
– Touring Club de France (T.C.F.), 65, avenue de la Grande-Armée – 75116 Paris

5. Water-skiing
Information:
– Fédération Française de Ski Nautique, 9, boulevard Péreire – 75017 Paris

6. Surfing
Information:
– Fédération Française de Surf-riding et de Skate-Board, Cité administrative, avenue Edouard VII – 64200 Biarritz

7. Sand-gliding
Information:
– Fédération Française de Char à Voile, 33, rue Mademoiselle – 78000 Versailles

8. Motorboating
Information:
– Fédération Française Motonautique, 6, place de la Concorde – 75008 Paris

Fishing
Information:
– Conseil Supérieur de la Pêche, 10, rue Péclet – 75015 Paris
– Union Nationale des Fédérations Départementales des Associations Agréées de Pêche et de Pisciculture, 17, rue Bergère – 75009 Paris

1. Fishing in rivers, lakes and ponds
For regulations apply to Préfectures, Mairies or Associations de Pêche for the relevant *département*.

2. Sea-fishing
Fishing in the sea is free and no special authorization is necessary along the whole coast, except for regulations concerning military zones or ports and conservation of fish stocks. It is advisable to check with the local Syndicat d'Initiative.

Horse-riding
Information:
– Association Nationale pour le Tourisme Equestre et l'Equitation de Loisirs (A.N.T.E.), 12, rue du Parc Royal – 75003 Paris
– Local Syndicats d'Initiative will provide itineraries as well as information on accommodation along routes.
– Fédération Equestre Française, 164, faubourg Saint-Honoré – 75008 Paris

1. Short riding holidays
– Touring Club de France, 65, avenue de la Grande-Armée–75016 Paris
– U.C.P.A. (Union Nationale des Centres Sportifs de Plein-Air), 62, rue de la Glacière – 75013 Paris
– Cheval Voyage 8, rue de Milan – 75009 Paris

Alsace-Vosges-Lorraine
Information:
– Association Alsacienne de Tourisme Equestre, 8, Grande-Rue, Andolsheim–68600 Neuf-Brisach
– Association Régionale de Tourisme Equestre Lorrain, 22, rue François de Neufchâteau – 88000 Epinal

Aquitaine
Information:
– Association Régionale de Tourisme Equestre, Domaine de Volcelest – 33830 Joué-Belin

Auvergne
Information:
– Association Départementale de Tourisme Equestre, Préfecture – 15000 Aurillac

Burgundy
Information:
– Maison du Parc Naturel Régional du Morvan Saint-Brisson – 58230 Montsauche

Brittany
Information:
– Association Régionale pour le Tourisme Equestre en Bretagne (A.R.T.E.B.), 1, rue Gambetta, BP 79 – 56300 Pontivy

Centre
Information:
– Association Régionale de Tourisme Equestre, rue Tournebride, BP 7 – 36600 Valençay

Champagne-Ardennes
Information:
– Association Champagne-Ardenne de Tourisme Equestre, Crédit Agricole – 08460 Signy-L'Abbaye

Corsica
Information:
– Association Régionale de Tourisme Equestre Corse, Casa di Muntagna, 9, rue du Colonel Ferraci – 20250 Corte

Franche-Comté
Information:
– Association Régionale de Tourisme Equestre de Franche-Comté – 25000 Besançon
– Association Départementale de Tourisme Equestre, Maison du Tourisme, rue des Bains – 70000 Vesoul

Ile-de-France
Information:
– Association Régionale de Tourisme Equestre Ile-de-France, 31, rue Chanez–75016 Paris

Languedoc-Roussillon
Information:
– Association Régionale de Tourisme Equestre, Chambre d'Agriculture, place Chaptal – 34076 Montpellier

Limousin
Information:
– Association de Tourisme Equestre du Limousin, 11, rue du Temple–87000 Limoges

Midi-Pyrénées
Information:
– Association Régionale de Tourisme Equestre, 61, allée de Brienne–31069 Toulouse

Nord-Pas-de-Calais
Information:
– Association Régionale de Tourisme Equestre, M.S. Bacquaert, 6, place Lisfranc – 59700 Marcq-en-Baroeul

Normandy
Information:
– Associations de Tourisme Equestre
Basse-Normandie
60, Grande-Rue – 61003 Alençon
Haute-Normandie
268, rue Jules-Ferry – 76480 Duclair

Pays-de-la-Loire
Information:
– Association Régionale de Tourisme Equestre, 5, rue de Santeuil–44000 Nantes

Picardy
Information:
– Association Régionale de Tourisme Equestre, 8, rue Saint-Jean, Vieux-Moulin – 60300 Cuise-La-Motte

Poitou-Charentes
Information:
– Association Régionale de Tourisme Equestre, Monsieur Arles-Dufour, Poursay-

Garnaud – 17400 Saint-Jean-d'Angély
– Haras National de Saintes, BP 174 – 17107 Saintes Cedex

Provence-Alpes-Côte-d'Azur
Information:
– Association Régionale de Tourisme Equestre, Monsieur G.-Maurice, quartier l'Islette – 84510 Caumont

Riviera-Côte-d'Azur
Information:
– Association Régionale de Tourisme Equestre, 19, boulevard Victor-Hugo–06130 Grasse

Rhône-Loire
Information:
– Association Régionale de Tourisme Equestre, 7, rue Major-Martin–69001 Lyon
– Fédération Equestre Française, 28, place Bellecour – 69002 Lyon

2. Horse-drawn carriage or caravan tours
Information:
– Cheval Voyage, 8, rue de Milan – 75009 Paris

Cycling
1. Hiring bicycles
– Information from local Syndicats d'Initiative and Offices de Tourisme
– French railways (S.N.C.F.) hire bicycles at more than 112 stations

2. Organized cycle tours
Information:
– Fédération Française de Cyclotourisme, 8, rue Jean-Marie Mégo – 75103 Paris

Clubs and associations:
– Bicyclub de France, 8, place de la Porte Champerret–75017 Paris
– Le Touring Club de France, 65, avenue de la Grande-Armée – 75116 Paris
– Le C.I.H.M. (Chalets Internationaux de Haute-Montagne), 15, rue Gay-Lussac – 75005 Paris

Alsace-Vosges-Lorraine
Information:
– Fédération Française de Cyclotourisme, ligue d'Alsace, 3, rue F. Kuhlmann – 68000 Colmar

Aquitaine
Information:
– Ligue Régionale de Cyclotourisme, Résidence Beausite, Bâtiment 1 – 33700 Mérignac

Auvergne
Information:
– Ligue Auvergne-Velay, Résidence 'Les Bouleaux', Bâtiment E,63, avenue Foch – 43000 Le Puy-en-Velay

Burgundy
Information:
– Ligue Régionale de Cyclotourisme, 5, rue du Puits-de-Têt – 21160 Marsannay

Brittany
Information:
– Ligue Régionale de Cyclotourisme, 11, rue des Cheminots – 22000 Saint-Brieucs

Champagne-Ardennes
Information:
– Ligue Régionale de Cyclotourisme, 3, rue Vieille-Rome – 10000 Troyes

Franche-Comté
Information:
– Ligue Régionale de la Fédération Française de Cyclotourisme, 14, rue de Doubs – 39500 Tavaux

Languedoc-Roussillon
Information:
– Association de Cyclotourisme, Direction Départementale de la Jeunesse et des Sports – 48000 Mende

Limousin
Information:
– Ligue Régionale de la Fédération Française de Cyclotourisme, 14, rue du Château-du-Theil – 19200 Ussel

Midi-Pyrénées
Information:
– Ligue Régionale et Union des Cyclotouristes Toulousains, 54, rue des Troubadours – 31000 Toulouse

Nord-Pas-de-Calais
Information:
– Ligue Régionale de Cyclotourisme, 7, rue de Picardie – 59510 Hern

Normandy
Information
– Amicale des Cyclotouristes Le Caennais, 148, rue Caponnière–14000 Caen

Pays-de-la-Loire
– Ligue de l'Atlantique de Cyclotourisme, Les Noues – 44850 Le Cellier

Picardy
– Ligue Régionale de la Fédération Française de Cyclotourisme, 29, rue Croix-Saint-Firmin – 80000 Amiens

Poitou-Charentes
– Ligue Poitou-Charentes de Cyclotourisme, 1, rue de l'Eglise–79230 Aiffres

Provence-Alpes-Côte-d'Azur
– Ligue Régionale de Cyclotourisme, Monsieur Exubis, La Cassette, avenue Saint-Véran – 04000 Digne

Riviera-Côte-d'Azur
– Maison des Associations, 9, rue Louis Braille – 06400 Cannes

Rhône-Loire
– Comité Départemental de Cyclotourisme de l'Ardèche, Domaine de Sagnes – 07000 Privas

Alpes-du-Nord
– Ligue Dauphiné-Savoie de Cyclotourisme, 8, cours Berriat–38000 Grenoble

Mountaineering
Information:
– Fédération Française de la Montagne, 20 bis, rue de La Boétie – 75008 Paris
– Club Alpin Français, 7, rue de la Boétie –

75008 Paris
– U.C.P.A. (Union Nationale des Centres de Plein-Air), 62, rue de la Glacière – 75013 Paris
– Touring Club de France, 'Groupe Montagne', 65, avenue de la Grande-Armée – 75782 Paris Cedex 16
– C.I.H.M. (Chalets Internationaux de Haute Montagne), 15, rue Gay-Lussac – 75005 Paris
– Groupe Universitaire de Montagne et de Ski (G.U.M.S.), 53, rue du Moulin-Vert – 75014 Paris
– Amis de la Nature, 197, rue Championnet – 75018 Paris

Skiing
Information:
– Fédération Française de Ski, 34, rue Eugène-Flachat – 75017 Paris
– Association des Mairies des Stations Françaises de Sport d'Hiver, 61, boulevard Haussmann – 75008 Paris
– France Ski International, aérogare des Invalides, 2 rue Esnault-Pelterie – 75007 Paris
Savoie
– Comité des Stations Savoyardes de Sports d'Hiver, Association Touristique Départementale, BP 348 – 74012 Annecy
Dauphiné
– Comité des Stations du Dauphiné, Maison du Tourisme, 14, place de la République – 38000 Grenoble

1. Summer skiing
Isère
– L'Alpe-d'Huez – Les Deux-Alpes
Savoie
– La Plagne, Les Ménuires, Val Thorens, Tignes, Val d'Isère (col de l'Iseran)
Haute-Savoie
– Chamonix (Grands Montets à Argentière)

2. Mountain Rambling
The following organize excursions from December to June:
– C.A.F., Touring Club de France, U.C.P.A., C.I.H.M., G.U.M.S. (see Mountaineering for addresses)

3. Cross-country Skiing
Information:
– Association Nationale des Centres Ecoles et Foyers de Ski de Fond, Secrétariat, BP 112 – 05000 Gap

Railways of Tourist Interest
Information:
– A.F.A.C. (Association Française des Amis des Chemins de Fer), Cour Souterraine Porte 9, Gare de Paris-Est – 75010 Paris
– A.J.E.C.T.A. (Association des Jeunes pour l'Entretien et la Conservation des Trains d'Autrefois), BP 1 – 77650 Longueville
– A.F.T. (Association pour le Tourisme Ferroviaire), BP 1431–92154 Suresnes
– F.A.C.S. (Fédération des Amis des Chemins de Fer Secondaires), 134, rue de Rennes – 75006 Paris

Grape-picking Festivals
These usually take place in September and October in most of the areas near vineyards. Some festivals are held in spring and summer, and on 22 January to celebrate Saint-Vincent, the patron saint of vine-growers.

Tourist Information

Alsace-Vosges-Lorraine
Grape-picking festivals:
Bas-Rhin
In October at Barr, Marlenheim, Obernai, Molsheim, Mutzig, Scherwiller
Haut-Rhin
At Whir, Riquewihr, Ribeauvillé, in August: wine fair at Colmar, in May: at Mulhouse, Guebwiller

Aquitaine
Dordogne
Wine festival at Sigoulès (summer)
Gironde
In June, wine festivals at Soulac, Montalivet, Carcans, Maubuisson, Lacanau, Arcachon, Le Pyla
In June, gathering of the *confréries vineuses*: at Saint-Émilion, in the Medoc and Graves, and end of July/beginning of August at Sauveterre de Guyenne, Castillon, Lesparre, Saint-Croix-du-Mont
In September, grape-picking festivals in Médoc, Saint-Émilion, Sauterne, Fronsade, Blaye
Landes
Beginning of October, grape-picking festival at Pouillon

Auvergne
End of August, wine festival at Saint-Pourcain-sur-Sioule (Allier)

Burgundy
Côte d'Or
In September, vine festival at Dijon and festival of Sauvignon at Saint-Bris-le-Vineaux
In November, 'Les Trois Glorieuses', wine festival at Clos-de-Vougeot, wine sale of Hospices à Beaune, *fête de la Paulée* at Meursault
Nièvre
In August, wine fair at Pouilly-sur-Loire
Saône-et-Loire
End of May, wine fair at Mâcon
Mid-September, wine festival at Saint-Jean-Devaux
End of October, Raclet festival at Romanèche-Thorins

Centre
Cher
In March, wine fair at Saint-Armand
Indre
In October, grape-picking festival at Pont-Chrétien-Chabenet
Indre-et-Loire
In March, wine fair at Chinon
15 August, wine festival at Amboise and Vouvray
Loiret
End of July, festival of Côteaux du Giennois

Champagne-Ardennes
Aube
22 January, festival of the Confrérie Saint-Paul, Saint-Vincent des Vignerons du Barsuraubois
End of August, grape-picking festival at Bar-sur-Aube (every 4 years)
Mid-September, fair of the wines of Champagne at Bar-sur-Aube
End of September, days of sauerkraut and Champagne
Marne
21 January, festival of Saint-Vincent at

Ambonnay
In May, Champagne fair at Rilly-la-Montagne

Franche-Comté
Haute-Saône
End of September, grape-picking festival at Champlitte
Jura
In July, grand wine festival at Arbois
Beginning of September, festival of new wines at Arbois

Languedoc-Roussillon
Aude
In August, wine festival at Largrasse and Narbonne
Gard
Mid-August, vine-growers' festival at Méjannes-le-Clap
End of September, grape-picking corrida at Nîmes
In April, wine fair of the Côtes du Rhône, fair of the wine of the Gard at Villeneuve-les-Avignons
In May, wine festival at Roquemaure
Hérault
In August, Muscat festival at Frontignan
In October, festival of new wine at Béziers, international wine fair at Montpellier
Pyrénées-Orientales
In August, Muscat festival at Rivesaltes, wine festival at Estagel and Baixas

Midi-Pyrénées
Gers
End of August, Armagnac fair
Tarn-et-Garonne
Beginning of September, wine festival at Fronton
End of September, chasselas festival at Moissac

Pays-de-la-Loire
Loire-Atlantique
Beginning of October, festival of grape-picking and new wine at Le Loroux-Botteraux, Haute-Goulaine, Paulx, Saint-Etienne de Montluc, Saint-Léger-les-Vignes, Ancenis, Chemere, Saint-Philbert-de-Grandlieu
Mid-November, wine fair at Nantes
Maine-et-Loire
In February, wine festival of Anjou wines at Angers, Chalonnes-sur-Loire, Saumur
Mid-June, festival of vintage wines of Côteaux de Layon at Saint-Aubin-de-Luigne

Poitou-Charentes
Deux-Sèvres
In March, wine fair at Thouars
End of November, grape-picking festival at Boullé-Loretz

Provence-Alpes-Côte-d'Azur
Bouches-du-Rhône
In September, grape-picking corrida at Arles
Var
In August, wine festivals at Cogolin, Sainte-Maxime
In September, grape-picking festival at Saint-Tropez
In October, grape-picking festival at La Motte
Vaucluse

In summer, festival of Côtes-du-Rhone Villages at Vacqueyras
End of September, grape-picking festival at Chateauneuf-du-Pape

Rhône-Loire
Ardèche
Beginning of September, wine festival at Saint-Peray
Loire
First weekend in November, wine fair at Saint-Haon-le-Vieux
Last weekend in November, wine fair at Chavannay

Museums of Unusual Interest
Alsace-Vosges-Lorraine
Baccarat (Meurthe-et-Moselle) – Musée de la Cristallerie
Domrémy (Vosges) – Maison natale de Jeanne-d'Arc
Epinal (Vosges) – Musée international de l'Imagerie Populaire
Marckolsheim (Bas-Rhin) – Mémorial Ligne Maginot
Marsal (Moselle) – Musée du Sel
Mirecourt (Vosges) – Musée de la Lutherie
Mulhouse (Haut-Rhin) – Musée de l'Impression sur Etoffes-Musée du Chemin de Fer – Musée du Sapeur-Pompier
Muhlbach (Haut-Rhin) – Musée de la Schlitte
Nancy (Meurthe-et-Moselle) – Musée du Fer
Pfaffenhoffen (Bas-Rhin) – Musée de l'Imagerie Peinte et Populaire Alsacienne
Riquewihr (Haut-Rhin) – Musée de l'Histoire des P.T.T. d'Alsace
Sarreguemines (Moselle) – Musée de la Faïencerie
Strasbourg (Bas-Rhin) – Musée Alsacien
Varennes-en-Argonne (Meuse) – Musée de la Guerre

Aquitaine
Dordogne
Bergerac – Musée du Tabac
Goranc – Musée de la Vigne
Mazères – Musée de Figures en Costumes d'Epoque
Margaux-Cussac – Musée du Cheval
Monbazillac – Musée du Meuble Périgourdin
Gironde
Arcachon – Musée de la Mer
Bordeaux – Musée de la Résistance
Carcans – Musée de la Forêt
Pauillac – Maison du Vin
Saint-Macaire – Musée Postal d'Aquitaine
Landes
Bascons – Musée de la Course Landaise
Luxey – Ecomusée
Sabres – Ecomusée de la Grande-Lande
Samadet – Musée de la Faïencerie
Lot-et-Garonne
Lauzun – Musée de l'Equipment Agricole
Montclar – Musée d'Armes Anciennes
Pyrénées-Atlantiques
Arudy – Musée de la Faune et de la Flore
Bayonne – Musée Basque
Biarritz – Musée de la Mer
Saint-Jean-Pied-de-Port – Musée de la Pelote Basque

Auvergne
Montluçon (Allier) – Musée de la Vielle
Aurillac (Cantal) – Maison des Volcans

Le Puy (Haute-Loire) – Maison de la Dentelle
Volvic (Puy-de-Dôme) – Maison de la Pierre
Loubaresse (Cantal) – Maison du Paysan
Faverolles (Cantal) – Les Compagnons du Buffadou
Salers (Cantal) – Maison des Templiers
Clavières (Cantal) – Musée National de la Résistance
Saugues (Haute-Loire) – Musée de la Forêt
Ambert (Puy-de-Dôme) – Musée du Papier
Saint-Anthème (Puy-de-Dôme) – Jasserie du Coq Noir Fabrication de la Fourme

Burgundy
Beaune (Côte-d'Or) – Musée des Vins de Bourgogne
Châlon-sur-Saône (Saône-et-Loire) – Musée de la Photographie
Le Creusot (Saône-et-Loire) – Musée de l'Homme et de l'Industrie
Digoin (Saône-et-Loire) – Musée de la Céramique
Château-Chinon (Nièvre) – Musée du Costume
Verdun-sur-Doubs (Saône-et-Loire) – Musée du Blé et du Pain

Brittany
Dinan (Côtes-du-Nord) – Musée des Oiseaux
Trégastel (Côtes-du-Nord) – Aquarium Marin
Tréguier (Côtes-du-Nord) – Musée Ernest-Renan
Brest (Finistère) – Musée Naval
Concarneau (Finistère) – Musée de la Pêche
Ouessant (Finistère) – Maison des Techniques et Traditions Ouessantines
Pont-l'Abbé (Finistère) – Musée Bigouden
Quimper (Finistère) – Musée de la Faïencerie
Dinard (Ille-et-Vilaine) – Aquarium Musée de la Mer
Fougères (Ille-et-Vilaine) – Musée de la Chaussure
Vannes (Morbihan) – Musée de l'Huître
Brech (Morbihan) – Ecomusée

Champagne-Ardennes
Fumay (Ardennes) – Musée de l'Ardoise
Novion-Porcien (Ardennes) – Musée des Trois Guerres
Brienne-le-Château (Aube) – Musée Napoléon
Troyes (Aube) – Musée de l'Outil et de la Pensée Ouvrière – Musée de la Bonneterie – Musée de la Pharmacie
L'Epine (Marne) – Musée Agricole de la Bertauge
Germaine (Marne) – Maison du Bûcheron
Prez-sous-Lafauche (Haute-Marne) – Zoo de Bois

Centre
Cher
Epineuil-le-Fleuriel – Musée Alain-Fournier
Lignières-en-Berry – Musée des Arts Populaires
Indre
Gargilesse – Maison de George Sand
La Châtre Nohant – Musée George Sand
Le Blanc – Musée des Oiseaux
Indre-et-Loire
Bourgueil – Musée de la Cave Touristique

Chenonceaux – Musée de Cires
Descartes – Musée René-Descartes et René-Boylesve
Tours – Musée des Vins de Touraine
Loiret
Checy – Musée de la Tonnellerie
Gien – Musée International de la Chasse – Musée de la Faïencerie
Orléans – Maison de Jeanne d'Arc
Eure-et-Loir
Illiers-Combray – Souvenirs de Marcel Proust

Franche-Comté
Arbois (Jura) – Musée de la Vigne et du Vin
Dôle (Jura) – Musée de la Maison Natale de Pasteur
Saint-Claude (Jura) – Maison de la Confrérie des Maîtres Pipiers
Haut-du-Them (Haute-Saône) – Musée de la Montagne
Ronchamp (Haute-Saône) – Maison de la Mine

Ile-de-France
Information:
Association pour la Promotion des Musées de l'Ile-de-France – Château de Sceaux – 92320 Sceaux
Gagny (Seine Saint-Denis) – Musée Français de la Spéléologie
Charenton-le-Pont (Val de Marne) – Musée du Pain
L'Haÿ-les-Roses (Val de Marne) – Musée de la Rose
Parmain (Val d'Oise) – Musée de la Coiffure
Poissy (Yvelines) – Musée du Jouet
Couilly-Pont-aux-Dames (Seine-et-Marne) – Musée du Théâtre
Melun (Seine-et-Marne) – Musée de la Gendarmerie
Coulommiers (Seine-et-Marne) – Musée du Papier
Conflans-Sainte-Honorine (Yvelines) – Musée de la Batellerie
Orgerus (Yvelines) – Musée du Papillon

Languedoc-Roussillon
Lézignan-Corbières (Aude) – Musée de la Vigne et du Vin
Nîmes (Gard) – Musée Taurin et Musée du Vieux Nîmes
Villeneuve (Gard) – Musée de l'Hospice
Mialet (Gard) – Musée du Désert
Saint-Jean-du-Gard (Gard) – Musées Cévenols
Vestric (Gard) – Musée Montcalm
Béziers (Hérault) – Musée du Vieux Bitterois et du Vin
Montpellier (Hérault) – Musée d'Anatomie
Banyuls (Pyrénées-Orientales) – Réserve Biologique Marine
Thuir (Pyrénées-Orientales) – Caves de la Maison Byrrh

Limousin
Aubusson (Creuse) – Musée du Vieux Tapissier
Bellac (Haute-Vienne) – Musée Jean-Giraudoux
Saint-Yrieix-la-Perche (Haute-Vienne) – Musée de la Porcelaine

Midi-Pyrénées
Aveyron
Salmiech – Musée des Charrois
Decazeville – Musée Régional de Géologie –

Musée de la Vigne et du Vin
Marcillac – Chapelle des Pénitents – Musée de la Vigne et du Vin
Naucelle – Musée de la Résistance
Haute-Garonne
Toulouse – Musée du Vieux Toulouse
Luchon – Musée du Pays de Luchon
Hautes-Pyrénées
Lourdes – Musée de Cire
Tarbes – Musée Foch – Musée des Hussards
Tarn
Ferrières – Musée du Protestantisme en Haut-Languedoc
Gaillac – Musée Folklorique et Compagnonnique
Mazamet – Musée du Catharisme
Tarn-et-Garonne
Auvillar – Musée du Vieil Auvillar
Grisolles – Musée du Terroir
Saint-Antonin-Noble-Val – Musée du Vieux Saint-Antonin

Paris
Maison de Balzac, 47, rue Raynouard – 75016
Musée de la Mode et du Costume, 10, avenue Pierre-1er de Serbie – 75016
Musée de la Chasse et de la Nature, 60, rue des Archives – 75003
Musée National de la Légion d'Honneur et des Ordres de Chevalerie, 2, rue de Bellechasse – 75007
Musée Postal, 34, boulevard Vaugirard – 75015
Maison de la Serrure, 1, rue la Perle – 75003

Nord-Pas-de-Calais
Lille (Nord) – Musée Industriel
Sars-Poteries (Nord) – Musée du Verre
Felleries (Nord) – Musée des Bois-Jolis
Calais (Pas-de-Calais) – Musée de la Guerre
Audinghem (Pas-de-Calais) – Musée du Mur de l'Atlantique

Normandy
Calvados
Cherbourg, Sainte-Mère-l'Eglise, Sainte-Marie-du-Mont, Arromanches, Ouistreham – Musées des Plages du Débarquement
Balleroy – Musée des Ballons
Crèvecoeur-en-Auge – Musée Schlumberger
Lisieux – Musée des Merveilles de la Mer
Soumont-Saint-Quentin – La Ferme de Saint-Quentin
Eure
Bernay – Musée de la 'Charrette'
La Couture-Boussey – Instruments de Musique
Manche
Saint-Michel-de-Montjoie – Musée du Granit
Valognes – Musée du Cidre et Costumes Normands
Villedieu–les-Poëles – Musée Vivant de la Poeslerie
Orne
Alençon – Musée de la Dentelle
Argentan – Exposition de Dentelle
Seine-Maritime
Fécamp – Musée de la Bénédictine
Rouen – Musée de la Ferronnerie
Moulineaux – Musée des Vikings

Pays-de-la-Loire
Loire-Atlantique
Bourgneuf-en-Retz – Musée du Pays de

Tourist Information

Retz
Le Croisic – Musée de la Marine –
Aquarium de la Côte d'Amour
Nantes – Musée Compagnonnique – Musée
Jules-Verne
Saille – Musée du Paludier
Saint-Joachim – La Chaumière Briéronne
Saint-Lyphard – Maison des Techniques et
Traditions
Saint-Malo-de-Guersac – Musée de Rosé –
Maison de l'Eclusier
Maine et Loire
Cholet – Musée des Guerres de Vendée
Déneze-sous-Doué – Caves Enigmatiques
Les-Ponts-de-Cé – Musée des Coiffes
Louresse-Rochemenier – Musée
Troglodytique
Montsorreau – Musée des Goums
Marocains
Saint-Hilaire-Saint-Florent – Musée du
Champignon
Saint-Laurent-de-la-Plaine – Musée des
Vieux Métiers
Saumur – Musée du Cheval
Sarthe
Fresnay-sur-Sarthe – Musée des Coiffes
Jupilles – Les Métiers du Bois
Vendée
Fontenay-le-Comte – Musée de Terre-
Neuve
Les Sables d'Olonnes – Zoo Marin
Monsireigne – Musée de la France
Protestante de l'Ouest
Saint-Jean-de-Monts – Bourrine des
Grenouillères
Saint-Michael-en-l'Herm – Musée des
Coiffes

Picardy
Château-Thierry (Aisne) – Musée Jean-de-
la-Fontaine
Corbeny (Aisne) – Musée Vivant de
l'Abeille
Montgobert (Aisne) – Musée Européen du
Bois et de l'Outil
Saint-Quentin (Aisne) – Musée
d'Entomologie
Compiègne (Oise) – Musée de la Figurine
Historique
Senlis (Oise) – Musée de la Vénerie
Millencourt-en-Ponthieu (Somme) – La
Grange aux Vieux Outils

Poitou-Charentes
Bourcefranc (Charente-Maritime) – Musée
d'Histoire de l'Huître
Marennes (Charente-Maritime) –
Diaporama sur l'Huître
Ile d'Oléron (Charente-Maritime) – Musée
Ostréicole sur le Port
Port-des-Barques (Charente-Maritime) –
Musée de la Percheronnerie
Saint-Martin-de-Ré (Charente-Maritime) –
Musée de la Marine
Rochefort (Charente-Maritime) – Musée
Pierre-Loti
Saint-Bris-Saint-Cézaire (Charente-
Maritime) – Musée de la 'Mérine à
Nasthasie' Habitation du Viticulteur
La Tremblade-Ronce-les-Bains (Charente-
Maritime) – Musée Maritime
Vandré (Charente-Maritime) – 'La Vie à
Vandré il ya a 100 ans'
Bressuire (Deux-Sèvres) – Musée de la
Céramique
Melle (Deux-Sèvres) – Musée des Mines
d'Argent

Thouars (Deux-Sèvres) – Musée de
Céramique
Cherves (Vienne) – Musée Paysan
Gençay (Vienne) – Musée l'Ordre de Malte

Provence-Alpes-Côte-d'Azur et Riviera
Arles (Bouches-du-Rhône) – Musée de la
Camargue
Fontvieille (Bouches-du-Rhône) – Moulin
d'Alphonse-Daudet
Marseille (Bouches-du-Rhône) – Musée des
Docks Romains
Toulon (Var) – Musée Naval
La Seyne-sur-Mer (Var) – Musée de la Mer
Saint-Tropez (Var) – Musée Naval
Les Embiez (Var) – Aquarium
Méditerranéen
Cap d'Antibes (Alpes-Maritimes) – Musée
Naval et Napoléonien
Nice (Alpes-Maritimes) – Musée Naval
Maillane (Bouches-du-Rhône) – Maison de
Mistral
Moustiers-Sainte-Marie (Alpes-de-Haute-
Provence) – Faïences

Rhône-Loire
Loire
Ambierle – Musée Forézien Alice-Taverne
Chazelles-sur-Lyon – Musée de l'Océanie
Marlhes – Musée de la Béate
Montbrison – Musée Minéralogique
d'Allard – Musée de la Poupée
Sauvain – La Maison Sauvagnarde
Saint-Etienne – Musée d'Art et d'Industrie
– Musée de la Mine
Villars – Musée de la Mine
Jonzieux – Musée de la Passementerie
Usson-en-Forez – Musée du Val d'Ance
Ardèche
Privas – Musée Agricole de Verdus-
Freyssenet
Rhône
Lyon – Musée International de la
Marionnette – Musée des Arts
Décoratifs – Musée de l'Imprimerie et de la
Banque

Alpes-du-Nord
Chambéry (Savoie) – Maison de J. J.-
Rousseau et de Mme de Warrens
Annecy (Savoie) – Musée Salésien
Chamonix (Haute-Savoie) – Musée Alpin –
Musée Loppé
Fessy-en-Chablais (Haute-Savoie) – Musée
de la Terre
Grenoble (Isère) – Musée Daughinois –
Musée Stendhal – Musée de la Résistance
Saint-Pierre-de-Chartreuse (Isère) – Musée
de la Correrie
La Côte-Saint-André (Isère) – Musée
Berlioz

Handicrafts
Information on courses held in various
parts of France can be obtained from the
Centre National d'Information et de
Documentation sur les Métiers d'Art, 107,
rue de Rivoli – 75001 Paris

Where to Obtain Information
1. In France: from the various offices of
France-Information-Loisirs (F.I.L.)
Bordeaux Office de Tourisme
12, Cours du 30 Juillet – 33000 Bordeaux

Calais Office de Tourisme
12, boulevard Clémenceau – 62100 Calais

Colmar Office de Tourisme
4, rue Unterlinden – 68000 Colmar

Evry Agora D'Evry
91000 Evry Ville Nouvelle

Grenoble Maison du Tourisme
Rue de la République – 38000 Grenoble

Lille Office de Tourisme
Place Rihour – 59800 Lille

Lyon Office de Tourisme
Place Bellecour – 69000 Lyon

Marseille Office de Tourisme
4, Canebière – 13001 Marseille

Metz Office de Tourisme
Porte Serpenoise – 57007 Metz Cedex

Nantes Office de Tourisme
Place du Change – 44000 Nantes

Paris Maison du Tourisme Vert
35, rue Godot-de-Mauroy – 75009 Paris

Paris Office de Tourisme
127, Champs-Elysées – 75008 Paris

Paris Centre National d'Art et de Culture
'Georges Pompidou' – 75191 Paris Cedex 04

Paris 8, avenue de l'Opéra
75001 Paris

Pontoise Préfecture du Val d'Oise
95010 Cergy Pontoise

Reims Office de Tourisme
3, boulevard de la Paix – 51100 Reims

Rosny/s/Bois Centre Commercial
Avenue du Général de Gaulle – 93110
Rosny-sous-Bois

Rouen Office de Tourisme
25, place de la Cathédrale – 76100 Rouen

Strasbourg Office de Tourisme
Pont de l'Europe – 67000 Strasbourg

Toulouse Office de Tourisme
Donjon du Capitole – 31000 Toulouse

2. In France: regional tourist offices
(Comités régionaux au tourisme)

Ile-de-France
101, rue de Vaugirard – 75006 Paris

Alsace-Vosges-Lorraine
10, avenue de la Paix – 67000 Strasbourg

Aquitaine
24, allées de Tourny – 33000 Bordeaux

Auvergne
Maison de la Règion, 43, avenue Julien
63000 Clermont-Ferrand

Burgundy
Préfect – 21034 Dijon Cedex

Brittany
3, rue d'Espagne – 35100 Rennes

Centre
10, rue du Colombier, BP 2412 – 45032
Orléans Cedex

Champagne-Ardennes
2 bis, boulevard Vaubécourt – 51000
Châlons-sur-Marne

Corsica
38, cours Napoléon, BP 162 – 2000 Ajaccio

Franche-Comté
Place de la 1re Armée Française – 25041
Besançon

Languedoc-Roussillon
12, rue Foch – 34000 Montpellier

Limousin
41, boulevard Carnot – 87000 Limoges

Midi-Pyrénées
3, rue de l'Esquile – 31000 Toulouse

Nord-Pas-de-Calais
157, boulevard de la Liberté – 59800 Lille

Normandy
35, rue Joséphine – 27000 Evreux

Pays-de-la-Loire
3, place Saint-Pierre – 44000 Nantes

Picardy
9, rue Allard, BP 0342 – 80003 Amiens

Poitou-Charentes
3, place Aristide-Briand – 86000 Poitiers

Provence-Alpes-Côte-d'Azur
372, rue du Paradis – 13008 Marseille

Riviera-Côte-d'Azur
55, Promenade des Anglais – 06000 Nice

Rhône-Loire
5, place de la Baleine – 69005 Lyon

Alpes-du-Nord
11 ter, avenue de Lyon – 73000 Chambéry

La Réunion
Prefecture de la Réunion – 97405 Saint-
Denis

3. **French Tourist Offices abroad**
Belgium
Bruxelles (1060), 21, avenue de la Toison-
d'Or
Brussels (1060), Guldenvlieslaan 21

Great Britain
London W1V 0AL, 178 Picadilly

Netherlands
Amsterdam (1017 KX), Prinsengracht 670

United States of America
New York (N.Y. 10020), 610 Fifth Avenue
Chicago (Illinois 60611), 6645 North
Michigan Avenue – Suite 430
Beverly Hills (California 90212), 9401
Wilshire Boulevard
Dallas (Texas 75258), World Trade Center,
No 103, 2050 Stemmons Freeway – PO Box
58610

West Germany
D6 Frankfurt 1, Kaiserstrasse 12, Postfach
2927
D4 Düsseldorf, Berliner Allee 26

4. Offices in Paris
Office de Tourisme de Paris-Accueil de
France, 127, avenue des Champs-Elysées –
75008 Paris
Bureaux d'accueil et d'information, Gare du
Nord; Gare de l'Est; Gare de Lyon
(S.N.C.F.), 127, avenue des Champs-Elysées
– 75008 Paris
Automobile Club de France, 6, place de la
Concorde – 75008 Paris
Touring Club de France, 65, avenue de la
Grande-Armée – 75782 Paris Cedex 16

The information listed above was correct at
the time of pubication. The French Tourist
Offices will supply telephone numbers and
more detailed information.

Bibliography

John Ardagh, *France in the 1980s*, Secker & Warburg and Penguin
Books, 1982

Suzanne Berger, *Peasants against Politics: Rural Organization in
Brittany, 1911–67*, Havard University Press, 1972

Collins Companion Guides (by various authors) to Burgundy,
the Ile-de-France, the Loire, the South of France, South-west
France; William Collins

Pierre Collombert and Louis Viry, *Le Cri des Paysans*, Editions
Sved, 1977

Anne-Marie Crolais, *L'Agricultrice*, Ramsay, 1982

Michel Debatisse, *La Révolution silencieuse*, Calmann-Lévy, 1963

Georges Duby and Armand Wallon (eds.), *Histoire de la France
rurale*, 4 vols., notably vol. 4, *La Fin de la France paysanne: 1914 à
nos jours*, by Michel Gervais, Marcel Jollivet and Yves
Tavernier, Le Seuil, 1977

Per-Jakez Hélias, *The Horse of Pride: Life in a Breton Village*, Yale
University Press, 1980

Emmanuel Le Roy Ladurie, *Montaillou*, Scolar Press, 1978;
Penguin Books, 1980

Henri Mendras, *Sociologie de la campagne française*, Presses
Universitaires de France, 1965

Henri Mendras and Marcel Jollivet, *Les Collectivités rurales
françaises*, Armand Colin, 1971

Michelin green guides, 19 to different French regions, 7 of them
available in English

Edgar Morin, *Plodémet*, Allen Lane, The Penguin Press, 1971

François de Virieu, *La Fin d'une agriculture*, Calmann-Lévy, 1967

Gordon Wright, *Rural Revolution in France*,
Oxford University Press, 1964

Laurence Wylie, *Village in the Vaucluse*, Harrap, 1961

Index

Index

Index

Index

W

Y

Z